Voices, Spaces, and Processes in Constitutionalism

Edited by

Colin Harvey, John Morison,
and
Jo Shaw

ISBN 0–631–21884–X

First Published 2000

Published simultaneously as Vol. 27 No. 1 of
Journal of Law and Society ISSN 0263–323X

Blackwell Publishers
108 Cowley Road, Oxford OX4 1JF, UK
and
350 Main Street, Malden, MA 02148, USA.

British Library Cataloguing in Publication Data applied for

Library of Congress Cataloguing-in-Publication Data applied for

Printed on acid free recycled paper 

Typeset by Poole Typesetting (Wessex) Ltd, Bournemouth, Dorset
Printed and bound in Great Britain by Whitstable Litho
Whitstable, Kent

Contents

JOURNAL OF LAW AND SOCIETY
VOLUME 27, NUMBER 1, MARCH 2000
ISSN: 0263–323X, pp. 1–3

Voices, Spaces, and Processes in Constitutionalism

COLIN HARVEY,* JOHN MORISON,* AND JO SHAW**

INTRODUCTION

Internal and external factors are presently inspiring a resurgence of interest in constitutionalism. This interest goes beyond the purely parochial concerns of traditional constitutional doctrine. We are experiencing a transition to a form of internationalization which is distinct from what has gone before. Globalization and europeanization are more than simply fashionable intellectual currency. They are impacting significantly on all areas of legal scholarship. The architecture of legal discourse is altering to reflect this and in the process new sites of constitutional contestation are opening up. Multi-layered governance is a reality which few can afford to neglect. This process will only intensify in the years to come. The title of this collection captures what we see as an exciting time for those prepared to engage with these trends on an inclusive basis.

Internally, competing claims to recognition by a variety of excluded and oppressed groups have challenged some of the old stories about constitutional traditions. These groups seek to expose the partial and distorted nature of concepts which claim universality in the constitutional state. In practice many of these 'internal' disputes are now effectively internationalized and thus problematize any simple notion of 'inside/outside'. New forms of regional co-operation have raised the spectre of a postnational constitutionalism which is rightly suspicious of the loaded language of the past. As the collection demonstrates, there are attempts to respond at the national level to these transnational processes. For example, the 'third way' proposed by 'new Labour' in Britain confronts these and the concept has clear implications for areas as diverse as: the voluntary sector; corporate governance; and devolutionary settlements. At the micro-level mediation raises familiar debates about the nature of the processes of constitutionalism. In particular, the work renews the informalism/formalism debate. This maps onto broader themes in, for example, regulatory law where proceduralization is discussed in response to the problematization of law's role.

* *School of Law, The Queen's University, Belfast BT7 1NN, Northern Ireland*
** *Centre for the Study of Law in Europe, Department of Law, University of Leeds, Leeds LS2 9JT, England*

Whatever view one takes of the substantive issues in these disputes it is evident that this is an important time in the debate on constitutionalism. Serious questions are being asked about traditional approaches. There are solid grounds for scepticism about our inherited vocabularies. It is questionable whether they continue to possess both explanatory and critical power. If they fail in both respects the issue for scholars is the troubling one of what it means, in precise terms, to be 'critical' in legal scholarship. The new critical voices entering this debate tend not to be solely concerned with advancing alternative models for their own sake. The work arises from dissatisfaction with the explanatory potential of the maps of legal and political knowledge that we have inherited. This new constitutionalism seeks both tools that will facilitate the work of scholarship but also a critical foothold that prevents us becoming enthralled by the force of the languages of constitutional law and politics that we possess.

The inherited concept of constitutionalism that we have is the doctrine that governments must act within the constraints of a known constitution whether this is written or not. It is a notion of government tied to an ordered framework of impersonal laws. This concept of constitutionalism can be traced to the seventeenth-century struggle between monarchist support for the doctrine of the divine right of kings and parliament and the judiciary's assertion of the primacy of a system of authority based on law. Since then, the concept has been put to use in a diverse range of ways depending on particular societal contexts. This diversity in usage raises difficult questions which are now being addressed. For there are clearly problems with purely static views of constitutionalism. It is no coincidence that the terms 'relational', 'constitutional conversations', 'dialogic constitutionalism', and 'proceduralism' recur in this collection. The new voices talk about constitutionalism as an interactive process of connectedness and thus they seek to disrupt traditional narratives of a settled constitutional order. Some will quite fairly cast suspicion on claims to novelty. Process-based theory is not new to law. But the basic terms of the debate have shifted to reflect specific historical contingencies. Others will simply overreact and even retreat to the classical texts to rekindle their faith.

The concept of constitutionalism faces in two directions at once. This is precisely because constitutionalism implies both a foundational act and an ongoing processes of contestation. One is always a backwards look at the historical fact of the founding act and the other is the normative task of continuing interpretation. To be sure, constitutionalism has a grand historical legacy but it is also an often mundane day-to-day activity. The 'constitution in practice' is an intricate web of lived experience and human interaction. Rather than a static exercise in historical retrieval, constitutionalism is an ongoing process which each new generation engages in and necessarily alters in the process of engagement. It is no longer best viewed exclusively as a means of limiting or controlling power for it is itself constituted by democratic struggles. Liberal constitutionalism has, in effect, collapsed into democracy. The emphasis on constitutionalism as an ongoing process gets us away from an obsessive concern with the historical facts of a constitutive act. Enactment becomes a part only of the story. However the problem that continues to haunt constitutionalism is the legacy of the 'wilfulness' of the constitutive act. By unearthing constitutionalism's historical specificity one is faced with the fact of force which often underpins it. Republicans, in particular, struggle with this because they have to contend with the accusation that the theory ultimately sanctions militarism and terror. And it is here that the politics of discourse raises old fears. If constitutionalism is an essentially contested concept and there are no universal criteria to settle the meaning of constitutionalism indefinitely upon what do we ground our criticism of pure unmediated power struggles?

This is where the governmentality literature is of interest. For this work argues that there is nothing rational or necessary about the constitutionalism that we have. There is less interest here in the reconstructive effort made by those who see constitutionalism as a continuing conversation. The governmentality literature instead reveals the strategies of power which maintain the unities of modernity. Constitutionalism is thus a discursive practice which we can probe for the purpose of unearthing the complex strategies of subjugation and domination which it contains. Modernity's narrative of progression is rejected in work that suspects that we have simply replaced old forms of tyranny with new mechanisms of enslavement. This exposes the contingency of our current practices but also the formations that constitute more sophisticated systems of domination. This is a less optimistic reading of our current practices which encourages constant vigilance.

These are only some of the themes to be found in the current literature and within this collection. Many more could be mentioned. The aim in this collection is to bring together in one place important critical voices in the current debate on constitutionalism. No attempt is made to claim a false unity. We prefer to allow the contributors to speak for themselves. Each of the contributions thus reflects the specific concerns of the author. We do however wish to advance this collection as a critical contribution to the current debate on our 'constitutional futures'.

JOURNAL OF LAW AND SOCIETY
VOLUME 27, NUMBER 1, MARCH 2000
ISSN: 0263–323X, pp. 4–37

Process and Constitutional Discourse in the European Union

JO SHAW*

The paper presents a three-step approach to key constitutional issues in the European Union. The first step introduces the main descriptive elements of EU constitutionalism, highlighting some of the principal fields in which constitutional debate is presently clustering. Step two elaborates upon the tensions within EU constitutionalism by presenting a conceptual approach focusing upon the 'postnational' and procedural questions. Finally, in the third step, the paper sets out examples in order to demonstrate how the conceptual framework fits more closely with the emerging empirical reality of EU constitutional practices. It focuses upon events surrounding the inter-governmental conferences at which amendments to the EU treaties are agreed by the member states. The aim of the paper is to locate some of the tensions and relations which hold EU constitutionalism in place, rather than to capture its 'essence'.

I. INTRODUCTION

This paper proceeds in three steps, the first one of which is essentially descriptive. In order to explain in brief terms the status quo of the constitutional question in the European Union, I initially introduce and then sketch the key descriptive elements of EU constitutionalism. This will highlight some of the principal areas where constitutional debate is clustering at the present time and offer a preliminary systematization of what I term the EU constitution 'in practice'. I term the elements discussed the 'pillars of EU constitutionalism'.[1] The presentation proceeds out of a general

1 I use this terminology in the knowledge that it might generate some confusion with the use of the term 'Pillar' to describe the different frameworks within the European Union: First

* *Centre for the Study of Law in Europe, Department of Law, University of Leeds, Leeds LS2 9JT, England*

An earlier version of this material was presented at a seminar at the University of Aberdeen in October 1999. My thanks to the participants in this seminar, and especially to Carole Lyons and Neil Walker, for their questions, comments, and suggestions.

problematization of the 'constitutional question' in the EU. The second step then elaborates upon some of the tensions in EU constitutionalism which emerge from this presentation by setting out a general conceptual framework for approaching EU constitutionalism in terms of its 'postnationalism'. Building on earlier work,[2] the argument suggests that the postnational 'positioning' of the EU, along with key procedural, dialogic, and relational aspects of the process of EU polity formation, assist in the task of understanding the emerging constitutional edifice as poised between important normative questions about states, polities, and citizens and longstanding questions about the nature and process of EU-based integration. In other words, the focus upon dialogue and process is not for its own sake, or pursued with a view to prescribing the correct direction which EU constitutionalism should take, but is linked to an argument which highlights the specific historically and geographically contingent features of the EU integration process.

The third step generates a number of examples which seek to demonstrate how the conceptual framework sketched in the second step enjoys a close fit with current practices of EU constitutionalism. To that end, it examines the more specific routine and rhythm of EU constitution-building, focusing upon the role of the inter-governmental conferences (IGCs) which lead to the member states making amendments to the treaties, upon the interventions of the Court of Justice and its various interlocutors, and upon the possibilities for non-élite and non-state actors within civil society to play a marginal but none the less discernible role in EU constitution-building and polity formation. In particular, it highlights key aspects of the Treaty of Amsterdam, which came into force in May 1999, and the events and issue discussions which preceded it and subsequent and potential outputs resulting from the Treaty as an ongoing process of constitutional settlement. Hence the focus is upon constitutional discourse.

In recent years, the range of thinking amongst lawyers about constitutionalism in the EU context has gradually grown much more adventurous, not least because of the emergence of the rather unusually structured EU and because of the impact which the changed institutional framework and operational modus with its greater variety of 'methods' has had upon the

Pillar: the EC, ECSC, and Euratom treaties; Second Pillar: Common Foreign and Security Policy; Third Pillar: pre-Amsterdam: Co-operation in Justice and Home Affairs and post-Amsterdam: Police and Judicial Co-operation in Criminal Matters. To distinguish the two uses, I have used capital letters to distinguish the Second Pillar and Third Pillar, and so on.

2 See, in particular, J. Shaw, 'Postnational Constitutionalism in the European Union' (1999) 6 *J. of European Public Policy* 579; J. Shaw, 'Constitutionalism and flexibility in the EU: developing a relational approach' in *Constitutional Change in the EU: from Uniformity to Flexibility*, eds. G. de Búrca and J. Scott (2000)(a); J. Shaw, 'Constitutional Settlements and the Citizen after the Treaty of Amsterdam' in *European Integration: Institutional Dynamics and Prospects for Democracy after Amsterdam*, eds. K. Neunreither and A. Wiener (2000)(b).

'old' European Community (EC) and its 'method' narrowly understood.[3] At the same time, a wider interest in constitutionalism in the EU has emerged also amongst political theorists, political scientists, and indeed, scholars of international relations.[4] Any number of exogenous factors can be identified as driving that turn: the rise of so-called 'world constitutionalism' with its new post-Cold War hegemonies in relation to the role of law, markets, and market-based institutions; simultaneous, sometimes countervailing, tendencies towards regionalism and globalization, along with the rise of identity politics and the idea of a constitutionalism of a 'bottom-up' variety driven by struggles for recognition and claim-making rather than élite conceptions of the nature of the polity. Internal factors are also relevant. For example, part of that interest in constitutionalism in the particular EU context continues to be driven still by a fascination most evident in relation to the Court of Justice itself as an international judicial body creating an international rule of law in transnational conditions, especially as other international judicial bodies begin to take on some of the same features.[5] Another part of the debate stems from a shift away from primary concerns with the descriptive and positivist features of the substantive and actually existing constitutional frame of the Union (the rules which make the system work) towards problematizing the constructive potential of 'the

3 See, for example, K. Armstrong, 'Legal Integration: Theorizing the Legal Dimension of European Integration' (1998) 36 *J. of Common Market Studies* 155; D. Curtin and I. Dekker, 'The EU as a "Layered" International Organization: Institutional Unity in Disguise' in *The Evolution of EU Law*, eds. P. Craig and G. de Búrca (1999); M. Everson, 'Beyond the *Bundesverfassungsgericht*: On the Necessary Cunning of Constitutional Reasoning' (1998) 4 *European Law J.* 389; C. Joerges, 'Taking the Law Seriously: On Political Science and the Role of Law in the Process of European Integration' (1996) 2 *European Law J.* 105; N. MacCormick, 'Democracy, Subsidiarity, and Citizenship in the 'European Commonwealth (1997) 16 *Law and Philosophy* 331; M. Poiares Maduro, 'Europe and the Constitution: *What if this is As Good As It Gets?*' in *Rethinking European Constitutionalism*, eds. J. Weiler and K. Wind (2000); N. Walker, 'European Constitutionalism and European Integration' [1996] Public Law 266; id., 'Theoretical Reflections on Flexibility and Europe's Future', in de Búrca and Scott, op. cit., n. 2; J.H.H. Weiler, *The Constitution of Europe* (1999).

4 R. Bellamy and D. Castiglione, 'Building the Union: The Nature of Sovereignty in the Political Architecture of Europe' (1997) 16 *Law and Philosophy* 421; R. Bellamy and D. Castiglione, ''A Republic, if you can keep it': The Democratic Constitution of the European Union' in *The European Union and its Order*, eds. Z. Bańkowski and A. Scott (2000); R. Bellamy and D. Castiglione (eds.), *Constitutionalism in Transformation: European and Theoretical Perspectives* (1996); R. Bellamy, V. Bufacchi, and D. Castigione (eds.), *Democracy and Constitutional Culture in the Union of Europe* (1995); A. Weale and M. Nentwich (eds.), *Political Theory and the European Union. Legitimacy, Constitutional Choice and Citizenship* (1998); D. Wincott, 'Does the European Union Pervert Democracy? Questions of Democracy in New Constitutionalist Thought on the Future of Europe' (1998) 4 *European Law J.* 411.

5 K. Alter, 'Explaining National Court Acceptance of European Court Jurisprudence: A Critical Evaluation of Theories of Legal Integration' in *The European Court and National Courts-Doctrine and Jurisprudence*, eds. A.-M. Slaughter, A. Stone Sweet, and J.H.H. Weiler (1998), K. Alter, 'Who Are the "Masters of the Treaty"?: European Governments and the European Court of Justice' (1998) 52 *International Organization* 121.

constitution' in its socio-political sense within the Union's governance structures. What does such a narrative of constitutionalism bring to the understanding of the Union? Inevitably such a debate must problematize the relationship between the EU and the notion of 'stateness', even though, thus far, most work has failed to adopt a critical perspective upon what constitutionalism might be or might mean. The generally accepted precept is that constitutionalism stands for the principle that government *ought* to be conducted in certain types of ordered and just ways, in the sense of conforming to the well-established and widely regarded principles of the rule of law, checks on powers, and the protection of individual rights. Overall, however, there is now a much wider agenda related to the challenge of fitting together constitutionalism, along with its complex and multi-textured heritage and, in particular, its uncertain relationship with the nation state, with the new post-national, post-state 'Euro-polity'.

The limited aim of this paper is to provide a description and redescription of EU constitutionalism, and its voices, spaces, and processes, in the context of the reformulated conceptual framework which I argue for. It does not claim, however, to capture an 'essence' of EU constitutionalism, but merely to locate some of the tensions and relations which hold it in place. Thus, links can be drawn between the largely descriptive presentation in section II and the dialogic conception sketched in section III, which in turn lead on to the examples presented in section IV. It does not seek to offer normative prescriptions on how to use constitutional thinking and constitutional processes to escape the EU's well-documented legitimacy or democracy gaps, although it is based upon practically inescapable normative assumptions about the utility of constitutional thinking in the promotion of order, justice, and civility in societies and polities, even (perhaps particularly?) outwith the bounds of the nation state.[6]

II. PILLARS OF EU CONSTITUTIONALISM

1. *Contexts of constitutionalism*

Presenting EU constitutionalism, whether in descriptive or conceptual terms, demands a certain preliminary definitional effort, principally in order to justify the use of the loaded terminology of constitution, constitutional law, and constitutionalism in relation to the EU. Self-evidently, the EU is not a state, and very likely will never become one – or at least not in the conventional Westphalian sense of a coincidence of legal authority over a given territory *and* an element of cohesive identity formation amongst

6 On the characterization of such thinking as 'meta-constitutional' see Walker, op. cit., n. 3.

'the people'.[7] However, it is as often distinguished by commentators from 'ordinary' or 'mere' international organizations as it is from the nation state.[8] Interestingly, as the focus of much research on the EU in political science has swung towards the use of the methodologies of comparative politics in order to increase understanding of its systems of governance, and away from an overwhelming interest in explaining its occurrence as a case of 'regional integration' in a world of nation states, a shared terrain of interest has emerged between lawyers and political scientists in relation to systemic questions about the framework of governance and how it works. For both lawyers and political scientists, however, the shift in focus has meant a more direct confrontation with the 'touch of stateness'[9] and the paradox which this imports into the study of the EU polity.

For lawyers, the study of the EU in 'constitutional' terms developed in the first years as the explication and elucidation of the treaty framework, notably the European Community treaty establishing the so-called supranational 'First Pillar'.[10] Legal scholars highlighted this framework as having been 'constitutionalized' by the Court of Justice through the application of notions such as the supremacy, direct applicability, and direct effect of EC law in relation to national law. Thus, according to the case law of the Court of Justice, EC law is part of national law and takes precedence over it, including over national constitutional provisions; enforceable rights under EC law are procedural claims which national courts must uphold for the benefit of an aggrieved individual as against an infringing member state, as well as embodying substantive benefits accorded by the EU treaties. The two systems are organically connected through the system of references for preliminary rulings under Article 234 EC, allowing the national court to pose questions to the Court of Justice on issues of EC law, and giving the Court the opportunity to give authoritative rulings which should be followed not only by the referring court but by all other national courts as well, to ensure the uniform application of EC law. In addition, the self-evident federalization of law suggested by this perspective has been buttressed by the Court's discovery and construction of a doctrine of fundamental rights *within* the EU legal order (as opposed to the imposition of external systems of fundamental rights based on the national constitutions and/or the European Convention on Human Rights and Fundamental Freedoms)

7 See, for more details on the question of 'stateness', J. Shaw and A. Wiener, 'The Paradox of the "European Polity"' in *State of the Union, Volume 5, Risks, Reforms, Resistance or Revival*, eds. M. Green Cowles and M. Smith (2000).

8 See, for two very recent assessments of the national/international parallel, E. Denza, 'Two Legal Orders: Divergent or Convergent?' (1999) 48 *International and Comparative Law Q.* 257, and M. Zürn and D. Wolf, 'European Law and International Regimes: The Features of Law Beyond the Nation State' (1999) 5 *European Law J.* 272.

9 The terminology is developed further in Shaw and Wiener, op. cit., n. 7.

10 The classic analysis is J.H.H. Weiler, 'The transformation of Europe' (1991) 100 *Yale Law J.* 2410.

and the articulation of the activities of the Community and its institutions as based on a system of autonomous and evolving (if limited) powers, rather than upon a notion of delegation.

However, there was always another dimension to the construction of the 'constitutionalized Treaty', and that is provided by the vision of the EU as legal order from the perspective of the national courts, in particular the constitutional courts of a number of member states. Thus, for the German Federal Constitutional Court, the image of the constitutionalized EC Treaty was not adequate alone to sustain the authority of the EC law and the Court of Justice. That Court has, for example, denied that the Court of Justice can have the so-called *Kompetenz-Kompetenz* to determine the final scope of EC law in relation to German law and the German state as sovereign entity.[11] A key factor will remain the absence of a people, as a vital prerequisite to sustaining a constitutional vision of the EU. In practical terms, these difficulties have frequently taken the form of resistance to the Court of Justice usurping national constitutional authority in relation to questions such as fundamental rights. Thus, a fuller perspective on the nature of the EU legal order would seem to need to take into account the competing and in some ways conflicting visions provided by the Court of Justice and (certain) national courts, avoiding a one-dimensional approach focusing on *either* jurisdictional authority to the exclusion of the other. To that end, there have been a number of useful expositions of EU constitutionalism which take into account a more sophisticated and differentiated understanding of the EU legal order. For example, some work draws upon pluralist theories of legal authority and of the institutions of law which posit the EU's legal order within a system of overlapping and heterarchical orders in which the nation state order is not automatically privileged.[12] There are theories of 'multi-level constitutionalism' which draw strength specifically from the multi-level ordering of EU constitutionalism as comprising both national and EU elements.[13] Finally, there are theories which are grounded in a reconceptualization of an EU legal order based on an explicitly unitary theory of the EU as a single legal order, encompassing both the European Communities, traditionally understood as supranational and 'federalized' in nature, as well as the more inter-governmental Second

11 *Brunner* [1994] 1 C.M.L.R. 57.

12 See, for example, the work of Neil MacCormick, op. cit., n. 3 and *Questioning Sovereignty* (1999); see also Z. Bańkowski and A. Scott, 'The European Union?' in *Constitutionalism, Democracy and Sovereignty: American and European Perspectives*, ed. R. Bellamy (1996), and Z. Bańkowski and E. Christodoulidis, 'The European Union as an Essentially Contested Project' (1998) 4 *European Law J.* 341.

13 See, for example, the work of Ingolf Pernice: 'Constitutional Law Implications for a State Participating in a Process of Regional Integration. German Constitution and "Multilevel Constitutionalism"', in *German Reports on Public Law. Presented to the XV International Congress on Comparative Law*, ed. E. Riedel (1998); 'Multilevel Constitutionalism and the Treaty of Amsterdam: European Constitution-Making Revisited?' (1999) 36 *Common Market Law Rev.* 703. See, also, Poiares Maduro, op. cit., n. 3.

and Third Pillars where the direct dependence of the EU upon the systems of the member states is even more evident.[14]

It is in reflecting upon these conceptions of EU constitutionalism that it becomes most evident that there is a need for a fresh start in relation to the systematic study of the central elements of EU constitutionalism in the formal sense of the current constitutional framework which sustains the polity. For it is clear that whatever the currency of the 'constitutionalized' EC Treaty in terms of either scholarly discourse or legal authority, it now represents an *incomplete* statement of the scope of EU constitutionalism, after the creation of the European Union by the Treaty of Maastricht in 1993, and its subsequent evolution and adaptation by the Treaty of Amsterdam in 1999. It does not capture the complexity of the constitutional framework of the Three Pillar system, or the (re)emerging activism of the Court of Justice in the constitutional domain as it generalizes the application of principles such as transparency across the Three Pillars[15] and in relation to institutional activities such as comitology not foreseen in the treaties,[16] and begins the task of policing the boundaries between the internal systems of an increasingly differentiated polity.[17] In what follows, the task is largely to open up questions rather than to provide a complete statement of the EU's existing constitutional framework.[18] It is, moreover, merely a sketch of the

14 See, for example, the work of Armin von Bogdandy: '*Die Europäische Union als supranationale Föderation*' (1999) 22 *Integration* 95; 'The European Union as a Supranational Federation. A conceptual attempt in the light of the Amsterdam Treaty', draft paper, June 1999; A. von Bogdandy and M. Nettesheim, 'Ex Pluribus Unum: Fusion of the European Communities into the European Union' (1996) 2 *European Law J.* 267.

15 See, for example, Case T-174/95, *Svenska Journalistforbundet* v. *Council* [1998] ECR II-2289; Case T-14/98, *Hautala* v. *Council*, judgment of July 19 1999, not yet reported.

16 Case T-188/97, *Rothmans International BV* v. *Commission*, judgment of July 19 1999, not yet reported.

17 Case C-170/96, *Commission* v. *Council (Air Transport Visas)* [1998] ECR I-2763; Case T-135/96, *UEAPME* v. *Council* [1998] ECR II-2335. See, generally, Curtin and Dekker, op. cit., n. 3.

18 There are few if any extended attempts, in the English-language literature at least, to describe the EU system in explicitly constitutionalist terms. So far, most of the textbooks avoid the large-scale adoption of constitutionalist terminology to offer a sense of systematization to aspects of the law of the EU, although, for exceptions, see D. Chalmers, *European Union Law, Vol. One: Law and EU Government* (1998) ch. 5 ('Constitutionalism and the European Communities'); J. Shaw, *Law of the European Union* (2nd edn., 1996) ch. 3 ('Constitutional Fundamentals of the European Union'); and F. Snyder, 'Constitutional Law of the European Union' in *Collected Courses of the Academy of European Law, Volume VI, Book I*, ed. Academy of European Law (1998). See, now, K. Lenaerts, D. Arts, and R. Bray (eds.), *Constitutional Law of the European Union* (1999), although this is translated from a work originally published in Dutch. Trevor Hartley's work, *Constitutional Problems of the European Union* (1999), is essentially oriented around a critique of the activism of the Court of Justice rather than being an attempt to articulate the EU in constitutional terms. Likewise, Joseph Weiler's *The Constitution of Europe* (1999) is analytical rather than expository.

main issues and not an attempt at a comprehensive restatement of the 'constitutional *acquis*'.[19]

Returning briefly to the definitional question in relation to constitutions and constitutionalism with which this section began, it is clear that while there is no single formalized concept of 'a European Union Constitution' akin to many national constitutions which could form the basis of study or comparison, none the less, there exists a set of basic ground rules which govern the exercise of the many governmental functions and powers which have been ascribed to the EU and its institutions. The EU also operates these ground rules on the basis of a number of key constitutional principles, which in turn are based upon recognizably 'constitutional' value systems and anchored into the constitutional heritages of the member states. The most notable example is to be found in Article 6(1) of the Treaty on European Union (TEU):

> The Union is founded on the principles of liberty, democracy, respect for human rights and fundamental freedoms, and the rule of law, principles which are common to the member states.

This sets the basic political conditions for accession to the EU (Article 49 TEU). Yet, in truth, the body of principles found in the treaties – and associated case law and legislation – is by no means as complete and coherent as one would anticipate with a full-function national constitution. Given, moreover, that the Court does describe the EC Treaty as the Community's 'constitutional charter',[20] the limited scope and extent of the existing principles might be apt to disappoint somewhat in comparison to expectation. It could, at best, be described as a 'constitution in practice', if not a 'constitution in form'.

Secondly, also for definitional purposes, it is rather important to distinguish in the EU context between the 'formal-legal' and 'real' elements of the constitution. Gráinne de Búrca has identified and discussed the relatively significant gap existing within the EU system of governance between 'the formal institutional picture presented by the treaties and the Court' on the one hand, and 'the more complex and nuanced reality of the evolving EU governance structure', in particular, 'the increase in formal and informal bodies playing a greater or lesser role within EU law-making and policy-making.'[21] In that context, she is referring in particular to the prolific system of 'comitology', comprising manifold committees of representatives of the member states chaired by a representative from the Commission,

19 A reference to that rather mythical concept of the *acquis communautaire* (the shared political and legal properties of the system) which is intended to protect the integrity of the system against the degradation of disintegrationist steps. It is guaranteed in general terms by Article 2, fifth indent TEU, and more specifically in relation to measures adopted pursuant to the principles of flexible integration or 'closer co-operation', by Article 43(1)(e) TEU.

20 Case 294/83, *Partie Ecologiste 'Les Verts'* v. *European Parliament* [1986] ECR 1339.

21 G. de Búrca, 'The Institutional Development of the EU: A Constitutional Analysis', in Craig and de Búrca, op. cit., n. 3.

which exercise many advisory and regulatory functions. Also to be included are agencies and other bodies, many of which are not formally provided for in the treaties. As de Búrca argues, this misfit between formality and reality has direct constitutional implications, for it can be used as the basis for denying the constitutional character of the EU as a whole (as opposed to the more limited EC Treaty), for example, using the argument that it is premature or wrong to do so as the treaty frameworks and institutional practices remain so far too provisional and shifting.[22] In addition, the complex, shifting and partial character of the treaties' rendering of the realities of institutional practices across the Three Pillars also poses a challenge to the capacity of the normative principles such as those contained in Article 6(1) TEU effectively to provide a framework of constitutional checks and balances.[23] In other words, is such a framework 'normatively constitutional' and, indeed, can it ever be so?

This leads to a third preliminary point about the framework of EU constitutionalism, namely, the heavy presence of aspects of flexibility and differentiation within the system. Elsewhere[24] I have argued for the flexibility which exists within the EU legal order not to be seen as necessarily in contradiction to adherence to ideas of constitutionalism. By 'flexibility' in this context is meant a rather broad-scale conception of the suppleness of the polity in many dimensions and at many levels. This includes the lack of permanent or even relatively permanent fixity of external boundaries and the fact that both the polity itself and its many possible futures escape definition in standard political and legal terms (its 'mixity'). It also covers the more 'traditional' legal meanings of the concept as applied to opt-outs/opt-ins, overlapping systems of authority, and asymmetrical and partial legal solutions and the legal conditions under which these can operate. Thus, it includes the Social Policy Agreement 1993–97, the Schengen Agreement aimed at the removal of internal borders and the creation of associated substitute systems of control, the new post-Amsterdam EC Title on immigration, asylum, and other matters related to free movement, and EMU (which together constitute the 'unplanned architectural sprawl of flexibility'[25]). In addition, it also covers the ordering principles of Articles 40, 43–45 TEU and 11 EC which attempt to set constitutional limits upon so-called 'closer co-operation' embarked upon in the future within the framework of the existing treaties. In arguing that flexibility and constitutionalism can be seen in the same plane, and not as competing principles of arbitrariness and certainty respectively, it is essential for a constitution to be seen as an evolving

22 id., p. 64.

23 Such doubts are expressed strongly by Deidre Curtin: 'The Constitutional Structure of the Union: A Europe of Bits and Pieces' (1993) 30 *Common Market Law Rev.* 69; 'Betwixt and Between: Democracy and Transparency in the Governance of the European Union' in *Reforming the Treaty on European Union – The Legal Debate*, eds. J.A. Winter, D.M. Curtin, A.E. Kellermann, and B. de Witte (1996).

24 Shaw, op. cit. (2000)(a), n. 2.

25 Walker, op. cit., n. 3.

project rather than as a perfect and immutable rendering at a fixed moment of the political will of a popular sovereign and the equally perfect translation of that will into the constitutional law. The argument relies also on conceptualizing the basis of the polity as its discursive practices, not its legal order. These points will be picked up again in Section III.

Finally, in terms of a preliminary attempt to ascertain the basic character of EU constitutionalism – prior to highlighting some of its key elements – it is important to ask the question 'what are the EC and the EU for?'; in other words, we must consider the functional properties of EU constitutionalism, and assess how these goals are given expression in the treaties. While ostensibly still a limited purpose entity, which for many years was called an 'association of functional integration' (*Zweckverband funktionationaler Integration*) by a leading German commentator,[26] the EU – in the fuller sense of encompassing EC and EU objectives – provides for the possibility of some form of governmental activity across a remarkably wide range of societal tasks. Since, of course, the overriding goal of creating an 'ever closer union' of the peoples of Europe remains untouched in the preamble to the EC Treaty and has now been picked up in Article 1 TEU, offering a concrete link to the foundational ideals of the European Communities associated with politicians such as Jean Monnet and Robert Schuman, this is not in a sense surprising. But it is still useful to remind ourselves that the 'official' goals of the EU as a whole encompass more than the economic objectives comprising economic integration of markets, the creation of the single market, and the establishment of the single currency, which are in turn associated with macro-economic objectives to achieve high, but sustainable, economic growth whilst simultaneously seeking a higher standard of living, the protection of the environment, higher employment, and 'social progress' (Article 1 TEU, first indent). The EU also has external objectives to 'assert its identity on the international scene', internal objectives to promote the rights and interests of nationals of the member states through the introduction of a concept of citizenship, and, since the Treaty of Amsterdam, the objective to:

> maintain and develop the Union as an area of freedom, security and justice in which the free movement of persons is assured in conjunction with appropriate measures with respect to external border controls, asylum, immigration and the prevention and combating of crime (Article 1 TEU, fourth indent).

This latter is the new 'internal market'[27] for the EU in terms of policy objectives, accounting for a considerable proportion of the time devoted to

26 H.P. Ipsen, *Europäisches Gemeinschaftsrecht* (1972); for commentary, see C. Joerges, 'Taking the Law Seriously: On Political Science and the Role of Law in the Process of European Integration' (1996) 2 *European Law J.* 105, at 108.

27 The reference back is to the so-called '1992 Programme', the attempt to complete the internal market by legislative means before the deadline of 31 December 1992 set by what was then Article 8A EEC, as amended by the Single European Act. See the comparison made by Home Secretary Jack Straw before the House of Lords Select Committee on the European Communities, a view with which the committee concurred: Select Committee on European Communities, *Nineteenth Report*, HL (1998–99) 101, para. 34.

policy-making within the institutions at present.[28] Further elucidation of the economic and social objectives of the EU, and in relation to questions such as citizenship and free movement, are to be found in the EC Treaty where the relevant competences are in practice located.

Because of the highly incremental and non-systematic character of much of the EU's constitutional development, it is relatively difficult to offer a coherent division of the basic principles of the EU Treaties concerned with definably constitutional questions. The systematization in relation to the existing *acquis* offered by the Treaty of Amsterdam in 1999 was extremely partial: some obsolete provisions were excised from the text, and the treaties renumbered in ways which cumulate uncertainty for observers and undermine the famed goal of transparency.[29] Moreover, as section IV will reiterate, it is important not to see the inter-governmental conferences, during the course of which member states negotiate amendments to the treaties, as the isolated constitutional conventions of the EU. They exist in a complex matrix or interpretative space. The role of the Court of Justice as a constitutional interlocutor is generally acknowledged – even if it remains contested in certain spheres – but there are many diverse influences upon the evolution of the EU's constitutional framework from the institutions, from national governments and courts, and even from 'private' actors such as non-governmental organizations, and many times and places where those influences make themselves felt. The evolutionary process is, therefore, highly incremental, and has involved multiple interlocutors. Consequently, what follows by way of a suggested categorization of key constitutional principles to be found in the EU treaties is provisional, and should not be seen as creating cast-iron rigid divisions. For simplicity's sake alone, moreover, the discussion is here largely limited to the provisions of the EU treaties, although in practice some reference to case law and other forms of institutional output is inevitable.

28 See, also, the Special European Council meeting devoted to the topic, Tampere, October 1999, under the Finnish presidency; Presidency Conclusions: *www.europa.eu.int* and SN 200/99. Measures akin to the internal market programme such as a 'scoreboard' managed by the Commission are envisaged.

29 For many years to come, those working with the law of the EU will need to hand a table of equivalences, setting out the pre-Amsterdam and post-Amsterdam numbering schemes. The point is complicated considerably by previous partial renumbering. A good example is provided by the case of *Wijsenbeek*, where the Court's judgment (phrased partially in post- and partially in pre-Amsterdam terms according to its new approach – although the facts pertain to the pre-Amsterdam era) where the judgment was partially in terms of the provision establishing the principle of the single market and freedom of movement (originally Article 8A EEC, renumbered as Article 7A EC after Maastricht), and partly in terms of the citizenship provision which likewise appears to guarantee a right of residence and free movement to EU nationals (Article 8A EC after Maastricht, and renumbered now Article 18 EC). (Case 378/97, *Wijsenbeek*, judgment of 21 September 1999, not yet reported.)

2. *Pillars of constitutionalism*

The first group of provisions is concerned with the nature of the polity, including its multilevel constitutional system, and the relations to the national polities and the international system. At first sight, this appears to be a contradictory statement since much of the discussion so far in this article has been preoccupied, directly or indirectly, with the non-specificity of the EU as a polity, with its 'betweenness', and with the difficulties and – I would argue – the undesirability of capturing its essence or nature. However, as I shall argue, these provisions are openings, not closures. The starting point must necessarily be the first articles of each treaty. Article 1 EC establishes the EC in simple unelaborated terms; Article 1 TEU is more illuminating:

> By this Treaty, the High Contracting Parties establish among themselves a European Union, hereinafter called 'the Union'.
> This Treaty marks a new stage in the process of creating an ever closer union among the peoples of Europe, in which decisions are taken as openly as possible and as closely as possible to the citizen.
> The Union shall be founded on the European Communities,[30] supplemented by the policies and forms of cooperation established by this Treaty.[31] Its task shall be to organise, in a manner demonstrating consistency and solidarity, relations between the member states and between their peoples.

Also to be included in this group of provisions are the preambles to the various treaties and their rhetorical references to 'unions', Article 6(1) TEU already discussed above, the functional provisions related to objectives and tasks also highlighted in the earlier discussion, as well as a number of other general provisions such as Articles 312 EC and 51 TEU which establish the treaties for an unlimited period, and Articles 48 and 49 TEU which set the conditions for amending the treaties and for enlargement respectively. It would also cover provisions for entry into force of the treaties. Overall, I would argue that such provisions offer not a closure of the pressing questions about the nature of the polity (or indeed a prejudgement about whether the polity has a 'nature' in that sense), but rather an opening of the debate, especially for academic scholars.[32] They do not preclude argument, for example, that the EU should be understood in a non-teleological way, rather than with a view to the processes of integration having a fixed and definable end.[33] They provide the basis for a number of productive debates about the precise 'differentness' of the EU.

30 That is, the so-called 'First Pillar'.

31 That is, the so-called 'Second Pillar' (Common Foreign and Security Policy) and 'Third Pillar' (the residual provisions – following substantial 'communitarization' of the post-Maastricht Third Pillar – on Police and Judicial Co-operation in Criminal Matters).

32 See, for example, the work of Curtin and Dekker, Pernice, and von Bogdandy, cited above at nn. 3 and 13–14.

33 Bańkowski and Christodoulidis, op. cit., n. 12.

Second, I would gather together the provisions related to the rule of law and its systemic properties, including the role of the Court of Justice. Thus, in addition to the very general statement about the rule of law in Article 6(1) TEU, central to this group of provisions is Article 220 EC which provides that 'The Court of Justice shall ensure that in the interpretation and application of this Treaty the law is observed.' Building on this, the Court binds the member states to the rule of law, in particular through Article 10 EC which establishes their loyalty to the treaties they have signed and their duty to comply with treaty-derived obligations and sets up the Commission's primary and centralized powers of enforcement of EC law against non-conforming member states in Articles 226 and 228 EC. But, in truth, the rule of law, in the sense of the binding of the member states to the law which they have created, is enforced as much in a decentralized way through the Court's evolutionary case law on the relationship between EC law and national law, especially the case law on direct effect and supremacy and the more recently obligation on national authorities to make good loss caused in certain circumstances by a failure to apply or properly to enforce EC law in breach of a treaty obligation.[34] Vital in this context is the co-optation of national courts as Community courts by the Court of Justice; they are drawn into the system of obligations under Article 10 EC and sustained by the organic link between national courts and the Court of Justice which is based upon the preliminary ruling jurisdiction in Article 234 EC.[35] In general terms, individuals are constructed as the subjects rather than the mere objects of EC law, a notable variation from the traditional patterns of international law. *Vis-à-vis* the other institutions, the rule of law is instantiated in the provisions on judicial review by the Court of Justice of the acts and omissions of the institutions, allowing for the annulment of unlawful acts, for sanctions upon unlawful failures to act, and binding the Community to a principle of tortious liability for certain limited types of loss (Articles 230–233, 235 and 288 EC).

The third group brings together the key values, principles, and norms within the system, including fundamental rights, non-discrimination, and the institutionalization of Union citizenship; in other words, all matters related to the delivery of ideas of justice and fairness as an outcome of legal and political deliberations and related to maintaining the status of the individual as a holder of substantive rights under the system. Again reference should be made to Article 6(1) TEU as a foundation stone, but in this context one must refer also to two other paragraphs of Article 6, which guarantee respect for fundamental rights as they result from the ECHR and the national constitutional traditions common to the member states as general principles of Community law (paragraph 2) and respect for the national

34 See, generally, B. de Witte, 'Direct Effect, Supremacy, and the Nature of the Legal Order' in Craig and de Búrca, op. cit., n. 3.

35 I. Maher, 'National Courts as European Community Courts' (1994) 14 *Legal Studies* 226.

identities of its member states (paragraph 3). The Court of Justice is given jurisdiction over Article 6(2) TEU on fundamental rights by Article 46 TEU, even though in most cases the general provisions of the TEU are outwith its jurisdiction. Fundamental rights also have an explicitly political dimension since the Treaty of Amsterdam, with Article 7 TEU allowing the Council to pursue a political process to sanction member states failing to comply with the Article 6(1) TEU guarantees, including human rights and fundamental freedoms.[36] Other key provisions in this field include Articles 12, 13, 17–22 EC, respectively covering non-discrimination on grounds of (EU) nationality as a general principle, the establishment of a power for the Council to adopt measures to combat discrimination on grounds of sex, racial or ethnic origin, religion or belief, disability, age or sexual orientation (yet to be exercised), and the status of and rights/duties associated with citizenship of the Union. Notably, Article 17(2) 'attaches' to the Union citizen all the rights and duties applying under the EC Treaty, a provision interpreted as being of significance in establishing a distinct legal figure of the Union citizen in the Court of Justice's first significant incursion into this field, the case of *Martínez Sala*.[37] Also to be included in this category are the provisions prohibiting sex discrimination in the field of employment (Article 141 EC), and the gender mainstreaming provision pushing the Community to aim to eliminate inequalities and to promote equality between men and women in relation to all its activities (Article 3(2) EC). Furthermore, Article 6 EC now centralizes environmental protection requirements in a similar way.

In the political domain, there are important general principles of 'transparency' and 'subsidiarity' (in the 'closeness to citizen' sense enunciated in Article 1 TEU, rather than the more technical sense of Article 5 EC which is covered in the next paragraph). Here, only the transparency principle has a direct significance for individuals, at least in the limited form of the right under Article 255 EC of access to documents, under conditions to be laid down by the Council and subject to the Rules of Procedure of the individual institutions. Finally, also protected as general principles of EC law under the Court's case law are principles of administrative and legislative legality such as the principles of legal certainty, non-discrimination and procedural fairness, which govern the ways in which the institutions may exercise their power. In that context, the Ombudsman appointed by the European Parliament can also uphold individual rights (Article 195 EC).

Finally, turning directly to those provisions which govern the exercise of power within the EU, these constitute the fourth discernible category of constitutional principles. Included here are those provisions granting specific or general competences to the EC, the EU, and the various institutions, and

36 P. Alston and J.H.H. Weiler, 'An "Ever Closer Union" in Need of a Human Rights Policy: The European Union and Human Rights', Harvard Jean Monnet working paper 99/1.

37 Case C-85/96, *Martínez Sala* v. *Freistaat Bayern* [1998] ECR I-2691.

those limiting the exercise of such competences. It also covers general concepts such as the principle of limited powers or *pouvoirs attribués* itself (Article 5 EC, first paragraph, for the whole EC; Article 7 EC so far as pertains to each individual institution), the notion of implied powers (Article 308 EC, and the Court's case law on implied powers[38]), 'interinstitutional balance' (an 'unwritten rule'), and the best known examples: subsidiarity and proportionality (Article 5 EC, second and third paragraphs). For the policing of many of these limits, reference must be made to the Court's powers of judicial review which allow it to annul an act based upon an insufficient or incorrect legal basis, and to ensure that the correct institutions participate in decision-making according to the correct procedures.[39] There are also many provisions in the treaties which organize the internal operation of the institutions, as well as their political and legal functioning within the system of the treaties, through, for example, the adoption of rules of procedure, and the basic terms of the employment of officials and the duties they hold to the interests of the Union as opposed to national interests. In addition, in an overarching statement of principle, Article 6(4) TEU mandates rather vaguely that 'The Union shall provide itself with the means necessary to attain its objectives and carry through its policies.' This should be seen as a general expression of the need for a fit between, on the one hand, the functional objectives of the EC/EU discussed earlier and the existence and exercise of powers necessary to achieve those objectives.

From this snapshot taken of the framing pillars of EU constitutionalism, what conclusions and reflections may be drawn? A first important conclusion from the weight of evidence regarding the existence of a 'constitution in practice' if not 'in form' concerns the inevitable observation that practical constitution-building and polity-formation within and in relation to the EU will invariably continue alongside any conceptual, theoretical or normative debate about the nature and future of EU constitutionalism. Any such constitutional debate or convention would have to proceed in the knowledge that practical constitutionalism carries on alongside in the form of the day-to-day practices of the EU institutions, working with and constructing constitutional resources into the formal and informal outputs which eventually become the *acquis*.[40]

The second point is to reinforce the insight that the image of the 'constitutionalised treaty' cannot – if it ever could – any longer sustain the EU as constitutional legal order. While this concept has been a force for cohesion

38 See, for example, Case 281, and so on/85 *Germany* v. *Commission (Migration Policy)* [1987] ECR 3203.

39 Case 45/86, *Commission* v. *Council (Generalised Tariff Preferences)* [1987] ECR 1493, at 1520: 'the choice of the legal basis for a measure may not depend simply on an institution's conviction as to the objective pursued but must be based on objective factors which are amenable to judicial review'.

40 A. Wiener, 'The Embedded Acquis Communautaire. Transmission Belt and Prism of New Governance' (1998) 4 *European Law J.* 294; Shaw and Wiener, op. cit., n 7.

in the formative years of the European Communities, a mature EU needs a form of constitutional glue which is based on more than formal legal legitimacy based principally on a vertical hierarchy. Third, and finally, on a closely related issue, there are many commentators who continue to argue for the constitutive force of a formative constitutional experience to bridge that same legitimacy gap.[41] Such a formative experience would inevitably involve the replacement, or at least the supplementation, of the traditional mode of treaty-making behind closed doors in IGCs. One might point to the small steps are being taken down this route in piecemeal areas, such as the proposal for a charter of fundamental rights under discussion through 1999 and 2000, which will be examined in section IV. Moreover, in more general terms it could be argued that IGCs have to be evaluated in the light of a wider context of interlocutors and events which act upon the negotiations. In any event, the sceptic would suggest that the hopes and expectations which would be built into a constitutional convention or similar process if it were conceived as a single, once-and-for-all, closing of 'Europe's constitutional gap' would be likely to be disappointed, in particular for reasons which will emerge in the course of section III. However, the shift to a more dialogic approach to constitution-making none the less demonstrated by such calls is, from the perspective of the argument pursued in this paper, part of the overall process of achieving constitutional maturity.

III. TOWARDS POST-NATIONAL CONSTITUTIONALISM

The attempt in this section to formulate a dialogic and procedural conception of EU constitutionalism is driven by three concerns.[42] The first is the intuition that the procedural deficits identified by those who call for a formative constitutional experience for the EU are more than simply anecdotal expressions of the self-evident inadequacies of EU processes which have resulted in high levels of Euro-scepticism not only in the United Kingdom, but also in member states where there has traditionally been strong support for integrationist objectives. Rather, they express a real need for a theorization of constitutional politics in which questions of dialogue and process are central to polity formation. Second, we need to be aware of the limited explanatory capacity of any dialogic conception, since dialogic constitutionalism does not explain all aspects of constitution-building at all times and in all places. None the less, I would contend above all that the reconceptualization attempted in this section in fact matches more closely the current reality of constitution-building and constitutional politics in the

41 For two recent examples from the German and United Kingdom press, see I. Pernice, '*Vertragsrevision oder Europäische Verfassungsgebung?*', *Frankfurter Allegmeine Zeitung*, 7 July 1999, 7; J. Freedland, 'This institution has failed. For we, the people, have not spoken yet. Europe in crisis', *Guardian*, 17 March 1999.

42 I develop this argument in more detail in Shaw, op. cit. (1999), n. 2, especially pp. 587–95.

EU than those conceptualizations which seek to force the EU more directly into the straitjackets of domestic state politics, or the politics of international diplomacy amongst states. However, the task of this paper is not to contend *prescriptively* that dialogue is the only form of acceptable constitution-building in the EU. On the contrary, bargains between the member states remain a primary source of constitutional outputs and it would be both naïve and wrong to ignore this point. Nor is it contended that all dialogue is 'good' in a normative sense, although keeping the conversation going is sometimes an acceptable minimum outcome in the EU context. Dialogic constitutionalism represents a useful reference point, therefore, to assess constitution-making endeavours in the EU.

The third concern regards the significance of the 'postnational' condition.[43] The fact that the EU is a non-state polity is more than simply a 'setting' for its constitutional practices and futures. The invocation of postnationalism suggests not abandonment of the anchoring of the national constitutions, which are hardly likely to be swept away in a Euro-philic tide of enthusiasm for building a United States of Europe, but rather the reinforcement of a constitutional politics which is specifically non-teleological and accepts contestation and non-fixity as a way of life, not a deviant practice. Thus Zenon Bańkowski and Emilios Christodoulidis have argued for the EU to be understood as an 'essentially contested project', drawing upon W.B. Gallie's idea of the 'essentially contested concept'.[44] They develop a crucial variation, however, by focusing on contestation rather than contestability or contestedness. Linking their argument to a pluralist and heterarchical conception of the EU legal order, they argue that:

> the whole point of trying to describe the EU in terms of 'interlocking normative spheres' is to be able to see the whole system as a continuous process of negotiation and renegotiation; one that does not have to have a single reference point to make it either a stable state system or one that is approaching that end.[45]

One of the key elements of that negotiation and renegotiation is the fact that the currency of the negotiation comprises emotionally charged and themselves contested concepts such as national identity and sovereignty, such that the 'statist heritage' is both carried forward into the evolution of the EU, and itself transmuted by the processes of transposition to the postnational dimension. Hence a dialogic conceptualization of constitutionalism in the EU is, in my view, fundamental precisely to conceiving of the EU's constitutionalism as postnational. This is not meant to indicate that the EU is 'after' the nation state, in either legal or political terms, but

43 In his paper in this issue, Damian Chalmers also addresses the postnational condition, but in the more abstract context of the history of the modern constitution and the emergence of 'constitutional substitutes'. Like this paper, his argument also focuses on questions of communication and, particularly, recognition, in constitutional contexts.

44 Bańkowski and Christodoulidis, op. cit., n. 12; the reference is to W.B. Gallie, 'Essentially contested concepts' (1955–56) 56 *Proceedings of the Aristotelian Society* 167.

45 id., p. 342.

precisely to capture the 'open-ended, indeterminate, discursive, *sui generis* and contested'[46] nature of the project. It problematizes, for example, linear assumptions about progress from a union of states to an integrated polity, and posits a reflexive critique of institutions, legal forms, and identity formations beyond statist limits, in which the nation state is one actor, but not a privileged one. Moreover, for these purposes, the national constitution is relevant to the development of EU constitutionalism, but it cannot make a privileged claim for recognition.[47] Hence the discourse of postnationalism is essentially interrogatory, demanding that the practical and intellectual challenges to nation states posed by the twin developments of globalization and regionalization are reflected back upon taken-for-granted assumptions about the Westphalian system of states.

The opening argument in this paper identified EU constitutionalism as poised between normative questions about states, polities, and citizens and the historical, geographical, and political contingencies of the EU as a polity-formation process which belies conventional categorization and cannot be simply captured by a straightforward formula of integration or federalization. The conventional tools of state-building, including constitutionalism, cannot be applied unchanged to the EU because they fail to grasp two crucial elements: its contingency in the sense of postnationalism as defined here; and the continuing contested nature of its politics, in which left/right cleavages are entwined with differing, shifting, and often strategically focused levels of support for 'more Europe' or 'less Europe', as well as interacting with the identity politics of a changing, globalizing, regionalizing, and localizing geo-political space in Europe. A dialogic understanding of constitutionalism becomes, on this view, more than just an attempt to civilize a space of constitutional politics by improving systems of communication and recognition, but the basis of constitutionalism itself in such a contested order.

The argument about constitutionalism can only move forward, I would suggest, if we focus upon key procedural, dialogic and relational elements in a reworked conception of constitutionalism as the framework within which differences and similarities between social groups are uncovered, negotiated, and resolved. Such negotiations and resolutions are themselves not necessarily to be understood as finally determinative, but as interim solutions within a continuing conversation.[48] Moreover, it is useful to draw parallels from other constitutional spaces in transition, and to that end the work of a number of Canadian writers, as well as the Canadian experience itself, is instructive.[49] In particular, the work of the Canadian political

46 A list of adjectives borrowed from Poiares Maduro, op. cit., n. 3.

47 id.

48 S. Chambers, 'Contract or Conversation? Theoretical Lessons from the Canadian Constitutional Crisis' (1998) 26 *Politics and Society* 143.

49 See, further, for a more extended Canadian comparison, Shaw, op. cit. (2000)(a), n. 2. Much of this section is based on that paper.

theorist James Tully proves to be particularly useful as a starting point for rethinking the EU's post-national constitutionalism since it is founded upon a linkage of constitutionalism and the negotiation of cultural recognition, as well as a normative presupposition of the acute need for 'diversity awareness' amongst participants in a constitutional process.[50] It provides both a statement of the conventions which should underpin a form of reworked constitutionalism which he terms 'common constitutionalism' and a method for theorizing constitutional dialogue in divided societies. Tully's argument is both explicit and prescriptive about the conventions which must – perforce – underlie a constitutional process which achieves cultural recognition, which is just, and which will lead to stability within divided societies. Hence he asserts that:

> A constitution should be seen as a form of activity, an intercultural dialogue in which culturally diverse sovereign citizens of contemporary societies negotiate agreements on their forms of association over time in accordance with three conventions of mutual recognition, consent and cultural continuity.[51]

These three principles are conventions in the sense that they are:

> norms that come into being and come to be accepted as authoritative in the course of constitutional practice, including criticism and contestation of that practice. They gradually gain their authority by acts in conformity with them and by appeals to them by both sides, as warrants of justification, when they are transgressed.[52]

Tully's conventions of common constitutionalism do not at first sight appear particularly controversial. Mutual recognition is distinguished from assimilation, consent from coercion, and cultural continuity from the *tabula rasa* notion which informed the unique moment of constitutional creation which occurred at Philadelphia on behalf of an essentially fictional 'we, the People'. The 'bite' of these ideas emerges more strongly when the details of Tully's intellectual method are fed into the debate. He proposes an approach to constitution-building derived from critical concepts of understanding, definition, and description drawn from the philosophy and philosophical practices of Ludwig Wittgenstein[53] specifically as an alternative worldview to that which informs so-called modern constitutionalism. The latter is harshly criticized by Tully as facilitating imperialistic cultural practices and substituting

50 J. Tully, *Strange Multiplicity. Constitutionalism in an age of diversity* (1995); 'Freedom and Disclosure in Multinational Societies' in *Justice and Stability in Multinational Societies*, eds. A. Gagnon and J. Tully (2000, forthcoming); 'Identity Politics and Freedom: the challenge of reimagining belonging in multicultural and multinational societies' (conference on Reimagining Belonging, Aalborg University, Denmark, May 1999); and 'The agonic freedom of citizens' (1999) 28 *Economy and Society* 161.

51 id. (1995), at p. 30.

52 id., at p. 116.

53 Tully's use of Wittgensteinian thinking to develop a political philosophy for constitutionalism can be contrasted with the use of Wittgensteinian ideas about speech-acts and language in the emerging tradition of constructivist studies of the EU: see T. Christiansen, K.E. Jørgensen, and A. Wiener, 'The social construction of Europe' (1999) 6 *J. of European Public Policy* 528, at 541.

the assimilation, integration, and transcendence of difference for its recognition and affirmation.[54] A Wittgensteinian approach supplies a way of understanding which is not a redescription of another's cultural situation in one's own language, but which reveals redescription as what it really is, namely 'one heuristic description of examples among others; one interlocution among others in the dialogue of humankind'. It also provides a 'philosophical account of the way in which exchanges of views in intercultural dialogues nurture the attitude of "diversity awareness" by enabling the interlocutors to regard cases differently and change their way of looking at things', and finally it links the real world and the philosophical world by showing 'how understanding occurs in the real world of overlapping, interacting and negotiated cultural diversity in which we speak, act and associate together'.[55] Significantly, the account supplies a duty to hear the other side, and to listen to arguments presented in the terminology and languages of others.

Simone Chambers offers general support to Tully's approach to constitutionalism as a dialogic and conversational process, rather than as a contractual one producing a fixed outcome.[56] However, she suggests that Habermasian discourse theory can provide an alternative grounding of the approach. But as she indicates, she and Tully agree upon the fundamental principle that 'constitutionalism in an age of democratic diversity is more about keeping a conversation going than getting all the parties to sign on the dotted line at one time and place'.[57] Chambers is addressing in particular the Canadian experience of failing to achieve a consensus across the relevant constitutional actors on what being Canadian and being subject to a Canadian constitutional settlement actually means. These problems have been acute ever since the repatriation of the Canadian constitution occurred in 1982 in circumstances which overrode the will of the province of Quebec, and have persisted through the course of the negotiations of, but subsequent failure to accept, the Meech Lake and Charlottetown accords which were intended to accommodate the situation of Quebec.[58] These constitutional problems

54 Tully, op. cit. (1995), n. 50, at p. 44.

55 All quotations drawn from id, p. 111.

56 Such arguments are implicitly deploying the concept of 'contract' in its classical or neoclassical sense of a discrete relationship with a high degree of fixity in relation to the participants, the procedures for entering and leaving, and the contents of the contract. Interestingly, debates about contractualism in constitutional politics rarely address the challenges of understanding a contract or network of contracts as 'relational', and thus as a complex and changing transaction rather than one with fixed terms, entries and exits: for example,. H. Abromeit and T. Hitzel-Cassagnes, 'Constitutional Change and Contractual Revision: Principles and Procedures' (1999) 5 *European Law J.* 23. On relational contract, see S. Wheeler and J. Shaw, *Contract Law*, (1996) ch. 2.

57 Chambers, op. cit., n. 48, at p. 155.

58 For brief accounts of this situation see, for example, id., at pp. 144–9; P. Oliver, 'Canada's Two Solitudes: Constitutional Law and International Law in *Reference re Secession of Quebec*' (1999) 6 *International J. on Minority and Group Rights* 63; M. Walters, 'Nationalism and the Pathology of Legal Systems: Considering the *Quebec Secession Reference* and its Lessons for the United Kingdom' (1999) 62 *Modern Law Rev.* 370, at 372–5.

continue against a backdrop of continuing arguments by separatists in Quebec promoting its secession from the rest of Canada, if need be by a unilateral act based upon the will of the people of Quebec. Better, in such circumstances of fundamental disagreement, Chambers suggests, to accept the new interpretation which Canada's situation seems to generate, that is, 'the idea of an ongoing open conversation between diversities rather than the idea of a unitary identity for a nation-state'.[59] Part of the problem, she argues, is overemphasis upon particular constitutional moments rather than the constitutional continuum. Thus, a different approach will be taken if it is accepted that constitutional issues are not settled once and for all, in a single constituting act. So, she argues, the referendum on the Charlottetown accord which formulated a complex and, some would argue, unwieldy notion of what it meant to be Canadian was lost, because it became divisive rather than discursive. It became a yes/no and win/lose scenario in which the adversarial is privileged over the discursive.

Chambers continues, and concludes – in a manner that has clear resonance for a polity as diverse as the EU – that:

> it is Canada's great achievement and strength that it has built a political association without imposing unitary identity on its diverse members . . . This is the constitutional model of the future – a constitutional model that can accommodate multiculturalism and diversity.

Clearly, the EU has not reached that stage of development, since the elements of 'political association' are by no means as strong as those existing in most parts of Canada as a federation, albeit that this federal nature is heavily contested in some parts of the country. However, the utility of these arguments – for the purposes of the exposition of this paper – is to suggest a different way of thinking about the rhythm and routine of the most public and widely discussed events in the evolving history of the EU constitution: the inter-governmental conferences. It offers a conceptual model where dialogue is the root of constitutional process which provides, I would argue, a more descriptively accurate framework for understanding evolving EU constitutional practices. It is useful because it does not seek to cover up or displace the 'open-ended, indeterminate, discursive, *sui generis* and contested'[60] nature of the constitutionalist project, but places those qualities at the centre of the debate.

59 Chambers, id., at p. 165.
60 Compare n. 46 above.

IV. IGCS AND POST-NATIONAL EU CONSTITUTIONAL SETTLEMENTS

1. *The evolution and transformation of the IGC as political event*

IGCs have become a significant part of the life of what is now the EU since 1985, which saw the successful conclusion of the first IGC to result in substantial amendments to the scope and objectives of the original treaties of Rome and Paris, and to alter the balance of powers between the institutions; it led to the adoption of the Single European Act (SEA) of 1986, famous in part because Margaret Thatcher later regretted signing what turned out to be a more *dirigiste* and federalist instrument than she originally thought. This was the beginning of an accelerating narrative of IGCs and the ideas which circulated in and around them. The completion of the internal market by the end of 1992 was the 'big idea' of that first IGC, although other changes of significance were introduced – for example, establishing the treaty basis of an environmental policy.

Sharing with the SEA the fact that they were primarily a product of the political vision of Jacques Delors for the evolution of European integration (coalescing with the political leadership of François Mitterand and Helmut Kohl), two further IGCs ran in parallel during 1990–91, covering monetary union and political union. They led to the conclusion of the treaty on European Union or Treaty of Maastricht, to the establishment of the EU itself and of the Second and Third Pillars, and to many significant amendments to what was then renamed the EC Treaty, especially the provisions on and timetable for the completion of economic and monetary union. The single currency timetable was, as is now well known, respected in very large part with the introduction of the euro from 1 January 1999; the ideals of 'political union' have proved to be more elusive as yet, although there has been a notable acceleration of activities in relation to foreign policy and internal security-related co-operation.[61]

The Treaty of Maastricht itself provided for the convening of a further IGC in 1996,[62] setting out a shopping list of matters to be considered by the politicians, conceived as being in large part unfinished business from the Treaty of Maastricht. These related in large measure to institutional questions, particularly with a view to the anticipated enlargement of the EU to include many of the recently democratized countries of east-central and eastern Europe, some of the Baltic states, and some of the Mediterranean applicants such as Cyprus and perhaps Malta. The IGC of 1996–97 leading to what became the Treaty of Amsterdam thus appeared to lack a 'big idea'; in practice, it came to be dominated at a political level by the possibilities of the rhetoric and practices of 'flexibility'. In terms of substantive

61 See Curtin and Dekker, op. cit., n. 3.

62 What was then Article N(2) TEU

amendments also, the 'achievements' were greater than expected, with the treaty setting in place the conditions not only for the 'communitarization' (that is, bringing within Community framework) of the Schengen agreement on open borders and its own '*acquis*' of inter-governmental agreements and other implementing measures between the participants and of large parts of the old Maastricht Third Pillar on free movement, asylum, and immigration into a new title, establishing an explicit timetable for the achievement of cross-EU free movement of persons (albeit with the United Kingdom, Ireland, and Denmark (partially) opted out). It provided, in addition, for the renovation and substantial extension of social policy, with the end of the United Kingdom social policy opt-out of 1993–97,[63] and for the introduction of a new set of provisions on employment policy.[64] Most notably, one outcome of the Treaty of Amsterdam appears to have been that it created the momentum allowing for the generation of a new 'big idea' for the Union: the development of the 'Area of Freedom, Security and Justice' (Article 1 TEU), which has been compared in terms of importance and scale to the project to complete the internal market.[65]

Finally, at least one more IGC is foreseen in the treaty documents, since a protocol on enlargement[66] annexed by the Treaty of Amsterdam to the TEU and the EC, ECSC, and Euratom treaties, provides for the convening of an IGC before the membership of the EU exceeds twenty, and articulates in a separate provision not specifically linked to an IGC (but requiring in practice treaty amendment to give it effect) a bargain between the member states in relation to enlargement which balances the reduction in the membership of the Commission to one member per country against the reweighting of voting in the Council. Motivated by this, the member states have convened another IGC for 2000, again appearing in the initial stages to be looking for a rather narrow agenda of housekeeping, review of the institutions, and simplification/transparency to give legal effect to these political bargains.

Since IGCs now appear to be deeply rooted into the EU's political cycle, with one academic commentator calling for them to be in permanent session 'with small batches of amendments submitted for approval to the regular summits',[67] it becomes important to interpret their significance. In

63 It ended in practice with the election of the Labour government on 1 May 1997, but the treaty provisions remained formally unchanged until the coming into force of the Treaty of Amsterdam on 1 May 1999.

64 These are intended in large part to set off some of the effects of economic and monetary union, which might give rise to asymmetric shocks and an undermining of labour market conditions in vulnerable countries or regions.

65 See the brief discussion of this question at n. 27 above. Action Plan of the Council and the Commission on how best to implement the provisions of the Treaty of Amsterdam on an area of freedom, security and justice, OJ 1999 C19/1; Presidency Conclusions, Tampere European Council, 15 and 16 October 1999, SN200/00.

66 Article 1 of Protocol no. 7 of 1997.

67 J.H.H. Weiler, 'Bread and Circus: the State of the European Union' (1998) 4 *Columbia J. of European Law* 223, at 224.

particular, do IGCs represent a damaging cycle of 'boom and bust' for big political ideas in the EU or are they in practice part of a process of incremental change? In her examination of the 'transmission belt of EU governance', Antje Wiener makes use of the concept of the 'embedded *acquis communautaire*' in order to explain the emergence of EU citizenship policy as a case of EU governance from idea to outcome.[68] This focuses upon 'the continuously changing institutional terms which result from the constructive process of "integration through law".'[69] Wiener examines EU citizenship policy from its emergence in the form of 'ideas and values', through its routinization in the form of 'practices and policy objectives', to its solidification as part of the shared legal properties of the Union – that is, the *acquis communautaire* itself – as 'rules, procedures and regulations'.[70] This represents a useful conceptualization of EU governance not as either the outcome of bargaining based solely on the preferences of the member states (the classic inter-governmentalist leitmotiv) or as a haphazard patchwork of ideas and ideologies circulating in the ether which from time to time realize expression in concrete outputs, but as a historically and institutionally contingent process. The case of the IGC as constitutional forum is particularly interesting in that context, because the beguiling simplicity of its status within the text of the treaties is in fact not a true picture.

For example, the work of the IGC of 1996–97 was prepared by a so-called reflection group, comprising representatives from the member states and the European Parliament and chaired by a representative of the Commission. It produced two influential reports, as did all the other EU institutions.[71] The Commission established a task force on the IGC which made significant inputs into the process both before and after the IGC was formally convened. Two Council presidencies (Ireland and the Netherlands) exerted a particular influence, as their national representatives chaired the crucial ministerial and working-group meetings in the second half of 1996 and the first half of 1997, and were also responsible for drafting the basic discussion documents.[72] All the other member states produced reports setting out their public thoughts on the revision process.

68 Wiener, op. cit., n. 40.

69 id., at p. 299.

70 id., at p. 302.

71 See G. de Búrca, 'The Quest for Legitimacy in the European Union' (1996) 59 *Modern Law Rev.* 349 which tracks key themes relating to legitimacy (citizenship; democracy; subsidiarity; and openness/transparency) through official reports relating to the convening of the 1996–97 IGC from the Reflection Group, the Council, the Commission, the European Parliament, the Court of Justice, the Committee of the Regions, and the Economic and Social Committee.

72 Irish presidency draft proposals for the amendment of the EC/EU Treaties: *The European Union Today and Tomorrow. Adapting the European Union for the Benefit of its Peoples and Preparing it for the Future. A General Outline for a Draft Revision of the Treaties*, Brussels, 5 December 1996, Conf. 2500/96.

On the other hand, the inputs into the IGC were not confined solely to the institutions, the member states, and other public authorities, such as national parliaments. There emerged in the shadow of the 1996–97 IGC a veritable 'cottage industry' of expressions of opinion, lobbying documents, and attempts to exert pressure from national and transnational private actors trying to be heard in the conference room. The extent to which such voices are in practice listened to by the relevant actors (and only the member states formally conclude the treaties, even though the Commission sits at the conference table as well) might well be doubted. But it is certainly true that since the debacle surrounding the ratification of the Treaty of Maastricht, including the two referendums needed to secure acceptance in Denmark, the very close referendum vote in France, and the problems which ratification caused for John Major's government in the United Kingdom, member states do have an increasing awareness that the wider public – at least at national level – do perceive behind closed doors negotiation to be an unsatisfactory way of proceeding with such important decisions. In the light of these many influences, it seems increasingly unsurprising, therefore, that the IGC of 1996–97 became concerned with more than dealing with the aftermath of the Maastricht process itself, and became a forum for debating a number of political questions about the future of the EU, such as flexibility.

Overall the significance of IGCs understood as constitutionally defining moments for all parties involved should not be overstated. As James Caporaso comments, 'viewed from a long-term perspective, the 1996 conference is likely to be but one punctuation mark in a long, meandering, often messy process of political change.'[73] The tendency is to assume that IGCs and treaties give the member states the invariable 'last say'.[74] Is it the correct interpretation to say that through inter-governmental conferences and new treaty provisions the member states recapture and redirect the integration process? A plausible alternative is to suggest that the ongoing rhythm of conferences and amendments visible throughout the 1990s, where one IGC has led onto the next, has allowed the institutions, which are the real repeat players in the context of European integration, to 'capture' and 'direct' the will of the member states. Equally, the ever wider discursive basis of IGCs – which will be evidenced in more detail by the examples given below – could be said to envision a more dialogic form of EU constitutionalism. Not only does such an interpretation take into account the increasing cacophony of voices seeking to be heard in relation to all IGC negotiations, but it is also sensitive to the significance of the post-IGC phase. Once the negotiations conclude and the doors to the conference open, the outputs of the IGC are exposed to the impact of a much

73 J. Caporaso, 'The European Union and Forms of State: Westphalian, Regulatory or Post-Modern?' (1996) 34 *J. of Common Market Studies* 29, at 30.

74 R. Dahl, *A Preface to Democratic Theory* (1956) 38, quoted in D. Chryssochoou, 'New Challenges to the Study of European Integration: Implications for Theory-Building' (1997) 35 *J. of Common Market Studies* 521, at 522.

wider interpretative community. That is self-evident during the ratification process, when all national parliaments and at least some electorates get the opportunity to have a say on the outcomes, if not to change what was decided. But the significance of the statement is wider. For IGCs occur alongside the ongoing and routinized governance processes of the EU. The management of the internal market, the customs union, and the common agricultural policy does not cease during an IGC. Treaties, once ratified, escape the exclusive control of the member states. It seems almost trite to point to the dramatic expansions or changes in meaning resulting from interpretations placed upon individual treaty provisions such as Articles 28 (free movement of goods) or 141 (equal pay) EC by the Court of Justice over the years, in particular changes which have resulted in conferring 'new' legal rights on individuals as subjects of law. New legislative powers and competences agreed in a treaty will also lead into a legislative process where those powers may or may not be exercised, and where the precise substantive outcomes cannot be predicted by reference to the contents of the treaty or the *travaux preparatoires* of the IGC alone. Treaty powers have to be managed, and the Council of the EU comprising the representatives of the member states is just one of the institutions involved in the management process.

Some examples will assist in making the point about the contextualization of IGCs in a wider network of discursive practices and a wider institutional frame. I shall discuss in turn the incorporation into the treaties of what are known as the 'Copenhagen principles' setting basic liberal standards for states wishing to accede to the EU, the inclusion of a statement in the citizenship provisions regarding the 'complementarity' of Union citizenship, amendments made to the sex discrimination provisions, in particular with regard to the legality of positive action in relation to employment especially for the benefit of women, and, taking an as yet unfinished example, the idea of developing and incorporating a charter of fundamental rights for citizens of the Union.

2. *The Copenhagen principles*

At the Copenhagen European Council meeting in 1993, where the prospect of accession to the EU was first entertained as a serious prospect for the then newly democratized countries of east-central and eastern Europe (rather than some form of continued association, halfway house or longer-term waiting room), the European Council set out the following conditions of membership:[75]

75 Copenhagen European Council, June 21/22 1993, Bull. EC 6-1993, para. I.13. The European Council also went on to state that: 'The Union's capacity to absorb new members, while maintaining the momentum of European integration, is also an important consideration in the general interest of both the Union and the candidate countries.'

The European Council today agreed that the associated countries in Central and Eastern Europe that so desire shall become members of the European Union. Accession will take place as soon as an associated country is able to assume the obligations of membership by satisfying the economic and political conditions required.

Membership requires that the candidate country has achieved stability of institutions guaranteeing democracy, the rule of law, human rights and respect for and protection of minorities, the existence of a functioning market economy as well as the capacity to cope with competitive pressure and market forces within the Union. Membership presupposes the candidate's ability to take on the obligations of membership including adherence to the aims of political, economic and monetary union.

Originally a 'mere' political declaration conditioning accession negotiations, which are now taking place, the core elements of that declaration were taken up in Article 6(1) TEU, which we examined earlier as a foundation stone and pillar of EU constitutionalism in the current era. The continuity of language between the Copenhagen principles and the text of Article 6(1) is a good example of how certain norms shift easily from political to the legal domain within the EU, because the cycle of regular treaty amendments keeps open access to the foundational documents.

3. *The complementarity of Union citizenship*

The Treaty of Amsterdam introduced a small textual amendment to Article 17(1) EC. After declaring the establishment of Union citizenship, which dates back to the Treaty of Maastricht, a new sentence now reads: 'Citizenship of the Union shall complement and not replace national citizenship.' It might be possible to dismiss this change as simply codifying or consolidating the previous legal position. This very point was made explicitly for the Danes in the aftermath of the first Danish referendum on the Treaty of Maastricht in the Edinburgh Summit communiqué, and on that reading, the formal change in the Treaty of Amsterdam is no more than the continuation of the time-honoured practice of legal formality catching up to political reality, not dissimilar to the Copenhagen principles. It is also possible to interpret the insertion of a new sentence as the member states recalling a vision of the EU as (only) a union of nations, and as a reassertion of national sovereignty in relation to the citizenship question by claiming a crucial power of definition.

It has not been seriously suggested in academic or popular literatures that EU citizenship indeed *replaces* national citizenship. The issue of 'complementarity' is, however, more complex. The constitutional settlement of the EU does not take place in isolation. As I have suggested, provisions once inserted in the treaties elude the tight control of the member states, and can take on their own institutionally-defined logic and meaning. At the conclusion of the IGC, the doors open to a much wider interpretative community comprising the EU institutions, national governments and other public bodies, judicial institutions at a variety of levels, social movements and interest groups, and even the wider 'European' electorate and public opinion. The interventions of members of that community validate a more contextual approach to EU citizenship which steps outside the constraints of the formal treaty-based figure. The Treaty of Amsterdam has also been agreed in a broader context of the transformation of the nation state, for reasons which are not solely related to the European integration process, but have to do with internal and external pressures of a socio-economic and cultural nature as well. It must be correct to assume that national citizenship is transforming as well, although that is not to say that as a cipher or signifier of *national identity* it is necessarily diminished. But that still begs the question: if Union citizenship is indeed *complementing* national citizenships, then precisely what job(s) is it doing? Complementarity does not assume unchanged national citizenships. Exactly what it might mean remains open, I would submit, until there is in place a fuller political theory of Union citizenship as a form of postnational membership, and for the construction of such a theory we must look elsewhere in the treaties and at other contextualizing materials.[76] By confirming its complementary nature, the member states are precisely reinforcing both the quality of Union citizenship as an open-textured concept and consequently the transformatory capacity which they may have thought they were closing off. That might then open the door to creative interpretation or application by the Court of Justice or the Commission.

4. *The positive action controversy*

For the background to the third example regarding the legality of positive action programmes pursued within member states for the benefit, in particular, of women employees suffering long-term disadvantage in the labour market, it is necessary to look at a number of cases which have come before the Court of Justice. Until the Treaty of Amsterdam the relevant legal framework was limited to a directive guaranteeing equal treatment on grounds of sex in matters of employment.[77] Until then, the only treaty-based guarantee of sex equality was Article 119 EC, which concerned the sole question of equal pay, and was therefore largely irrelevant to the affirmative action debate so far as it pertained to access to employment, training, and promotion. Instead, for support for the legality of positive action as an anti-discrimination policy it was necessary to look at Article 2(4) of the Equal Treatment Directive which provides that the Directive – while guaranteeing equal treatment in all non-pay matters related to employment – shall none the less be 'without prejudice to measures which promote equal opportunity for men and women, in particular by removing existing inequalities which affect women's opportunities.' It is evident from these measures that there may be a conflict between the EU-level guarantee of equality contained in the Equal Treatment Directive, read in the light of

76 For a more extended excursus on this question, see Shaw, op. cit. (2000)(b), n. 2, especially pp. 305–13; J. Shaw, 'The Interpretation of European Union Citizenship' (1998) 61 *Modern Law Rev.* 293.

77 Directive 76/207 OJ 1976 L39/40.

this saving clause, and national and regional legislative frameworks which seek to establish, for example, quota systems to promote women's employment in areas where they have been underrepresented. Such systems are particularly common in the Germany, where each of the *Länder* has some form of legislative framework for using the *Land* public service as a laboratory for equal opportunities.[78]

The first challenge by a disappointed male applicant for promotion who blamed the effects of a positive action programme to reach the Court of Justice was the case of *Kalanke*. The outcome dismayed feminist campaigners, the Commission, and a number of member states. The applicant in *Kalanke* argued that his (EC) right to equality was infringed when he and a female co-worker applied for a promotion to a post of section manager within the public service of the City of Bremen.[79] A tiebreak situation emerged, because it was decided that the two applicants were equally qualified for the post, and the female applicant was given preference in accordance with the Bremen *Land* law on positive action. This provided that 'in the case of an assignment to a position in a higher pay, remuneration and salary bracket, women who have the same qualifications as men applying for the same post are to be given priority if they are underrepresented.' This was a radical variant of the tiebreak and preference rule, first, because underrepresentation was defined at 50 per cent and secondly, because it did not contain an *explicit* hardship clause allowing the balance to be tipped back in favour of men where circumstances required this.

In answer to questions posed by the national court about the relationship between this rule and the EC equal treatment guarantee, the Court found that applying the strict quota rule would be unlawful discrimination against the man because it was incompatible with the EC guarantee of equal treatment. It reached this conclusion notwithstanding the strong majoritarian and (national) constitutional legitimacy of the measure (agreed within regional and national legislatures, accepted as lawful under the German constitution). The Court was unable – or unwilling – to bring the Bremen clause within the scope of the limited Article 2(4) exception for equal opportunity measures.

There was a strong negative reaction to the Court's judgment in Germany (and indeed elsewhere[80]) – where affirmative action measures

78 C. Barnard and T. Hervey, 'Softening the approach to quotas: Positive action after *Marschall*' (1998) 20 *J. of Social Welfare and Family Law* 333; D. Schiek, 'Sex Equality Law after Kalanke and Marschall' (1998) 4 *European Law J.* 148.

79 Case C-450/93, *Kalanke* v. *Freie Hansestadt Bremen* [1995] ECR I-3051.

80 The academic comment was predominantly negative: for examples, see E. Szyszczak, 'Positive Action after *Kalanke*' (1996) 59 *Modern Law Rev.* 876; S. Prechal, 'Case note on Case C-450/93 *Kalanke* v. *Freie Hansestadt Bremen*' (1996) 33 *Common Market Law Rev.* 1245; S. Moore, 'Nothing Positive from the Court of Justice' (1996) 21 *European Law Rev.* 156; H. Fenwick, 'Perpetuating Inequality in the Name of Equal Treatment' (1996) 18 *J. of Social Welfare and Family Law* 263. In an interesting example of academic-judicial interaction, Advocate-General Jacobs's opinion in *Marschall* is heavily laced with negative reactions to those criticisms by academic feminists.

have become very much an accepted part of equal opportunity policies, and many public and private interests and groups including local and regional women's bureaux, trades unions, and other groups have invested considerable energy in attempts to enshrine positive action into national and regional laws. The Court's ruling was felt to be insufficiently respecting of national and regional policy choices, and difficult to reconcile with the principle of subsidiarity (Article 5 EC) which should precisely protect the autonomy in such matters of sub-units of the European Union. Measures were proposed to change the Equal Treatment Directive to ensure that at least the softer variants of national affirmative action programmes were safe from the scrutiny of the Court of Justice (perceived now to be a negative influence, after so many years of being held up as the great hope of liberal rights-based feminism).[81] More dramatically, agreement was reached at the immediately following (1996–97) IGC to amend the treaties themselves to protect equal opportunities measures. A new paragraph 4 was added to what is now Article 141 on equal pay, extending its reach into equal treatment generally, and apparently elevating the status of equality of result or outcome, at the expense of 'mere' equality of opportunity:

> With a view to ensuring full equality in practice between men and women in working life, the principle of equal treatment shall not prevent any Member State from maintaining or adopting measures providing for specific advantages in order to make it easier for the underrepresented sex to pursue a vocational activity or to prevent or compensate for disadvantages in professional careers.

In a declaration attached to the EC Treaty, the conference directed the member states in taking such positive action measures to 'aim at improving the situation of women in working life.' These new developments are backed up by a more general change, namely, the gender mainstreaming provision included in Article 3(2) EC.[82]

Of course, the 'women's lobby' is noticeably more organized and more closely keyed into the decision-making centres at national and supranational levels than almost any other social movement within the EU.[83] Certainly, it demonstrated an enviable capacity to translate its objections to the *Kalanke* judgment into concrete proposals then adopted at the highest level in the EU.[84] Perhaps it was in response to these types of reactions that when the Court was faced shortly after the Amsterdam agreement, but before its entry into force, with another affirmative action case – but this

81 Proposal for a Council Directive amending Directive 76/207 COM(96) 93; OJ 1996 C179/8.

82 See, further, for the role of this provision within the pillars of EU constitutionalism the text following n. 37 above.

83 On the many successes in relation to the politics of women's rights, see, generally, C. Hoskyns, *Integrating Gender. Women, Law and Politics in the European Union* (1996).

84 U. Liebert, 'Gender politics in the European Union: the return of the public', paper presented to the 1998 annual meeting of the American Political Science Association, Boston, September 1998; S. Mazey, 'The European Union and women's rights: from the Europeanization of national agendas to the nationalization of a European agenda?' (1998) 5 *J. of European Public Policy* 131.

time involving the more common variant of affirmative action legislation which included a hardship clause to protect the interests of men finding themselves in specific problematic circumstances – it concluded that such a measure *did not* conflict with the EC guarantee of equal treatment. Thus, in contrast to the negatively worded opinion of Advocate-General Jacobs in the *Marschall* case, the Court's rhetoric in its judgment was markedly changed from the formalism of *Kalanke*. It reminded its readers that:

> . . . even where male and female candidates are equally qualified, male candidates tend to be promoted in preference to female candidates particularly because of prejudices and stereotypes concerning the role and capacities of women in working life and the fear, for example, that women will interrupt their careers more frequently, that owing to household and family duties they will be less flexible in their working hours, or that they will be absent from work more frequently because of pregnancy, childbirth and breastfeeding.
>
> For these reasons, the mere fact that a male candidate and a female candidate are equally qualified does not mean that they have the same chance'[85]

So, in deference to a sense of the exclusion of female citizens from the full enjoyment of membership within the polity, the Court concluded in favour of a *restriction* in the scope and reach of EC law and the EC constitutional guarantee of formal equality, by allowing legislative freedom to the German *Länder*. Ulrike Liebert[86] identifies lobby politics as one of a number of linked answers to the puzzle of why gender policies should have been advanced in the Treaty of Amsterdam, notwithstanding the weight of the so-called 'joint decision trap' which focuses on the difficulties of achieving unanimity to change the status quo.[87] She cites also the influence of small Nordic states who placed this issue on their IGC agenda, the responsiveness of the Commission as a strategic actor to changes in public opinion which include approval of equal opportunities policies alongside a growing gender gap in approval ratings for the EU, the role of the European Parliament, and more general cultural changes in values and attitudes towards gender and equality issues. These are factors which operate in addition to the role of the Court of Justice, the national court, and the national and regional legislatures, all of which can be seen operating as a discursive community around these questions.

5. *Towards an EU Charter of fundamental rights*

The final example concerns the working methods of a recently established body working to elaborate a draft EU Charter of fundamental rights, building on the political will of the member states expressed in the conclusions to

85 Case C-409/95, *Marschall* v. *Land Nordrhein-Westfalen* [1997] ECR I-6363, at paras. 29–30.

86 Liebert, op. cit., n. 84.

87 F. Scharpf, 'The joint-decision trap: lessons from German federalism and European integration' (1988) 66 *Public Administration* 239.

the Cologne European Council of June 1999. The need for a statement of fundamental rights within the EU order which goes beyond the treaty guarantees discussed in section II, the references to and usage of the European Convention on Human Rights and Fundamental Freedoms, especially by the Court of Justice, and the Court's own case law has been a political hot potato within the EU for a number of years. The European Parliament, in particular, has been providing reports on fundamental rights questions for a number of years,[88] and this initiative has now been picked up by the Council of the EU itself.[89] The Commission has sponsored research on this question, and the drawing up of a number of experts' reports, most recently a 1999 report on *Affirming Fundamental Rights in the European Union: Time to Act*.[90] Many of these papers have concerned questions internal to and external to the EU in relation to fundamental rights. The German presidency resuscitated the narrower question of fundamental rights *within* the EU, giving it a prominent place on the agenda of the European Council in Cologne. The presidency conclusions contain a decision on the drawing up of a Charter of Fundamental Rights of the European Union.

The interesting question here concerns not the timing or scope of this initiative, both of which could be said to be driven by primary considerations of expediency rather than pure moral imperative. Rather, the question is that of process. First, the elaboration is taking place outside an IGC. It can be assumed, at this stage, that its status will be declaratory, like the Community Charter of Fundamental Social Rights for Workers, which was originally adopted – without the United Kingdom's participation – in 1989. But might its outputs, like those of that first charter, at some stage in the future, be formalized in a treaty, or quasi-treaty document such as a protocol? The Social Charter was originally made an explicit inspiration by the Social Policy Agreement attached to the Treaty of Maastricht, from which the United Kingdom opted out, and is referred to now in Article 136 EC as the basis for the EU's reformulated social policy provisions, so a similar destiny for the Fundamental Rights Charter must be a possibility. It could be taken further, and given a more explicit status with the rights taking on a legally enforceable character.

Second, in its Cologne decision the European Council determined the framework for the elaboration of the charter:

> a draft of such a Charter of Fundamental Rights of the European Union should be elaborated by a body composed of representatives of the Heads of State and Government and of the President of the Commission as well as of members of the European Parliament and national parliaments. Representatives of the European Court

88 Committee on Civil Liberties and Internal Affairs (Rapporteur, Anne-Marie Schaffner), *European Parliament Annual Report on respect for human rights in the European Union* (1997).

89 Council of the European Union, *Draft EU Annual Report on Human Rights*, 11350/99, 1 October 1999.

90 Report of the Expert Group on Fundamental Rights, *Affirming Fundamental Rights in the European Union: Time to Act*, Brussels, February 1999, European Commission, DGV.

of Justice should participate as observers. Representatives of the Economic and Social Committee, the Committee of the Regions *and social groups as well as experts should be invited to give their views*. Secretariat services should be provided by the General Secretariat of the Council' (emphasis added).

The Presidency conclusions of the Tampere European Council of October 1999 formalize this further in an annex regarding the *Composition, Method of Work and Practical Arrangements for the Body to Elaborate a Draft EU Charter of Fundamental Rights*, with 'other bodies, social groups and experts' to be invited to give their views. Moreover, 'in principle, hearings held by the body and documents submitted at such hearings should be public', and a 'complete language regime' will be applicable to meetings, making them accessible in all the official languages of the EU. The non-governmental interests will not be slow to respond to such an initiative. Within a few days, a response from the Platform of European Social NGOs and the European Trade Unions Confederation welcoming the initiative and insisting that they should be fully consulted had appeared on the Platform website,[91] and was given quasi-official sponsorship by appearing also on the website of the Social Affairs Directorate of the European Commission.[92] Making the dialogue with non-governmental interests a possibility dramatically opens upon the dialogic potential of this particular proto-constitutional process.

V. CONCLUSIONS

The task of this paper has not been to try to capture the 'essence' of constitutionalism, but to suggest a redescription and reconceptualization which contextualizes it against a backdrop of key normative theories about dialogic constitutionalism and an understanding of the so-called 'new governance' of the EU as an emerging non-state multi-level polity. Thus it is the relations and tensions which hold the constitutional endeavour in place which have been the primary focus of attention, with examples drawn from recent and ongoing constitutionalist processes. If the side effect of this analysis is to suggest new ways forward which do help to close the EU's legitimacy gap because they increase possibilities of participation and can help to engender a sense of 'belongingness', then so be it. That, however, was not the primary objective of the paper. Rather, the attempt to demonstrate the creative and positive dimensions of understanding constitutionalism in process-oriented terms informed by the types of intellectual frameworks sketched in section III is justified, most strongly, by the closer fit which section IV has sought to show between the 'empirical reality' of constitution-building at the present time and the normative preconditions

91 *www.platform-ngos.org* (consulted on November 2 1999)
92 *www.europa.eu.int/comm/dg05* (consulted on November 2 1999).

of fostering justice and stability in divided societies. Thus the paper has not been about a wish-list or shopping list of legitimacy demands from national parliaments, NGOs or even a wider, if diffuse, euro-sceptic electoral public, but about the constructive interaction between the ideas, norms, standards, and principles which a constitutionalist turn in law and politics bring into the EU policy process and the evolution of the EU as a non-state polity with postnational governance arrangements and an indeterminate form. What the outcomes of these processes might be, and how they will be evaluated by the wider audience of Euro-watchers, is a question which remains to be answered.

JOURNAL OF LAW AND SOCIETY
VOLUME 27, NUMBER 1, MARCH 2000
ISSN: 0263–323X, pp. 38–60

Accountability in the Regulatory State

COLIN SCOTT*

Accountability has long been both a key theme and a key problem in constitutional scholarship. The centrality of the accountability debates in contemporary political and legal discourse is a product of the difficulty of balancing the autonomy given to those exercising public power with appropriate control. The traditional mechanisms of accountability to Parliament and to the courts are problematic because in a complex administrative state, characterized by widespread delegation of discretion to actors located far from the centre of government, the conception of centralized responsibility upon which traditional accountability mechanisms are based is often fictional. The problems of accountability have been made manifest by the transformations wrought on public administration by the new public management (NPM) revolution which have further fragmented the public sector. In this article it is argued that if public lawyers are to be reconciled to these changes then it will be through recognizing the potential for additional or extended mechanisms of accountability in supplementing or displacing traditional accountability functions. The article identifies and develops two such extended accountability models: interdependence and redundancy.

* *Law Department, London School of Economics and Political Science, Houghton Street, London WC2A 2AE, England*

Much of the data for this paper is drawn from two collaborative empirical projects on the regulation of the public sector (ESRC grant no. L124251015) and of the UK Office of Telecommunications (funded by the Leverhulme Trust, the Centre for the Study of Regulated Industries, and the Suntory and Toyota International Centres for Research in Economics and Related Disciplines). I am indebted to my collaborators, in particular to Christopher Hood. I am also grateful to the following for comments on earlier drafts of this article: participants in a LSE Law Department staff seminar, May 1999, a LSE MSc Regulation programme seminar, May 1999, and the Law and Society Association annual meeting in Chicago, June 1999; and Julia Black, Martin Loughlin, Imelda Maher, James Penner, Richard Rawlings, and the editors. I remain responsible for errors.

INTRODUCTION

The central problem of accountability arises from the delegation of authority to a wide range of public and some private actors, through legislation, contracts or other mechanisms. Debates over accountability have to grapple with the uncomfortable dilemma of how to give sufficient autonomy to these actors for them to be able to achieve their tasks, while at the same time ensuring an adequate degree of control.[1] Trust in mechanisms of accountability is thus a central precondition for the legitimate delegation of authority. In light of this analysis the distinction sometimes drawn between accountability and control – control implying *ex ante* involvement in a decision, while accountability is restricted to *ex post* oversight[2] – is not particularly helpful. This distinction, often found in public law accounts,[3] appears to neglect the observation that there is implicit in the capacity to call to account some element of control capacity.[4] It seems better to see control and accountability as linked concepts,[5] operating on a continuum. If we were to redraw the distinction it might be in terms that *managerial* control refers to the right to *ex ante* involvement in decision making, while *accountability-based* control refers to *ex post* oversight.

Accountability has long been both a key objective and key problem for the constitutional law analysis of the British state.[6] The ill-defined objectives lying behind the accountability concerns include the holding of public actors to the democratic will (through a concept of legality) and promoting fairness and rationality in administrative decision making. Central to this concern has been the concept of ministerial responsibility.[7] The problem derives from an acknowledgement that traditional mechanisms of accountability within the British state are weak instruments for achieving these objectives, and the problem is perceived to grow in scale the more state authority is delegated.

1 B. Smith and D.C. Hague (eds.), *The Dilemma of Accountability in Modern Government: Independence Versus Control* (1971).

2 P. Birkinshaw, 'Decision-Making and its Control in the Administrative Process – An Overview' in *Law, Legitimacy and the Constitution*, eds. P. McAuslan and J. McEldowney (1985) 152.

3 Compare R. Baldwin and C. McCrudden who treat control and accountability as synonyms: *Regulation and Public Law* (1987) 35–45.

4 P. Day and R. Klein suggest that holding to account is always likely to be premised upon some capacity to control: *Accountabilities: Five Public Services* (1987) 227–9. G. Craig, a public lawyer, argues for the retention of a distinction between control and accountability: *Administrative Law* (3rd edn., 1994) 88–9.

5 B. Stone, 'Administrative Accountability in the 'Westminster' Democracies: Towards a New Conceptual Framework' (1995) 8 *Governance* 505.

6 Notwithstanding the importance accorded to the concept of accountability in contemporary political and legal discourse, neither A.V. Dicey, *An Introduction to the Study of the Law of the Constitution* (10th edn., 1959) nor I. Jennings, *The Law and the Constitution* (5th edn., 1959) showed much interest in the accountability in these terms.

7 Stone, op. cit., n. 5, p. 506.

Setting out an agenda for the reform of public law in Britain in the mid-1980s, Martin Partington called on public lawyers to develop extended conceptions of accountability in order to be able to cope better with the transformation of the British state.[8] Subsequently public lawyers have paid more attention to accountability mechanisms going beyond the parliament and the courts, including grievance-handling, audit and internal review.[9] But such analysis has persisted in a linear and partial view of accountability, and been overtaken by the new challenges presented to public law by transformations in public administration associated with the New Public Management (NPM) revolution, 'a strategy driven and fashioned almost entirely by a political-economic impetus and with virtually no legal or constitutional consciousness'.[10]

This article deploys a concept of 'extended accountability' to argue that the fragmentation of the public sector associated with public sector reforms, loosely referred to under the rubric of 'the regulatory state', has made more transparent the existing dense networks of accountability associated with both public and private actors concerned with the delivery of public services. Traditional accountability mechanisms are part, but only part of these complex networks, which have the potential to ensure that service providers may be effectively required to account for their activities.

DEFINING AND MAPPING ACCOUNTABILITY

Accountability is the duty to give account for one's actions to some other person or body. Normanton once offered a somewhat more expansive definition:

> a liability to reveal, to explain, and to justify what one does; how one discharges responsibilities, financial or other, whose several origins may be political, constitutional, hierarchical or contractual.[11]

The concept of accountability has traditionally been drawn somewhat narrowly by public lawyers, to encompass the formal duties of public bodies to account for their actions to ministers, Parliament, and to courts. Changes in accountability structures since the Second World War have resulted in a recognition of some extended forms of accountability, as

8 M. Partington, 'The Reform of Public Law in Britain: Theoretical Problems and Practical Considerations' in McAuslan and McEldowney, op. cit., n. 2, p. 196.

9 See, generally, C. Harlow and R. Rawlings, *Law and Administration* (1st edn., 1984, 2nd edn., 1997). On grievance-handlers, see M. Seneviratne, *Ombudsmen in the Public Sector* (1994); on audit see F. White and K. Hollingsworth, *Audit, Accountability and Government* (1999); on internal review, see R. Sainsbury, 'Administrative Justice: Discretion and Procedure in Social Security Decision Making' in *The Uses of Discretion*, ed. K. Hawkins (1992), and J. Hanna, 'Internal Resolution of N.H.S. Complaints' (1995) 3 *Medical Law Rev.* 177.

10 M. Loughlin, *Public Law and Political Theory* (1992) 260.

11 E.L Normanton, 'Public Accountability and Audit: A Reconnaissance' in Smith and Hague, op. cit., n. 1, p. 311.

courts have been supplemented by a growing number of tribunals (for example, in the immigration and social security domains) and new or revamped administrative agencies such as grievance-handlers and public audit institutions have played a greater role in calling public bodies to account.[12] Simultaneously Parliament has enhanced its capacity for holding ministers and officials to account through the development of select committee structures,[13] in some cases linked to new oversight bodies such as the Parliamentary ombudsman and the National Audit Office.[14]

It is helpful to keep distinct the three sets of accountability questions: 'who is accountable?'; 'to whom?'; and 'for what?'. With the 'who is accountable?' question, the courts have been willing to review all decisions involving the exercise of public power, even where exercised by bodies in private ownership.[15] In the utilities sectors the exercise of public privileges, such as monopoly rights, by private companies carry with them responsibilities to account for their activities, both in domestic fora and EC law. In some instances, the receipt of public funds by private bodies renders recipients liable to public accountability through audit mechanisms.[16] Considerable attention has been paid to this issue in the literature, with a consensus for the view that simple distinctions between private actors (not publicly accountable) and public actors (subject to full public accountability) are thus not sustainable.[17]

12 For example, Craig, op. cit., n. 4 , pp. 88–9 uses a concept of traditional accountability to refer to accountability of public sector organizations to ministers, parliamentary select committees, and the Parliamentary Commissioner for Administration (the Ombudsman). A helpful taxonomy of traditional accountability mechanisms in United Kingdom government is found in P. Birkinshaw, I. Harden, and N. Lewis, *Government by Moonlight* (1990) app. 2. An excellent account of the development of the Parliamentary Ombudsman's jurisdiction, the development of audit, and the rise of the courts in reviewing administrative decisions is D. Woodhouse, *In Pursuit of Good Administration* (1997).

13 G. Drewry (ed.), *The New Select Committees* (2nd edn., 1989); N. Lewis notes the parliamentary Public Accounts Committee has been pre-eminent in this aspect of the development of Parliament's capacity for calling public bodies to account, in particular because of its relationship with the National Audit Office which publishes reports which form the basis for subsequent PAC investigations: 'Regulating Non-Government Bodies: Privatization, Accountability, and the Public Private Divide' in *The Changing Constitution*, eds. J. Jowell and D. Oliver (2nd edn., 1989) 228–9.

14 M. Elliott argues that in the financial sphere it was government not Parliament which led reforms in the accountability for public expenditure, as the relative financial autonomy of nationalized industries and local authorities became intolerable due to the fiscal problems faced by government from the mid-1970s: 'The Control of Public Expenditure' in Jowell and Oliver, id., p. 188.

15 *R.* v. *Panel on Takeovers and Mergers ex p. Datafin* [1987] Q.B. 815. See, generally, J. Black, 'Constitutionalizing Self-Regulation' (1996) 59 *Modern Law Rev.* 24.

16 White and Hollingsworth, op. cit., n. 9, pp. 88–9.

17 Lewis, op. cit., n. 13; Black, op. cit., n. 15; J. Freeman, 'Collaborative Governance in the Administrative State' (1997) 45 *University of California Law Rev.* 1; M. Aronson, 'A Public Lawyer's Response to Privatisation and Outsourcing' in *The Province of Administrative Law*, ed. M. Taggart (1997); J. McLean, 'Intermediate Associations and the State' in Taggart, id.; G. Teubner, 'After Privatization? The Many Autonomies of Private Law' (1998) 51 *Current Legal Problems* 393.

The 'to whom?' question has often been mingled with the 'for what?' question, for example in the distinction between legal accountability (to the courts in respect of the juridical values of fairness, rationality and legality) and political accountability (to ministers and to Parliament or other elected bodies such as local authorities and via these institutions ultimately to the electorate). Furthermore, while it might be helpful to think of 'administrative accountability' as accountability to administrative bodies such as grievance holders and auditors, in fact these mechanisms for accountability have conventionally been distinguished, with administrative accountability only indicating the former, while financial accountability is used for the latter.

Separating the 'to whom?' and 'for what?' we find three broad classes within each category. Thus accountability may be rendered to a higher authority ('upwards accountability'), to a broadly parallel institution ('horizontal accountability') or to lower level institutions and groups (such as consumers) ('downwards accountability').[18] The range of values for which accountability is rendered can be placed in three categories: economic values (including financial probity and value for money (VFM)); social and procedural values (such as fairness, equality, and legality); continuity/security values (such as social cohesion, universal service, and safety).[19] Figure 1 sets out the possible configurations of the 'to whom?' and 'for what?' questions, producing nine possible pairs of co-ordinates.

The final remark to be made about traditional approaches to accountability mechanisms is that public lawyers almost universally regard them as inadequate.[20] This dissatisfaction exists notwithstanding the remarkable expansion of accountability mechanisms applied to the United Kingdom public sector in recent years.[21] It is rarely possible to discern how adequacy

18 This distinction between 'downward', 'upwards', and 'outwards' accountability is made by H. Elcock, 'What Price Citizenship? Public Management and the Citizen's Charter' in *The Citizen's Charter*, ed. J. Chandler (1997) 33–7. Birkinshaw's (op. cit., n. 2, p. 153) distinction between vertical and horizontal accountability is also helpful, but I have split the vertical accountability into the distinct upwards and downwards forms. An alternative way to classify the 'to whom?' question is set out by Stone, op. cit., n. 5, pp. 510–11 and 522, in a five-fold classification. Thus, he splits 'upwards accountability' into Parliamentary control and judicial and quasi-judicial review; 'horizontal accountability' into constituency relations and managerialism, and has market mechanisms in what I call the 'downwards accountability' strand.

19 I base this classification on C. Hood, 'A Public Management for All Seasons' (1991) 69 *Public Administration* 3,11. See, also, C. Harlow, 'Public Service, Market Ideology and Citizenship' in *Public Services and Citizenship in European Law*, eds. M. Freedland and S. Sciarra (1998) 51–2.

20 Representative of this view is C. Graham, *Is There a Crisis in Regulatory Accountability?* (1995, reproduced in R. Baldwin, C. Scott, and C. Hood, *Reader on Regulation* (1998)) who argues that if there is a crisis of accountability in respect of the utilities sectors this is simply a product of a wider problem of poor accountability structures in the United Kingdom. See, also, Woodhouse, op. cit., n. 12, p. 37.

21 R. Baldwin and M. Cave, for example, note with approval the development of the select committee structures within the House of Commons, but also suggest that its capacity to call ministers and officials to account is limited due to lack of time, resources, and expertise: *Understanding Regulation* (1999) 288.

For what? **To whom?**	Economic Values	Social/Procedural Values	Continuity/ Security Values
'Upwards' accountability	Of departments to treasury for expenditure	Of administrative decision-makers to courts/ tribunals	Of utility companies to regulators
'Horizontal' accountability	Of public bodies to external and internal audit for probity and VFM	Review of decisions by grievance-handlers	Third-party accreditation of safety standards
'Downwards' accountability	Of utility companies to financial markets	Of public/ privatized service providers to users	Consultation requirements re: universal service requirements

Figure 1. Examples of linkages between values and accountability institutions

is actually being assessed. In its narrowest form, an adequate accountability system would ensure that all public bodies act in ways which correspond with the core juridical value of legality, and thus correspond with the democratic will.[22] Such a Diceyan conception of accountability was already in severe difficulty within Dicey's lifetime as discretionary authority was more widely dispersed with the growth of the welfare state. Even with the extension of juridical concerns to encompass rationality and fairness in decision making, and thus concerns to improve the quality of discretionary decisions,[23] this narrow model is also very weak at holding public bodies to account for decisions which affect the collectivity, but have little bearing on the welfare of any individual.[24] A broader approach might look for correspondence with a range of other values, such as value for money or openness. But such substantive tests of the effectiveness of accountability mechanisms create difficulties of measurement and do not indicate any appropriate way to recognize the conflict between desired values which is inevitable within particular domains.

22 This standard seems to be at the core of D. Woodhouse's 'public sector model of good administration', which she argues is being displaced by the New Public Management: op. cit., n. 12, p. 37. See, also, J. Jowell, 'The Rule of Law Today' in Jowell and Oliver, op. cit. (3rd edn., 1994), n. 13, p. 63.

23 Sainsbury, op. cit., n. 9, pp. 305–6.

24 Birkinshaw, op. cit., n. 2, p. 159.

We are said to live in the age of the regulatory state. This refers to a shift in the style of governance away from the direct provision of public services, associated with the welfare state, and towards oversight of provision of public services by others.[25] This shift is, in part, a response to the recognition that 'total control' models of state activity fail to deliver desired outcomes. The problem can be expressed in a number of ways: the limited capacity of central-state institutions to know what is best provided by state intervention[26]; the tendency of highly active states towards fiscal crisis[27]; the risk that state actors will be diverted from pursuit of public interest outcomes to the exercise of public power for the pursuit of narrower private interests[28]; and the limited capacity of the instruments of state activity (and notably law) to effect change in social and economic systems.[29]

The response to these disparate concerns has been a withdrawal of central-state institutions from much 'operational' activity (a trend mirrored in local government, and to a lesser extent in other public institutions such as the National Health Service), with the reservation to the centre of certain policy tasks, and a marked expansion in central oversight mechanisms.[30] In Osborne and Gaebler's phrase, this is a shift from rowing to steering.[31] Figure 2 identifies the main characteristics of regulatory state governance and offers examples.

The most obvious and fundamental feature of regulatory state governance is fragmentation of responsibility for provision and oversight of public services such as prisons and telecommunications. With prisons, the welfare-state model was reflected by the monolithic structure of the Prisons Department within the Home Office, responsible not only for its main tasks of containing and rehabilitating prisoners, but also the inspection and grievance-handling functions over its own service. Fragmentation of the

25 G. Majone, 'The Rise of the Regulatory State in Western Europe' (1994) 17 *West European Politics* 77; F. McGowan and H. Wallace, 'Towards a European Regulatory State' (1996) 3 *J. of European Public Policy* 56; M. Loughlin and C. Scott, 'The Regulatory State' in *Developments in British Politics* 5, eds. P. Dunleavy, A. Gamble, I. Holliday, and G. Peele (1997).

26 F. Hayek, *Law, Liberty and Legislation Vol. 2* (1976) 1–2.

27 J. O'Connor, *The Fiscal Crisis of the State* (1973); C. Offe, *Contradictions of the Welfare State* (1984). A more detailed examination of the linkage between fiscal crisis and accountability mechanisms in the United Kingdom is provided by Elliott, op. cit., n. 14.

28 J. Buchanan and G. Tullock, *The Calculus of Consent* (1962); G. Stigler, 'The Economic Theory of Regulation' (1971) *Bell J. of Economics and Management Science* 3.

29 N. Luhmann, *The Differentiation of Society* (1982); G. Teubner, 'Juridification: Concepts, Aspects, Limits Solutions' in *Juridification of Social Spheres*, ed. G. Teubner (1987).

30 C. Hood and C. Scott, 'Bureaucratic Regulation and New Public Management: Mirror-Image Developments?' (1996) 23 *J. of Law and Society* 321; J. McEldowney, 'The Control of Public Expenditure' in Jowell and Oliver, op. cit. (3rd edn., 1994), n. 13, p. 206.

31 D. Osborne and T. Gaebler, *Reinventing Government* (1992).

Characteristics	Examples
1. Separation of policy from operation	NHS internal market Next Steps agencies Contracting out/market testing Utilities privatization
2. Creation of free-standing regulatory institutions	Utilities regulators (for example, OFTEL, OFGEM, OFWAT, OFREG) National Audit Office, Audit Commission Prisons Inspectorate, Social Services Inspectorate Service First Unit, Better Regulation Unit Financial Services Authority
3. Increased formality/shift from discretion to rules	Financial services Service First (formerly Citizen's Charter)

Figure 2. Main characteristics of regulatory state developments

United Kingdom prisons sector has taken a number of forms. First, there was in 1993 a separation within the Home Office of responsibility for policy (which is reserved to Ministers and their rump civil servants in Queen Anne's Gate) and responsibility for operational matters which has been delegated, via a 'framework document', to the Prison Service, legally still part of the Home Office, but located separately and with its own chief executive. Second, there has been a policy of contracting out the operation of prisons by a variety of mechanisms to private companies under legislation passed in 1991.[32] Additionally the inspection function was separated from the Prisons Department in 1981, though maintained within the Home Office, and a separate grievance-handling mechanism (the Prisons Ombudsman) established in 1993.

A different form of fragmentation has occurred in the telecommunications sector. Within the welfare-state model the key actors responsible were the minister and a public corporation, British Telecom, the board of which was appointed by and answerable directly to the minister. The minister was accountable in the legal, financial, political, and administrative senses noted above (Figure 3, left hand side). Fragmentation in telecoms is a product of policies of privatization of BT (1984), re-regulation of the sector through the creation of a semi-independent regulator, OFTEL (1984),

32 Criminal Justice Act 1991, ss. 84–8; Criminal Justice Act (Contracted Out Prisons) Order 1992 (S.I. no. 1656); R. Harding, *Private Prisons and Public Accountability* (1997).

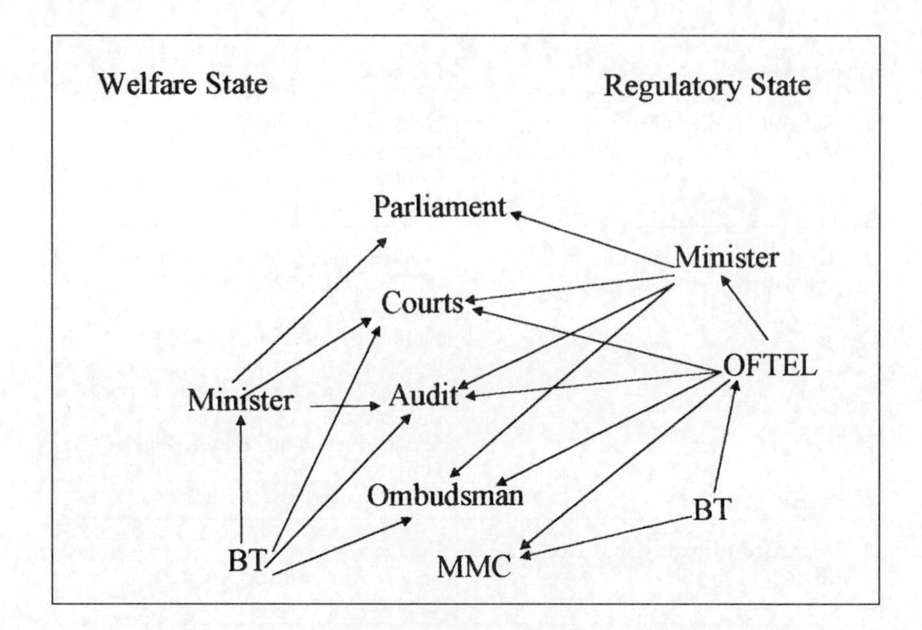

Figure 3. Accountability for provision of telecoms services 1. A public lawyer's model

and liberalization, under which many new firms have entered the market, particularly since 1992.[33]

Some public lawyers suggest that the transparency and need for specification of service standards associated with such innovations as creation of executive agencies and contracting out may 'sharpen accountability by defining goals, setting targets and monitoring performance.'[34] Such sharpened accountability may support traditional parliamentary oversight, but is more likely to enhance accountability to other, intermediate institutions. Furthermore it seems clear that fragmentation is more a cause of concern than satisfaction both to public lawyers and to labour lawyers.[35] The role of traditional accountability mechanisms appears to be diminished, it is no longer clear who is accountable, and there are problems with tracing the accountability linkages to the organizations who do the holding to account.[36]

33 M. Cave, 'The Evolution of Telecommunications Regulation in the UK' (1997) 41 *European Economic Rev.* 691.

34 Craig, op. cit., n. 4, p. 110.

35 Interestingly among the most anxious are scholars combining interests in public law and labour law: G. Morris, 'Fragmenting the State: Implications for Accountability for Employment Practices in Public Services' [1999] *Public Law* 64–83; M. Freedland, 'Government by Contract and Public Law' [1994] *Public Law* 86–104.

36 C. Harlow, 'Accountability, New Public Management, and the Problems of the Child Support Agency' (1999) 26 *J. of Law and Society* 150.

Returning to the telecommunications example, privatization of BT removed it from the sphere of the orthodox mechanisms of Parliamentary, legal, administrative, and financial accountability, apparently replacing these mechanisms with accountability to a regulatory agency for compliance with licence conditions (Figure 3, right hand side). The new regulator, OFTEL is subject to traditional mechanisms of legal, financial, and administrative accountability and additionally has to present an annual report to the minister,[37] and refer its proposals on modifying licence conditions to a third party, the Monopolies and Mergers Commission (MMC[38]) if the licensee does not consent to them.[39]

With prisons, the extent of accountability of the minister and the chief executive is blurred.[40] Under the last Conservative administration ministers required the chief executive of the Prison Service to answer parliamentary questions about prisons where they were deemed to relate to 'operational matters'[41] causing considerable frustration to parliamentarians who felt unable to pin responsibility on anyone. The Labour government elected in 1997 relocated responsibility for answering such questions with the minister.

Contracting out raises similar issues for advocates of traditional accountability models.[42] With prisons neither the directors of contracted-out prisons nor the chief executives of the companies employing them are directly accountable to Parliament (though this is true for governors of publicly

37 Telecommunications Act 1984, s. 55.

38 The Monopolies and Mergers Commission has been reformed and re-titled the Competition Commission under the Competition Act 1998, s. 45.

39 Telecommunications Act 1984, ss. 12–15.

40 This is a criticism extended more generally to the development of Next Steps or executive agencies by specialists in both public law and public administration. Woodhouse, op. cit., n. 12, p. 9 is critical of the distinction argued for by the Cabinet Office of a distinction between responsibility, which often lies with officials in executive agencies, and accountability which remains with the minister. Craig, op. cit., n. 4, p. 91 cites Drewry and Butcher for the proposition that ministers have used Next Steps agencies to delegate responsibility while retaining a monopoly over accountability to Parliament.

41 Craig, id., p. 91.

42 For M. Hunt, focusing on problems of legal accountability, the worry is about 'the capacity of English public law to respond appropriately to contractualisation by ensuring that constitutional values are observed by private actors performing public functions.' M. Hunt, 'Constitutionalism and the Contractualisation of Government in the United Kingdom' in Taggart, op. cit., n. 17, p. 38. But, chiming with some of the themes of this article, he hopes that the courts will be able to adapt, taking up an opportunity 'to assert their general public law principles over all exercises of power, regardless of the source of the power.' (at p. 38). Thus, he puts the need for accountability of private actors for exercises of public power centre stage. See also Dawn Oliver's attempts to express the common values underlying public and private law: 'The Underlying Values of Public and Private Law' in Taggart, id.; 'Common Values in Public and Private Law and the Public/Private Divide' [1997] *Public Law* 630; *Common Values and the Public-Private Divide* (1999). See, also, Freedland, op. cit., n. 35. Freedland is perhaps most representative of those so wedded to traditional accountability mechanisms (in this case legal accountability of contractors) that they downplay the potential for other mechanisms to act as functional substitutes (see, especially, pp. 101–4). See, also, Woodhouse, op. cit., n. 12, p. 14.

operated prisons too), though they are subject to each of the conventional forms of legal, financial, and administrative accountability mechanisms for the public sector. We return to the analysis of the prisons and telecommunications sectors in the next section of this article, to show how the (inadequate and possibly diminishing) traditional accountability mechanisms are being supplemented by new forms which enable us to conceive of an 'extended accountability' applying to actors within these policy domains.

EXTENDED ACCOUNTABILITY

The fragmentation of responsibility and accountability associated with the regulatory state has brought with it important new developments in all three of the dimensions of accountability discussed earlier (who? for what? to whom?). Indeed, extending accountability (of various forms) to actors previously immune, extending the range of values accounted for, and introducing new and more formal bodies for calling to account are central, instrumental features of regulatory governance. If we think of traditional accountability as encompassing the 'upwards' mechanisms of accountability to ministers, Parliament, and courts, with some recognition of the more formal horizontal mechanisms (such as grievance-handlers and auditors) then it is possible to conceive of a concept of 'extended accountability' within which traditional accountability is only part of a cluster of mechanisms through which public bodies are in fact held to account.[43]

We need to be clear that the extended accountability structures identified in this article, while they do not correspond to a traditional public law model, equally are not simply the product of an alternative neo-liberal model.[44] To be sure, the neo-liberal model of accountability through

43 Klein and Day contrast simple modern models of accountability (loosely approximating to the traditional accountability of public lawyers) with complex modern models of accountability which recognize both the fragmentation of traditional service delivery mechanisms (for example, through contracting out) but also new accountability mechanisms associated with them (for example, through contractual relations between service provider and purchaser and between service provider and professional bodies): Klein and Day, op. cit., n. 4, p. 11. Mark Freedland recognizes also a potential for extended accountability in his critique of the Private Finance Initiative (PFI – by which private sector funds are brought into public sector capital projects by means of a leasing by private organizations to the public sector). He suggests that the key issue is amenability of PFI to parliamentary and judicial control but that other mechanisms of accountability, notably 'open government mechanisms are sufficiently well-developed in this context so as substantially to supplement and reinforce the more traditional mechanisms of accountability'. M. Freedland, 'Public Law and Private Finance – Placing the Private Finance Initiative in a Public Law Frame' [1998] *Public Law* 288, 294–5. See, also, M. Aronson, 'A Public Lawyer's Response to Privatisation and Outsourcing' in Taggart, op. cit., n. 17.

44 Woodhouse, op. cit., n. 12, p. 58; L. Deleon, 'Accountability in a "Reinvented Government"' (1998) 76 *Public Administration* 539.

market mechanisms has been important. We need only think of the creation of internal markets (for example in the National Health Service), the changes to accountability for local service provision through the introduction of Compulsory Competitive Tendering (CCT),[45] encouraging users to hold service providers to account through league tables and enforceable quality standards, and the introduction of capital market disciplines through privatization. Such market or 'downwards accountability' structures are often characterized by a lack of distinctive normative content, effectively leaving the 'for what?' question to be filled in by the 'discovery procedure' of competition.[46] But the development of 'downwards accountability' mechanisms has not displaced the more traditional accountability mechanisms described above.[47] Market accountability forms have frequently been laid over hierarchical structures.[48] The investigation of any particular policy domain reveals complex structures of extended accountability, best characterized as hybrid in character.[49]

The extended mechanisms of accountability in the regulatory state are not linear in the way anticipated either by the public law literature[50] or

45 K. Walsh, N. Deakin, P. Smith, P. Spurgeon, and N. Thomas, *Contracting for Change: Contracts in Health, Social Care and Other Local Government Services* (1997); P. Vincent-Jones, 'The Regulation of Contractualisation in Quasi-Markets for Public Service' [1999] *Public Law* 304.

46 F. Hayek, *Law, Legislation and Liberty, Vol. 3* (1979) 67–70.

47 We may note also that 'downwards accountability' is not restricted to market forms. Hood's egalitarian model of public management anticipates the maximization of what he calls 'face-to face' accountability mechanisms, which include election of officials, and scrutiny of their conduct in community fora: C. Hood, *The Art of the State* (1997) 127–8. It seems fair to say that market mechanisms of downwards accountability have received more emphasis in the British NPM revolution, though recent commitments by the new Labour government indicate a tendency towards more participation in standard setting among user groups and employee groups in the Service First programme than was found in the Citizen's Charter programme which it replaces: C. Scott, 'Regulation Inside Government: Re-Badging the Citizen's Charter' [1999] *Public Law* 595.

48 Competing norms and institutions have often arisen over particular sectors because of a reluctance or lack of capacity for following through on the logic of liberal reforms. A classic example is provided by rail privatization which was intended to free rail operating companies to decide on the frequency with which they ran trains on particular routes according to commercial criteria (and thus introducing downwards accountability to the market). However, this aspect of rail operation was also to be regulated, and to quell anxiety in Parliament, the minister issued statutory directions to the regulator, the Office of Passenger Rail Franchising (OPRAF), indicating that he should approve frequencies of trains only where they did not deviate unduly from 'minimum service levels' based on previous, publicly operated timetables. When judicially reviewed, OPRAF was held to have acted outside the terms of these directions in approving timetables which deviated too much from previous timetables. See *R.* v. *Director of Passenger Rail Franchising ex p. Save Our Railways*, (*Independent*, 20 December 1995); Baldwin and Cave, op. cit., n. 21, p. 301.

49 Teubner, op. cit., n. 17, p. 406.

50 Woodhouse, op. cit., n. 12, pp. 8–9 notes the development of supplementary mechanisms of accountability, for example to consumers, and of chief executives of Next Steps agencies to ministers, but is critical of the fact that this brings us no closer to her ideal of a 'coherent set of arrangements'.

neo-liberal prescription.[51] Rather, they are premised on the existence of complex networks of accountability and functional equivalents within the British state structure.[52] Close exploration of the structures of extended accountability in the United Kingdom reveals at least two different models which have developed which feature overlapping and fuzzy responsibility and accountability: interdependence and redundancy. No domain is likely to precisely correspond to one or other of these models. There are likely to be elements of both identifiable in many policy domains but, for reasons of clarity, the examples used in the following sections are presented in somewhat simplified and ideal-type form.

1. *Interdependence*

The identification and mapping out of relationships of interdependence within policy domains has been one of the key contributions of the recent pluralist literature in public policy.[53] The identification of interdependence has important implications for accountability structures. Interdependence provides a model of accountability in which the formal parliamentary, judicial, and administrative methods of traditional accountability are supplemented by an extended accountability. Interdependent actors are dependent on each other in their actions because of the dispersal of key resources of authority (formal and informal), information, expertise, and capacity to bestow legitimacy such that each of the principal actors has constantly to account for at least some of its actions to others within the space, as a precondition to action.[54] The executive generally, and the Treasury in particular, has long had a central role in calling public bodies to account over a range of values, in a way that is often less transparent in the case of the more dignified, but arguably less efficient parliamentary mechanisms of accountability.[55] But these less formal and more hidden accountability mechanisms extend well beyond the capacities of central government, extending potentially to any actors, public or private, within a domain with the practical capacity to make another actor, public or private, account for its actions. Within the pluralist political science literature

51 Summarized in id., p. 46 as the 'New Public Management Model of Good Administration'.
52 Birkinshaw, op. cit., n. 2, pp. 165–6; N. Lewis, 'De-Legalisation in Britain in the 1980s' in McAuslan and McEldowney, op. cit., n. 2, p. 114.
53 See, for example, D. Marsh and R. Rhodes (eds.), *Policy Networks in British Government* (1991); M. Thatcher, 'The Development of Policy Network Analyses – From Modest Origins to Overarching Framework (1998) 10 *J. of Theoretical Politics* 389.
54 Compare D. Galligan, *Discretionary Powers* (1986) 128–40 for a discussion of the practical constraints on the discretion exercised by administrative actors. D.C Hague discussed the role of 'social accountability' in supplementing formal accountability mechanisms, to connote circumstances where there was some form of accounting to a community affected by decisions in a particular policy domain: 'The Ditchely Conference: A British View' in Smith and Hague, op. cit., n. 1, p. 76.
55 Elliott, op. cit., n. 14, p. 191.

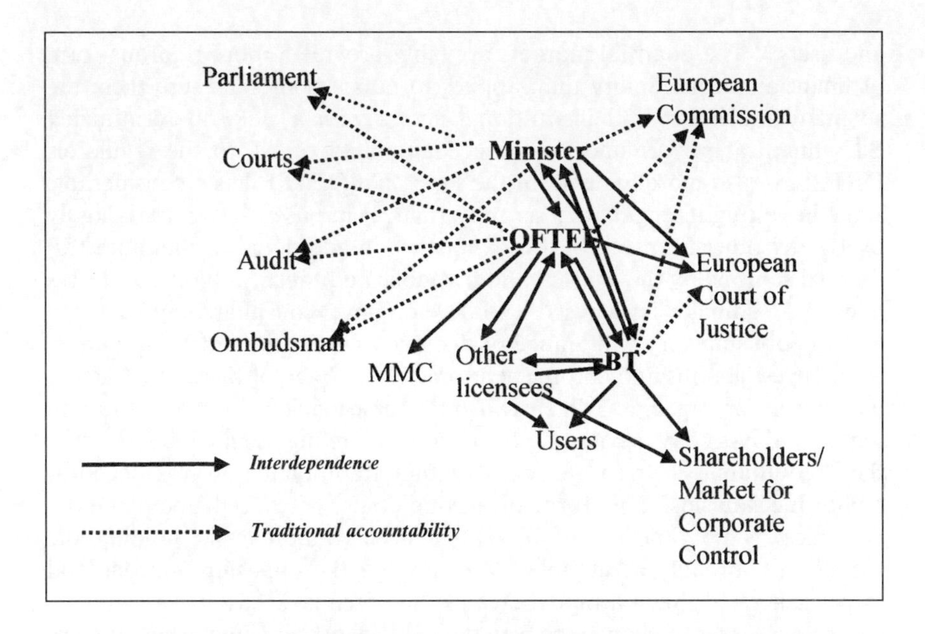

Figure 4. Accountability for provision of telecoms services 2. Interdependence model

this conception is sometimes referred to as 'constituency relations' or 'mutual accountability'.[56] Indeed it may be that the simple monolithic structures presented as the welfare state model are too simple, that they disguise intricate internal and opaque webs of control and accountability that are functionally equivalent to the new instruments of the regulatory state, but are less formal and transparent.[57] Among the more obvious examples were the consumer committees established for the nationalized industries with a brief to hold those public corporations to account from a collective consumer viewpoint.[58]

This model is exemplified by the United Kingdom telecommunications sector (figure 4). Figure 4 shows that though BT is subject to diminished upwards accountability to parliament and courts (noted above), it has a new forms of accountability in each dimension – upwards to a new regulator, horizontally to the mechanisms of corporate governance, and downwards to shareholders (and possibly also the market for corporate control)

56 Stone, op. cit., n. 5, p. 517.

57 For example, Hugh Heclo and Aaron Wildavsky's ethnographic study of Whitehall in the early 1970s found a village life regulated by informal accountability mechanisms of peer review: *The Private Government of Public Money* (1974). Day and Klein's study of accountability in five public services in the mid-1980s also found more complex models of accountability than a simple monolithic structure might imply: op. cit., n. 4.

58 Lewis, op. cit., n. 13, pp. 236–7; T. Prosser, *Nationalized Industries and Public Control* (1986).

and users.[59] The financial markets arguably provide a more rigorous form of financial accountability than applies to public bodies because there are so many individual and institutional actors with a stake in scrutinizing BT's financial performance.[60] The accountability of BT to the regulator, OFTEL, is also more focused, in the sense that OFTEL has a considerable stake in getting its regulatory scrutiny right, being itself scrutinized closely by BT, by other licensees, and by ministers, in additional to the more traditional scrutiny by the courts[61] and by public audit institutions.[62] OFTEL's quest for legitimacy has caused it to develop novel consultative procedures, and to publish a very wide range of documents on such matters as competition investigations and enforcement practices.[63] Each of these other actors has powers or capacities which constrain the capacities of the others and require a day-to-day accounting for actions, more intense in character than the accountability typically applied within traditional upwards accountability mechanisms. This form of accountability, premised upon interdependence, is not linear, but more like a servo-mechanism holding the regime in a broadly acceptable place through the opposing tensions and forces generated. Such a model creates the potential to use the shifting of balances in order to change the way the model works in any particular case.

2. *Redundancy*

A second extended accountability model is that of redundancy, in which overlapping (and ostensibly superfluous) accountability mechanisms reduce the centrality of any one of them. In common parlance, redundancy is

59 C. Hall, C. Scott, and C. Hood, *Telecommunications Regulation: Culture, Chaos and Interdependence Inside the Regulatory Process* (2000) ch. 5.

60 C. Scott, 'Privatization, Control and Accountability' in *Corporate Control and Accountability*, eds. J. McCahery, S. Picciotto, and C. Scott (1993).

61 *R.* v. *Director General of Telecommunications Ex p. Cellcom Ltd* (1999) 96(6) L.S.G. 31; *R.* v. *Director General of Telecommunications Ex p. British Telecommunications Plc*, (Q.B.D.) 20 December 1996; *Mercury Communications Ltd* v. *Director General of Telecommunications* 1996] 1 W.L.R. 48; [1996] 1 All E.R. 575; C. Scott, 'The Juridification of Regulatory Relations in the UK Utilities Sectors' in *Commercial Regulation and Judicial Review*, eds. J. Black, P. Muchlinski, and P. Walker (1998).

62 OFTEL has been subjected to a remarkable degree of scrutiny by the National Audit Office and consequently also by the parliamentary Public Accounts Committee: National Audit Office, *The Office of Telecommunications: Licence Compliance and Consumer Protection* HC 529 (1993); National Audit Office, *The Work of the Directors General of Telecommunications, Gas Supply, Water Services and Electricity Supply: National Audit Office* HC 645 (1996); National Audit Office, *Countering Anti-Competitive Behaviour in the Telecommunications Industry* HC 667 (1998).

63 Generally on this point, see J. Black, 'Talking about Regulation' [1998] *Public Law* 77 103–4. The interdependent relations of OFTEL in creating effective accountability are important notwithstanding recent evidence of a tightening of the traditional mechanisms of both juridical and audit accountability over OFTEL's activities: Hall, Scott, and Hood, op. cit., n. 59, ch. 5.

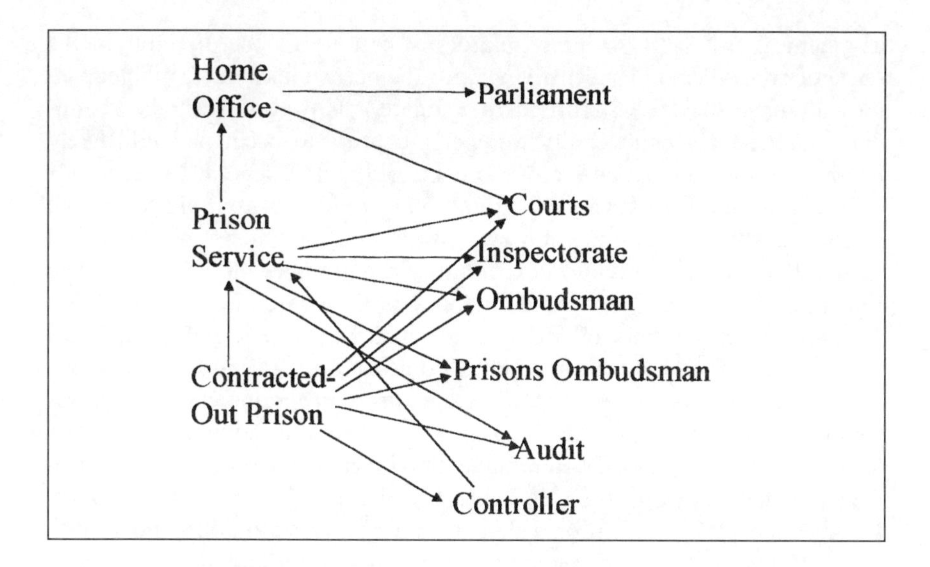

Figure 5. Accountability for prisons provision: redundancy model

represented by the 'belt and braces; approach, within which two independent mechanisms are deployed to ensure the system does not fail, both of which are capable of working on their own. Where one fails the other will still prevent disaster. Redundancy in failsafe mechanisms is a common characteristic of public sector activities generally, and can be threatened by privatization. Equally explicit concern about risks associated with change may cause redundancy to be built in to oversight structures. Redundancy can be an unintended effect of certain institutional configurations. In practice, examples of redundancy in accountability regimes appear to be a product of a mixture of design and contingency.

There are at least two forms to the redundancy model: traditional and multi-level governance. The traditional redundancy model is exemplified by the accountability mechanisms for contracted-out prisons in the United Kingdom (figure 5).[64] Directors of contracted-out prisons are subject to all the forms of accountability directed at publicly operated prisons: upwards (legal, to the courts); financial (to the National Audit Office)); and horizontal (to the Prisons Inspectorate, the Prisons Ombudsman, and prison visitors). But, contracted-out prisons are additionally subject to a further form of horizontal accountability with a requirement to account, day-to-day to an on-site regulator (called a controller), appointed by the Prison Service to monitor compliance with contract specification. Unusually within the prisons sector, controllers wield the capacity to levy formal sanctions for breach of contract. Some commentators have suggested that there is

64 C. Hood, C. Scott, O. James, T. Travers, and G. Jones, *Regulation Inside Government* (1999) 118.

a structural risk with on-site regulators of capture by the director, in the sense of controllers over-identifying with the needs and limits to the capacities of those they are supposed to regulate.[65] However, with the redundancy model of accountability were such capture to occur it would likely be identified by one or more of the others holding the director to account.[66]

The multi-level governance accountability model is exemplified by the mechanisms for accounting for expenditures made under jointly funded national and European Union expenditure programmes, notably under the European Structural Funds. Redundancy is built into the accountability mechanisms deliberately by EU decision makers, by requiring joint funding, and therefore ensuring that both domestic and EU audit institutions necessarily take an interest in single expenditure programmes within member states.[67] It will be seen from Figure 4 that there is a redundancy element to the United Kingdom telecommunications regime because of the involvement of the EC institutions in the oversight of EC competition policy. Infringements of competition rules are potentially actionable under both United Kingdom and EC regimes. The element of redundancy is likely to be enhanced as United Kingdom competition rules are aligned with those of the EC by the Competition Act 1998, and competition and utilities regulators exercise concurrent jurisdiction.[68]

The multi-level governance redundancy model of extended accountability is likely to see further development in the United Kingdom arising out the devolution of considerable powers to a new Scottish Parliament and Northern Irish and Welsh Assemblies. In each of these jurisdictions new executives and parliamentary/assembly committees have the potential to develop and reinvent the parliamentary oversight already exercised over United Kingdom-wide or multi-jurisdiction public functions.[69]

HARNESSING EXTENDED ACCOUNTABILITY AND BALANCING ITS NORMATIVE CONTENT

The two extended models of accountability identified in this article operate not in the linear fashion advocated by public lawyers, in which particular

65 Harding, op. cit., n. 32, pp. 42–50.

66 id., p. 160 recognizes the importance of the Chief Inspector of Prisons, though not other aspects of the accountability structure, in reducing what he sees as the considerable risks that contracted-out prisons regimes will be captured by private sector interests. Further redundancy is likely to be introduced in the United Kingdom by the extension of accountability in the downwards dimension with the drafting of a Prisoners' Charter proposed by the government: Cabinet Office, *Service First: The New Charter Programme* (1998) para. 4.22.

67 Hood et al., op. cit., n. 64, p. 175.

68 T. Prosser, 'Competition, Regulators and Public Service' in *The Competition Act: A New Era for UK Competition Law*, ed. B. Rodger (forthcoming).

69 R. Rawlings, 'The New Model Wales' (1998) 26 *J. of Law and Society* 461, 500–1.

institutions hold service providers to account for particular values. Rather, the various accountability networks which operate uniquely within each policy domain have the character of a complex system of checks and balances in which particular forms of behaviour are inhibited or encouraged by the overall balance in the system at any particular time. In practice it is possible to see numerous examples of 'opposed maximizers' holding one another in check and how changes in one aspect of an accountability regime affects the overall balance.[70] This analysis does not judge whether the outcomes in any particular system at any particular time in terms of accountability are negative or positive but, rather, offers a frame within which the mechanisms of accountability may be examined, and some idea as to how strategic interventions, through shifting of balances, might be made in order to correct a system which is malfunctioning (in terms of a failure to secure effective accountability).

Law is an important aspect of shifting balances in both the telecommunications and prisons sectors. The utilities regimes established on privatization have long been criticized for the inadequacy of their accountability mechanisms.[71] Liberalization in telecommunications tended to reduce the consensual nature of regulatory relations and has promoted increased incidences of judicial review and other litigation. The threat of judicial review, considered on its own, might be expected to act as a significant constraint on a regulator like OFTEL, and certainly there is evidence of such a constraining influence, found particularly in the way that major decision processes are built up with a clear eye on being able subsequently to demonstrate the fairness, rationality and legality of such procedures, and in some instances with frequent trips to counsel to seek opinions on how to draft policies in such a way as to be 'judge-proof'.[72] But, considered in the round, judicial review actions may reduce the power of others to hold OFTEL to account. Where BT uses its resources to challenge OFTEL by judicial review, this may reduce the capacity of other firms to hold OFTEL to account for its actions, as judicial review is seen to trump more immediate policy considerations. Other public bodies also may find that judicial review, paradoxically (and contrary to conventional administrative law wisdom), trumps policy. Following an unsuccessful action by BT to judicially review OFTEL's decision to introduce new controls on anti-competitive conduct, the Director-General of Telecommunications was able to see off the Public Accounts Committee's criticism of the licence modification that it would give him powers 'to become prosecutor, judge and jury' by pointing out:

70 A. Dunsire, 'Tipping the Balance: Autopoiesis and Governance' (1996) 28 *Administration and Society* 299, 312–4.

71 See the summary in Graham, op. cit., n. 20.

72 Hall, Scott, and Hood, op. cit., n. 59, ch. 9.

> The people who matter, the judges, have denied all of that, so it is not a matter of what I think or what the *Daily Telegraph* thinks, it is a matter of what the courts of the land have decided about what the Telecommunications Act means, how I should exercise the discretion and how I should pursue my duties under that Act. That issue is now resolved, and I hope that some of that language that you quote will go away.[73]

Balances of accountability are shifting in telecommunications in other ways. Accountability to consumers is likely to be enhanced through the creation of a separate Telecommunications Consumer Council.[74] Arguably, the more robust public oversight by ministers of the conduct of regulation by regulators enhances the accountability of such regulators to ministers. Since the election of the Labour government in 1997, the first rail regulator has been the subject matter of a number of public warnings in the media that the Secretary of State expected him to take a tougher line,[75] and the Director-General of the National Lottery was first publicly warned and then removed by the minister. Such unprecedented incidents must affect the perceptions of each of the utilities regulators of the accountability they owe to ministers.[76] The precise effect of such interventions on the overall accountability network remains to be seen.

With prisons, the development of litigation strategies has been both supportive of and supported by the work of the prisons humanity regulators, and notably the inspectorate and the ombudsman, the regulators providing better information which may be used in litigation, litigation providing more robust definitions of appropriate norms relating to the treatment of individual prisoners. The contracting out process too has had marked effects not only on the accountability of the contracted-out prisons themselves but also on the normative structure of oversight for prisons remaining subject to public operation. The more precise specification of standards associated with contracting out has spilled over into public prisons, giving a somewhat more precise normative structure for those involved in calling prisons to account,[77] while at the same time creating the potential for a form of 'yardstick competition' as bodies like the National Audit Office can directly compare the performance of comparable contracted-out and public prisons.[78]

73 Trade and Industry Select Committee, Third Report, *Telecommunications Regulation* HC (1996/97) 254, 48.

74 Department of Trade and Industry, *Consumer Councils: The Response to the Consultation* (1999). On the general argument that consumer capacities in the utilities sectors should be enhanced, see A. McHarg, 'Separation of Function and Regulatory Agencies: Dispute Resolution in the Privatized Utilities' in *Administrative Justice in the 21st Century*, eds. M. Harris and M. Partington (1999).

75 For example, the *Guardian*, 3 November 1997. John Swift QC subsequently resigned at the end of his five year contract as rail regulator.

76 Baldwin and Cave, op. cit., n. 21, pp. 292–3.

77 Hood et al., op. cit., n. 64, p. 126.

78 National Audit Office, *Report by the Comptroller and Auditor General: Wolds Remand Prison* (1994).

The challenge for public lawyers is to know when, where, and how to make appropriate strategic interventions in complex accountability networks to secure appropriate normative structures and outcomes. What I have in mind here is something like process of 'collibration' described by Andew Dunsire. Dunsire sees collibration as a stratagem common to a wide variety of processes by which balances are shifted to change the nature of the way that control systems (such as accountability mechanisms) work.[79] Such interventions may be applied to any of the three accountability parameters: who is accountable? for what? to whom? This offers the possibility of meeting Martin Loughlin's challenge for public law to 'adopt as its principal focus the examination of the manner in which the normative structures of law can contribute to the guidance, control and evaluation in government.'[80] The value of such changes may lie not directly in the development of a single accountability mechanism, but rather in the effects on the overall balance within the regime.[81] The logic of the argument presented here is that conflict and tension are inevitable within the complex accountability webs within any particular domain, and that the objective should not be to iron out conflict, but to exploit it to hold regimes in appropriate tension.

To take an example, within a redundancy model of accountability for contracted-out prisons, how do we ensure proper accountability for the range of values, such as humanity, efficiency, and security which might be deemed appropriate desiderata for a prisons regime? The orthodox answer would be to say that we have an inspector with a specific mandate to check on the humanity of prison regimes, and auditors to assess efficiency, and security people overseeing security. But this is only a partial answer. Within the redundancy model we have other mechanisms which directly or indirectly check on each of these values – the controller, company management, the Prisons Ombudsman, the European Committee for the Prevention of Torture, and the courts. These mechanisms are in tension with another, in the sense of having different concerns, powers, procedures, and culture, which generate competing agendas and capacities.[82] Within contracted-out prisons, corporate governance structures will hold directors to account for the expenditure of money, so that within an efficient redundancy system

79 Dunsire, op. cit., n. 70, pp. 318 ff. See, also, Normanton, op. cit., n. 11, p. 313 (referring to the 'readjustment' of the 'balance of accountability' and, bringing in the accountability of private actors, J. Braithwaite, 'On Speaking Softly and Carrying Big Sticks: Neglected Dimensions of a Republican Separation of Powers' (1997) 47 *University of Toronto Law J.* 305.

80 Loughlin, op. cit., n. 10, p. 264.

81 Compare Black, op. cit., n. 63, p. 105: She argued that 'there is a need to structure the distribution of authority and the forms and occasions of participation and accountability in such a way that they do not operate in conflict with each other or with the willingness and commitment of regulator and regulated alike to the conversation.'

82 Hood et al., op. cit., n. 64, p. 119.

enough money but no more than is necessary to provide a humane regime will be spent. We might expect periodically that value for money norms or security norms might inhibit the achievement of humanity norms. The solution would not necessarily be to crank up the humanity regime, but rather to apply techniques of selective inhibition to the other norm structures so that their pull on the overall system was diminished somewhat. This might, for example, be through changing financial incentives or oversight structures, or through enhancing access of prisoners to grievance-handlers or judicial review.

There are some rather obvious problems with relying on dense webs of accountability or functional equivalents to secure the achievement of key public law objectives in respect of governance regimes. Chief among these is a marked lack of transparency in the traditional informal arrangements of government, and in many of the new mechanisms such as contracting out,[83] and a lack of scope for broad participation in decision making.

As with other values over which accountability is sought, there have been marked changes in respect of transparency accountability. As noted above, NPM reforms of the United Kingdom public sector have increased transparency in some aspects of public service provision, such as quality and value for money. But, for the public lawyer, the difficulty lies in securing an overview of any policy domain, rather than a perspective on one set of values. NPM reforms, because they fragment responsibility, may threaten this general transparency. The Freedom of Information Bill introduced by the Labour government will make changes in all three facets of accountability for transparency, extending requirements to submit to the openness regime to various private actors, creating accountability for openness to a new commissioner (who will take over the responsibility for overseeing the code of practice on open government currently exercised by the Parliamentary Ombudsman),[84] and redefining the normative content with new rules on what information must be made available to the public. But this accountability mechanism does not have a monopoly even over the accountability for openness. Openness is likely to be an important value, to a lesser or greater extent, in the existing formal and informal accountability mechanisms which involve Parliament, ministers, agencies, courts, tribunals, auditors, and so on. The new regime is likely to bring changes to each of these other parts of the accountability structure, quite possibly shifting the balance towards openness values, and bolstering the requirements to account for openness in all parts of the domain. We may note however that one of the central mechanisms of accountability affecting agencies and

83 Lewis, op. cit., n. 52, p. 115.
84 Freedom of Information Bill, cl. 7.

non-departmental bodies, the informal influence of ministers (with 'lunch-table directives'[85]), is unlikely to be touched by the new openness regime.[86]

Other values are also being pursued by the Labour government with renewed vigour. The Cabinet office is both encouraging and policing the development of participatory structures for standard setting within the Service First programme (which replaces the Citizen's Charter programme) and has introduced a new co-ordination principle ('joined-up government') which is intended both to improve the co-ordination of policy across departments and to reduce the transaction costs for citizens dealing with the state.[87] Again, the effects of these interventions are not clearly predictable and public lawyers will want to monitor and evaluate them for their effects in shifting the normative balance within particular domains.

CONCLUSIONS

The transformation of public administration in the United Kingdom has made more transparent the dense networks of accountability within which public power is exercised. The constitutional significance of this observation is to suggest that there is a potential to harness these networks for the purposes of achieving effective accountability or control, even as public power continues to be exercised in more fragmented ways. Outstanding questions for this analysis are whether there are other models of accountability in the regulatory state not captured by the interdependence and redundancy models,[88] and whether it is possible to capture the complete set within an overall theory of extended accountability. Areas requiring further exploration are the role of voluntary organizations (such as prisons campaigners and consumer groups) and the media in rendering public and quasi-public bodies accountable.

Each of the two models of extended accountability discussed in this article presents difficulties for public lawyers and more generally. Neither model is directly 'programmable' with the public law norms (fairness, legality, rationality, and so on). Interventions to secure appropriate normative

85 Baldwin and McCrudden, op. cit., n. 3, p. 40.

86 An exception to this is in the utilities sectors, where the government has undertaken to publish ministerial guidance on social and environmental matters, making such ministerial influence more transparent: Department of Trade and Industry, *A Fair Deal for Consumers* (1998; Cm. 3898).There is some scepticism as to whether this measure will really reduce the extent to which ministers wield informal influence over agencies.

87 Cabinet Office, *Modernising Government* (1999; Cm. 4310).

88 Freedland, op. cit., n. 43, pp. 296–7 hints at a transparency model which includes the commitment of the Treasury to publish on its web-site a wide range of documents (including articulations of the regulatory framework) relating to the Private Finance Initiative. A problem with this transparency as a form of accountability is that it does not indicate to whom the Treasury and others are to be accountable, and, relatedly, indicates no conception of control.

outcomes must necessarily be indirect and unpredictable in their effects.[89] The interdependence model carries with it the risk that special interests, such as those of a particular firm or group of firms, may capture the regime through their overall weighting of power within it.[90] The redundancy model presents particular problems. If redundancy *per se* is a good characteristic for an accountability regime, it is difficult to calculate how much redundancy is sufficient and how to know when an additional layer of accountability is inefficient and to be removed. Equally, there is also the risk within a redundancy model of simultaneous failure of different parts of the system for the same reason. Where, for example, information is successfully hidden from more than one part of the accountability network, there is a risk of complete failure in respect of the matters for which that information is relevant.

Close observation of the structures of accountability in the regulatory state suggests that the public lawyer's concerns, premised upon an over-formal conception of accountability, if not unfounded are then neglectful of the complex webs of extended accountability which spring up in practice. Indeed, these extended accountability mechanisms already evidence a capacity to hold not only public but also private actors accountable for the exercise of power which is broadly public in character. Whilst not agreeing with Wilks and Freeman that it is possible to conceive of the accountability of a regulatory regime,[91] it is nevertheless helpful to think in terms of the *aggregate* accountability of each of the actors exercising power within a regime.[92]

89 Dunsire, op. cit., n. 70, p. 321.

90 Compare L. Hancher and M. Moran, 'Organising Regulatory Space' in *Capitalism, Culture and Regulation*, eds. L. Hancher and M. Moran (1989) 274.

91 S. Wilks, 'Utility Regulation, Corporate Governance, and the Amoral Corporation' in *Changing Regulatory Institutions in Britain and North America*, eds. S. Wilks and G.B. Doern (1998) at 140; J. Freeman, 'Private Parties, Public Functions and the New Administrative Law' (paper presented at the Law and Society Association Annual Conference, 1999) 47. See, also, Braithwaite, op. cit., n. 79.

92 See Hall, Scott, and Hood, op. cit., n. 59, ch. 5.

Journal of Law and Society
Volume 27, Number 1, March 2000
ISSN: 0263–323X, pp. 61–97

Governing after the Rights Revolution

Colin Harvey*

In this paper I explore the relevance of neo-republican thinking for current debates in constitutional law. In particular, I am interested in how deliberative forms of law and democracy might be grounded in real-world institutional contexts. My thesis is that the neo-republican model, underpinned as it is by the values of equality, participation, and accountability, has both explanatory and critical potential when exploring the voices, spaces, and processes of constitutionalism. I test this argument with reference to constitutional change in Northern Ireland. It is evident that equality is the core value in the settlement reached but it is in the combination of values that the potential and tensions will arise in the future. The provisions of the Northern Ireland Act 1998 on equality are useful examples of how law might be shaped to include the voices of affected groups in the process of enforcing change in public administration. Law's role in this process is, however, more problematic than is often assumed. In this, and in other aspects of the settlement, there are lessons for others who are presently reflecting on the constitutional future in the new devolutionary contexts.

INTRODUCTION

The United Kingdom, as part of a more comprehensive process of reform (and rather late in the day), is following other liberal democracies into the formal enactment of human rights guarantees.[1] This is the result of two

1 See J. Morison, 'The Case Against Constitutional Reform?' (1998) 25 *J. of Law and Society* 510, at 512: 'The reforms on offer at best would seem to bring the United Kingdom into line with other constitutions that were founded in the eighteenth and nineteenth centuries and are now beginning to feel their age.'

* *School of Law,The Queen's University, Belfast BT7 1NN, Northern Ireland*

This is based on a paper presented at the University of Michigan Law School, 5 October 1999. I would like to thank Professor John Morison for commenting on a draft of this paper and Professor Christopher McCrudden for encouraging me to look more closely at equality. Errors are mine alone.

developments. First, a political struggle by advocates of human rights to mainstream legal protection in the constitution and, second, the election of a government responsive to these demands.[2] Law's empire is presently being re-clothed and lawyers will have a new language in which to construct their arguments. Whether this will have a radical impact on the British constitution is yet to be seen.[3] There is much to learn from the success of this political campaign to give formal recognition to human rights. For it is always instructive to observe struggles for reform and how and why they succeed. While the strategic skills of the human rights movement is an interesting theme it will not be pursued in any depth. The concern here is to probe where we might venture after the 'rights revolution'.[4] The United Kingdom is currently experiencing a period of constitutional transition to what has been described as a form of 'quasi-federalism'.[5] This is not to overstate the significance of the constitutional reform project or to suggest that there is dearth of literature on new forms of governance.[6] That is patently not so. It is to give recognition to a problem that has been apparent for some time. The problem is reflected in the expressed desire of public lawyers for a perspective that possesses both explanatory and critical potential. There is a consensus of sorts that the old stories no longer possess the explanatory power they once did. New stories are being forwarded, some of which are explicitly meant to persuade institutional actors to change direction.[7] What is evident is that a partial conceptual framework will distort any practical analysis of change. If one is interested in addressing partiality then this requires an openness to new forms of constitutionalism that is occasionally lacking in the literature.[8] A critical model must be explicitly defended rather than assumed to exist free of normative commitments.

2 See D. Feldman, 'The Human Rights Act 1998 and Constitutional Principles' (1999) 19 *Legal Studies* 165; J. Young, 'The Politics of the Human Rights Act' (1999) 26 *J. of Law and Society* 27; I. Leigh, 'Horizontal Rights, the Human Rights Act and Privacy: Lessons from the Commonwealth' (1999) 48 *International and Comparative Law Q.* 57; K.D. Ewing, 'The Human Rights Act and Parliamentary Democracy' (1999) 62 *Modern Law Rev.* 79; M. Hunt, 'The Human Rights Act and Legal Culture: The Judiciary and the Legal Profession' (1999) 26 *J. of Law and Society* 86; M. Hunt, 'The "Horizontal Effect" of the Human Rights Act' [1998] *Public Law* 423

3 See R. Hazell, 'Reinventing the Constitution: Can the State Survive?' [1999] *Public Law* 84.

4 I borrow this title from C.R. Sunstein, *After the Rights Revolution: Reconceiving the Regulatory State* (1990) and recognize that he uses the term 'rights revolution' quite differently.

5 R. Hazell, 'The New Constitutional Settlement' in *Constitutional Futures: A History of the Next Ten Years*, ed. R. Hazell (1999) 230.

6 See, generally, R.A.W Rhodes, *Understanding Governance: Policy Networks, Governance, Reflexivity and Accountability* (1997). The absence of reference to social and economic rights in the constitutional reform debate is telling; see K.D. Ewing, 'Social Rights and Constitutional Law' [1999] *Public Law* 104.

7 For analysis of one in particular, see M. Loughlin, 'Rights Discourse and Public Law Thought in the United Kingdom' in *Rights and Democracy: Essays in United Kingdom-Canadian Constitutionalism*, ed. G.W. Anderson (1999) 193.

8 See, for example, E. Barendt, *An Introduction to Constitutional Law* (1998).

One of the continuing problems with new forms of constitutionalism is the failure to demonstrate how they might shape or provide tools to critique, political and legal practice. The focus of this paper is on Northern Ireland and the argument is that this provides a concrete example of how institutional structures can be created to facilitate deliberation and participation. In particular I use a case-study of constitutional change to test a conception of democratic law grounded in the value of equality. The argument advances in two basic stages. First, after surveying relevant literature I defend a conception of democratic law. This excursus is necessary in order to flesh out a conception of legality based on the value of equality. Any such argument in support of constitutionalism must confront some powerful criticism. The early stages of the paper are an attempt to survey the state of play but, in particular, I want to stress the importance of an argument I have advanced more fully elsewhere.[9] That is the importance of bringing neo-republican thinking into the debate on the future of United Kingdom constitutional law. Second, I explore constitutional reform in Northern Ireland in order to test the theory against practical developments on the ground. In particular, I focus on developments since the Belfast Agreement 1998 (the Agreement).[10] My thesis is that the constitutional settlement in Northern Ireland reflects a primary commitment to the value of equality. This value is fundamental to a defensible concept of neo-republicanism. This is not to argue that the settlement is unproblematic. There are aspects of the 'two communities' model which are questionable. Equality norms, of various types, structure the settlement reached. I argue that with enhanced democratic accountability and human rights guarantees the Agreement is based on a potentially instructive model of constitutionalism.

RENEGOTIATING CONSTITUTIONALISM

1. *The return of deliberative democracy*

The proliferation of perspectives is the most notable trend in recent thinking about constitutionalism and in public law generally.[11] Critical scholars have subjected traditional forms of constitutionalism to sustained criticism from a variety of perspectives. These long overdue critiques has focused on subjugated knowledges and the voices that are repressed within traditional narratives. In this new context public lawyers in particular crave a paradigm to orient practice. The new critical voices entering the field have inspired a renewed focus on the values which underpin the subject. It is now at least accepted that the partial nature of the conceptual framework

9 C.J. Harvey, 'The Politics of Legality' (1999) 50 *Northern Ireland Legal Q.* 528.

10 *The Belfast Agreement* (1998; Cm. 3883).

11 For an excellent example of the diversity even within perspectives see S. Millns and N. Whitty (eds.), *Feminist Perspectives on Public Law* (1999).

adopted impacts on what is seen and not seen in the empirical world. The framework of particular interest for the purpose of this paper is 'deliberative democracy'. The rise of dialogic or communicative models of law and democracy have revitalized the search for a defensible radical democratic model of legal discourse. Understanding law as a conversation or dialogue is useful in exploring the ways that discourses flow between intersecting legal orders. While dialogic understandings prove useful for grasping the internal nature of governance they are also yielding insights into the transnational nature of networks of governance.[12] Proponents of multi-layered and cosmopolitan democracy are heavily indebted to the current popularity of conversational models which stress the connectedness of discourses of law and politics.[13] For legal scholars, there are interesting themes to be explored which draw on this framework of analysis. For example, it opens up space for reflection on transnational legal activism and what I term the globalization[14] of 'judicial conversations'. What I mean by this is that it provides tools to capture the interactions between participants in law's community in a more convincing way. If there is a proposition that has rapidly gained acceptance it is that the dialogic model grasps the nature of modern or postmodern discourses about law in more convincing ways than monological approaches.

Just as Rawls[15] led the return to normative political philosophy, Habermas is the dominant figure in the resurgence of interest in deliberative democracy.[16] The model referred to throughout this paper is heavily influenced by Habermas's work on law and democracy. As we will see, his continued insistence on universalism and proceduralism is however problematic. The firm belief in deliberative democracy is at the core of his thinking and it informs, but does not determine, the neo-republican perspective

12 J. Habermas, 'The European Nation-State and the Pressures of Globalisation' (1999) 235 *New Left Rev.* 46–61. See U. Beck, 'Democracy Beyond the Nation-State: A Cosmopolitical Manifesto' *Dissent*, Winter 1998, 53–5; he rather aptly asks: 'can there be some form of transnational procedural legitimation?' (p. 53). For a discussion of the process of legal globalization, see G. Teubner, '"Global Bukowina": Legal Pluralism in the World Society' in *Global Law Without a State*, ed. G. Teubner (1997) 3–28.

13 See D. Held, *Democracy and the Global Order: From the Modern State to Cosmopolitan Governance* (1995); D. Held, 'From City-states to a Cosmopolitan Order?' in *Prospects for Democracy: North, South, East and West*, ed. D. Held (1993) 13. See, also, A. Giddens, *The Third Way: The Renewal of Social Democracy* (1998) 129–53.

14 On globalization, see the impressive D. Held et al., *Global Transformations: Politics, Economics and Culture* (1999).

15 J. Rawls, *Political Liberalism* (1993); J. Rawls, *A Theory of Justice* (1972). See, also, J. Rawls, 'The Idea of an Overlapping Consensus' (1987) 7 *Oxford J. of Legal Studies* 1.

16 See, in particular, J. Habermas, *Between Facts and Norms: Contributions to A Discourse Theory of Law and Democracy* (1996); J. Habermas, *The Structural Transformation of the Public Sphere: An Inquiry into a Category of Bourgeois Society* (1989); J. Habermas, *The Theory of Communicative Action. Vol. 2. Lifeworld and System: A Critique of Functionalist Reason* (1987). For an introduction, see S.K. White (ed.), *The Cambridge Companion to Habermas* (1995); W. Outhwaite (ed.), *The Habermas Reader* (1996).

presented in this paper. After several unsuccessful attempts to 'ground' critical theory in constitutive interests he eventually followed others in the turn from labour to language.[17] The communicative model has a number of distinct advantages over previous versions of critical theory. The one that is of most interest is the re-introduction of normative questions into political and legal thought. With the exception of Neumann and Kirchheimer, earlier critical theorists did not take normative questions surrounding legitimacy seriously.[18] They perpetuated the historicist problems with Marxism that the communicative model attempts to address. This transition to language has not been a smooth one and there are dangers. The main difficulty with the turn to discursive rationality is that it may become a form of 'transcendentalism', and thus exclusively reconstructive. For public lawyers, the problem here is the promotion of approaches which lose the value that can come from situated critique which recognizes historical contingency.[19] For example, this 'transcendentalism' and idealism is a real problem for those who are concerned with local and concrete forms of resistance.

Although Habermas has followed the turn to language, he has not joined other critical theorists on the path to what he pejoratively labels neo-conservatism.[20] Habermas has remained within a rationalist tradition and deeply suspicious of romantic rejections of modernity.[21] This is not because he is unaware of the destruction wrought by the process of modernization or because he has an inflated view of what theory can achieve. The concept of the 'colonization of the lifeworld' was early recognition of the destructiveness of modernity.[22] For Habermas, the answer is not to join the growing band of sceptics but to recognize the trend for what it is: a symptom of the exhaustion of subject-centred reason.[23] In an unusually strong attack on some modern intellectual trends Habermas has defended modernity against it critics.[24] At the core of his theoretical edifice is the belief that rationality requires a reconstruction not confined to the Weberian cage of instrumental reason.[25] From this a concept of communicative rationality has emerged

17 See D. Ingram, *Habermas and the Dialectic of Reason* (1987) 1–19.

18 S. Benhabib, *Critique Norm and Utopia: A Study of the Foundations of Critical Theory* (1986) 348.

19 id.

20 J. Habermas, *The New Conservatism: Cultural Criticism and the Historians' Debate* (1989).

21 See J. Habermas, *The Philosophical Discourse of Modernity* (1985).

22 Habermas, op. cit. (1987), n. 16.

23 Habermas, op. cit., n. 21.

24 id.

25 For further discussion see J.P. McCormick, 'Max Weber and Jürgen Habermas: The Sociology and Philosophy of Law During Crises of the State' (1997) 9 *Yale J. of Law and the Humanities* 297, at 298; he makes the now common argument that the ghost of the collapse of the Weimar Republic is what has haunted virtually all of Habermas's endeavours and that his work cannot be seen other than within the framework Weber left behind. As he further notes, the context has rather changed. For Weber wrote during the transition from non-interventionist to welfare state. We are now, however, poised at another transition to internationalization.

and it is to this that he recommends we look for more penetrating insights into the nature of modernity. His embrace of subjectless communication can be viewed as part of a larger body of work that has shifted in this basic direction. There is no need to explore the system-lifeworld distinction here although it is worth noting that some, like McCarthy, question the reliance on systems theory in his work.[26] It is also notable that Habermas accords law an important place in his reformulation of social theory. The result is a discourse theory of law and democracy which is highly ambitious in scope.[27] In his reconstruction of law and the constitutional state he effectively attempts a bridge-building exercise between what were considered previously to be both methodologically and substantively distinctive positions.[28] What is most striking about the work is the integrative role accorded to law.[29] Engagement with legal discourse would appear to have inspired a shift from his previous concern with the stages and impact of juridification.[30] In earlier work he noted the importance of protecting areas of life that were integrated through values, norms, and consensus formation from colonization by the system imperatives of economic and administrative subsystems.[31] In particular he suggests that these areas of life must be defended against being converted through law, acting as a steering mechanism, to a damaging form of socialization.[32] Procedural law is not novel, even if the Habermasian version is, but it does reflect what is an important strand in modern legal scholarship.[33] It is one among a number of such democratic theories which stress the importance of proceduralism.

There is no consensus about the most appropriate model of deliberative democracy or whether the project is in itself worthwhile. To borrow from Cover, it is perhaps important to remember that legal communications 'take place in a field of pain and death' even after the linguistic turn.[34] There are recurring themes in this literature critical of both this model and the resurgence of interest in deliberative democracy generally. Goodrich suggests that underpinning Habermas's work is a desire to bring communication to an

26 T. MacCarthy, *Ideals and Illusions: On Reconstruction and Deconstruction in Contemporary Critical Theory* (1991) 152–80.

27 See Habermas, op. cit. (1996), n. 16.

28 See J.P. McCormick, 'Habermas' Discourse Theory of Law: Bridging Anglo-American and Continental Legal Traditions' (1997) 60 *Modern Law Rev.* 734.

29 Compare J. Bohman, 'Complexity, Pluralism and the Constitutional State: On Habermas's *Faktizität und Geltung*' (1994) 28 *Law and Society Rev.* 897.

30 Habermas, op. cit. (1987), n. 16.

31 See J. Habermas, 'Law as a Medium and Law as Institution' in *Dilemmas of Law in the Welfare State*, ed. G. Teubner (1986) 203–20.

32 id., p. 220.

33 Although the theoretical edifice is distinctive it is interesting to contrast it with US process-based legal scholarship, see N. Duxbury, *Patterns of American Jurisprudence* (1995) 205–99.

34 R. Cover, 'Violence and the Word' in M. Minow, M. Ryan, and A. Sarat (eds.), *Narrative, Violence, and the Law: The Essays of Robert Cover* (1993) 203.

end.[35] This chimes with the concern that these theorists begin from the premise that pluralism is somehow troubling or problematic.[36] The attempt to ground the theories with the counterfactual 'veil of ignorance' or the normative presuppositions of communicative action appears both quaint and potentially dangerous to those who have abandoned the search for an 'other worldly' grounding for our current democratic practices. Even those sympathetic to the Habermasian project have wavered on his strong commitment to universalism and context-transcending norms. Mouffe prefers the poststructuralist emphasis on contingency and contradiction and the ways in which tensions can be operationalized for radical democratic practices.[37] In this she has, like several others, found engagement with the ideas of Schmitt useful.[38] In her 'agonistic' version of deliberative democracy the problem is excessive consensus.[39] Conflict is always present, even in cases where it is actively submerged. Mouffe wants us to break with rationalism, individualism, and universalism in the name of a truly radical democratic theory.[40]

Another criticism will appeal immediately to anyone who has attempted the practical 'application' of Habermasian thought.[41] As one approaches the concrete through the lens of this work, severe problems emerge. Luhmann, for example, notes that if facticity and validity are to have any meaning then communication must take place.[42] But if the legitimacy of arrangements is tied to norms of undistorted communication, can we ever be reasonably sure that our current mechanisms possess legitimacy? Is unanimity an appropriate standard in this regard? Habermasian proceduralism appears content with the prospect of continuing democratic dialogue with embedded normative constraints. This shares some characteristics with Rorty's conversational model.[43] Both are eager to see philosophy dethroned albeit to very different degrees. Habermas is content to supply a model which reconstructs the normative presuppositions of our communicative practices and demonstrates the universalism of a reason that holds itself to account. Rorty does not see the need to 'ground' his approach and is content with the contingency which this implies.

There are, of course, those who reject this democratic thinking and/or who view it as a naïve response to the current complex problems faced by society. Whereas deliberative democracy pins its hopes on the integrative

35 P. Goodrich, 'Habermas and the Postal Rule' (1996) 17 *Cardozo Law Rev.* 1457.

36 C. Mouffe, *The Return of the Political* (1995) 136.

37 id.

38 This might be contrasted with Habermas's treatment of Schmitt, see Habermas op. cit., n. 20, pp. 128–139.

39 See Mouffe, op. cit., n. 36.

40 id., p. 8.

41 See J. Dryzek, *Discursive Democracy: Politics, Policy and Political Science* (1990).

42 N. Luhmann, '*Quod Omnes Tangit*: Remarks on Jürgen Habermas's Legal Theory' (1996) 17 *Cardozo Law Rev.* 883.

43 R. Rorty, *Contingency, Irony and Solidarity* (1989); R. Rorty, *Essays on Heidegger and Others: Philosophical Papers Vol. 2* (1991) 164–76.

functions of law and democratic process, others are more inclined to see the aggregative nature of the democratic process as key. From this perspective democracy is about the aggregation of existing preferences and should not involve excessive focus on the conditions of possibility for preference formation. The typical plea of the radical democrat for more participation is rejected by system theorists as inadequate given the functional differentiation of modern society and the new evolutionary phase of reflexive law.[44] The answer lies not in more participation but in the self-reflection of the legal system.[45] The democratic project faces formidable difficulties. If it is to escape from accusations of pure idealism and nostalgia, it must demonstrate how its value commitments can shape real-world institutional contexts.

2. *Problematizing law*

Public lawyers do not remain immune to the surrounding intellectual climate. We are living in an era marked by a profound lack of faith in rationalism and our ability to achieve substantive goals through traditional tools of law and policy. This 'mood' has been influential in legal scholarship in often disparate ways. Many scholars have simply not been prepared to take the 'leap of faith' necessary to endorse uncritically a new schema. Yet, one finds the themes from the critical literature in work from almost every substantive area of modern legal scholarship. The clearest example of the impact on the general intellectual climate is a tendency to problematize 'law' and question traditional assumptions about its role and impact. Here, I attempt to draw together separate strands of thought to illustrate precisely what I mean by this. Those working in these areas might not agree with the links I make here. But they strike me as ones which are instructive. In particular I want to focus on three themes that raise related issues: law and discretion; post-instrumental law; and legality and indeterminacy. At first sight these are disparate areas involving quite distinct issues. It is suggested that in fact contemporary debate in these fields share an anxiety about law's current role. While participants in this debate all reject simplistic understandings of law there remains a problem in specifying precisely the role that law now has. I draw these debates together for illustrative purposes and I do not intend this to be exhaustive.

First, the law-discretion debate. Lawyers continue to function with a simplistic understanding of the relationship between law and discretion. Dworkin's description of discretion as the hole in the doughnut is about as deep as some lawyers will venture.[46] This is unsurprising for a field which

44 See G. Teubner, 'Substantive and Reflexive Elements in Modern Law' (1983) 17 *Law and Society Rev.* 239, at 242: 'This stage, in which law becomes a system for the co-ordination of action within and between semi-autonomous social sub-systems, can be seen as an emerging but as yet unrealised possibility . . .'

45 id.

46 See R.M. Dworkin, 'Is Law a System of Rules?' in *The Philosophy of Law*, ed. R.M. Dworkin (1977) 38.

promotes its own self-understanding as the master discipline. Lawyers desire, and are led to believe that they can have, the final word on the regulation of our common existence. In the social conversation it is lawyers' voices which are often the most piercing. For in orthodox legal scholarship it is law which brings communication to an end. The traditional view of legality which underpins this has its roots in a conservative fear of democracy and the contested nature of the political. Discretion is inherently objectionable and to be avoided wherever and whenever possible. The rejection of this thinking is a common theme in modern socio-legal scholarship. This work raises serious questions for the legal paradigm's insistence on pre-judging discretion. At the very least, this encourages a more sophisticated understanding of the nature of discretion which views law within the context of competing social, political, and cultural norms. In other words, law forms a part of an ongoing social conversation. As Black has noted, viewing rules as one more set of norms competing with others is the new orthodoxy.[47] What follows is the belief that the interpretation of rules is dependent on interpretative contexts to the extent that they will not act as constraints.[48] The end product is not chaos but the importance of adopting what Black has called a 'social paradigm' for understanding law and legal processes.[49] She raises a question that is relevant here. In this new paradigm how does law fare?[50] In order to explore this, and other issues, she focuses on institutionalism. Although this is forwarded as a potentially fruitful paradigm, her conclusion is that the legal paradigm should not be too quickly abandoned. The interest in law and discretion aids in locating law in its institutional context and thus within the social, political, and cultural norms that it must compete against in practice. But one wonders whether this avoids a paradigmatic understanding of law's role that can account for the fact that in practice law does appear to change the terms of the social conversation. In other words, it remains unclear what role law has and how this role is to be justified. I would suggest that we should be careful of too readily abandoning the concept of legality.

Secondly, we have explorations of post-instrumental law. Again, the insight that underpins much of the work is that the inherited languages of analysis are too simple and unsophisticated to capture the complexity of the relationship between law and society. The renewal of interest in general systems theory, and specifically autopoietic law, has added a new dimension to the debate.[51] Its importation into law arose from a concern with

47 J. Black, 'New Institutionalism and Naturalism in Socio-Legal Analysis: Institutionalist Approaches to Regulatory Decision-Making' (1997) 19 *Law and Policy* 51, at 52.

48 id., p. 53.

49 id.

50 id.

51 See, generally, G. Teubner (ed.), *Autopoietic Law: A New Approach to Law and Society* (1988); G. Teubner, 'Autopoiesis in Law and Society: A Rejoinder to Blankenburg' (1984) 18 *Law and Society Rev.* 291. See, also, H. Baxter, 'Autopoiesis and the "Relative Autonomy" of Law' (1998) 19 *Cardozo Law Rev.* 1987.

regulatory law and its failures and a general dissatisfaction with existing debates on deformalization and/or delegalization. Teubner seeks to contextualize this debate within evolutionary theory, arguing that we have reached a new evolutionary stage of 'reflexive law'.[52] Luhmann's description of law as normatively closed and cognitively open is now well known but what is interesting is the closed, circular, and self-referential nature of the system. The legal system produces and reproduces its own elements from itself. The result is a sophisticated version of legal autonomy. This is not intended as an apologetic return to legal formalism. Given that the basic element of the social system, viewed from this perspective, is communication and not the person, it differs markedly from traditional versions of legal positivism. In fact, advocates claim that it may be more responsive to social reality than other approaches.[53] By examining law as a functional system, existing horizontally with other systems, it claims to have the intellectual tools to grasp the complexity of some of the problems discussed above. For legal scholars this has involved exploring 'how the law thinks about X' but also problematizing traditional views about how change can be facilitated or encouraged through the use of law.[54] This work can begin to tell us what is happening when social discourses immunize themselves against law as well as give an interesting account of legal blindness.[55] Again, the attractiveness of the theory rests in the fact that it offers a new and more sophisticated way of thinking about some very old socio-legal problems. Despite reservations about the abstraction of the conceptual framework, its deployment can yield real insight into regulatory failure.

The third, and final, theme might appear at first glance an unlikely addition to this discussion. But I suggest it raises precisely the same general issues as those discussed above. The work in question traces a different path in the critical tradition back to scholars such as Heller, Kirchheimer, and Neumann who retained a democratic faith in legality. Habermas is arguably the modern representative of this school of thought which draws it inspiration from social democratic thinking. What emerges is concern with the implications of aspects of the current critical agenda. Some of this can be rather melodramatic and overstated. Scheuerman has, for example, made the following bold claim:

> As the ideal of the rule of law loses its status as an icon in American jurisprudence, those who traditionally have benefited most from it – the pariah, the economically vulnerably, the criminally accused, the dissenter – are now likely to suffer most.[56]

52 Teubner, op. cit., n. 44, p. 242.

53 Teubner, op. cit. (1988), n. 51, p. 2.

54 See J. Black, 'Talking about Regulation' [1998] *Public Law* 77; J. Black, 'Constitutionalising Self-regulation' (1996) 59 *Modern Law Rev.* 24.

55 G. Teubner, 'Regulatory Law: Chronicle of a Death Foretold' (1992) 1 *Social & Legal Studies* 451.

56 This quotation comes from a critique of law and economics but it clearly is intended to have wider implications, see W.E. Scheuerman, 'Free Market Anti-Formalism: The Case of Richard Posner' (1999) 12 *Ratio Juris* 80, at 94.

Scheuerman provides little support for the contention. The commitment which underpins this argument is a belief shared by many who retain faith in the ability of legal discourse to offer protection to the disadvantaged. The fear is that exposing indeterminacy does not benefit the disadvantaged and may in practice make their plight much worse. Scheuerman has taken a leading position on this issue and against some new versions of constitutionalism. For example, against Tully's[57] rejection of basic concepts of modern constitutionalism he argues that the legacy of constitutional theory is more open-ended than he suggests.[58] Scheuerman underestimates the value of Tully's version of dialogic constitutionalism. By collapsing comprehensive liberal theories of justice into discursive democracy Tully unearths their partial nature and thus the importance of subjecting them to negotiation and mediation.[59] This process is governed by the three conventions of: mutual recognition; continuity; and consent.[60] Tully is not proposing the 'end of constitutionalism' but the relevance of amendment to a form of constitutionalism that has had a damaging impact on the process of cultural recognition.

Scheuerman makes the equally contentious claim that Schmitt's marriage to national socialism stemmed from core elements of his jurisprudence and that there are connections between the themes he examined and contemporary critical legal scholarship.[61] The suggestion is that Schmitt sided with the Nazis because he saw them as a force that could 'solve' the indeterminacy dilemma. Now there are two ways to read this. One is that the authoritarian consequences rested not in the diagnosis of indeterminacy but in the attempt at reconstruction. Critical scholars might use this as an example of the problems with the formalist quest. The other interpretation, and the one favoured by Scheuerman, it would appear, is that Schmitt simply pushes the radical indeterminacy thesis to its radical limit.[62] Basically, Scheuerman is defending the resources of constitutionalism and its universalist core against what he views as a basic attack on its fundamental principles. What is of interest in this at times overstated work is that this critique comes from within the critical legal tradition in law. Here he draws on a critical theoretical tradition that does not abandon the basic tenets of modernism.[63] In particular he has defended the importance of the work of

57 J. Tully, *Strange Multiplicity: Constitutionalism in the Age of Diversity* (1995); J. Tully, 'Freedom and Disclosure in Multinational Societies', paper delivered at the Rights, Identities and Communities of the European Union workshop held at the University of Leeds in April 1999.

58 W.E. Scheuerman, 'Constitutionalism and Difference' (1997) XLVII *University of Toronto Law J.* 263.

59 Tully, op. cit. (1995), n. 57, p. 209.

60 id.

61 W.E. Scheuerman, 'After Legal Indeterminacy: Carl Schmitt and the National Socialist Legal Order' (1998) 19 *Cardozo Law Rev.* 1743.

62 id.

63 See W.E. Scheuerman, *Between the Norm and the Exception: The Frankfurt School and the Rule of Law* (1994).

Neumann and Kirchheimer.[64] This has similarities with Dyzenhaus in that both believe that the resources of social democratic legal theory have not been exhausted.[65] After an early preoccupation with Dworkin, Dyzenhaus now finds Heller to be a more sympathetic figure.[66] The work of Scheuerman and Dyzenhaus represents an important emerging strand of legal scholarship critical of the indeterminacy thesis and the general drift of critical legal scholarship. Of the three themes discussed it is here that the most traditional understanding of law is to be found. For both wish to demonstrate that the law does indeed constrain the powerful and that it can make a difference. Underpinning this scholarship is a fear of where the indeterminacy thesis might lead, and it is no coincidence that Dyzenhaus's argument comes from knowledge and experience of law and practice in South Africa. This is a fear which, in the case of Scheuerman and Dyzenhaus, is based on examinations of the historical legacy of constitutionalism. Are we so sure that liberating those in power from the notion that they are constrained by law will have a progressive impact? To what extent do the disadvantaged depend on a belief in the legitimacy of law with its implied and explicit promises? The relevance of this work is in the fact that it takes normative questions seriously and, from a critical perspective, attempts to demonstrate the difference that law can make. The suggestion in the work is that we should be careful not to collapse legality into a story of pure power relations and conflict. I believe that the resources supplied in this social democratic tradition must be taken seriously in any democratic reconstruction of legality. Public lawyers should, in particular, be interested in mining these valuable resources.

All three trends express anxiety about the explanatory power of traditional understandings of law. I suggest that these are all essentially disputes about what it means to be critical in modern legal scholarship. This is not a problem that is confined to law, it is a general problem for any social science. As Santos has noted:

> If at the close of the century we live in a world where there is so much to be criticized, why has it become so difficult to produce a critical theory? By critical theory I mean a the theory that does not reduce "reality" to what exists.[67]

Santos has captured precisely the dilemma faced by public lawyers at present.

64 id. See, also, W.E. Scheuerman (ed.), *The Rule of Law Under Siege: Selected Essays of Franz L. Neumann and Otto Kirchheimer* (1996).

65 See D. Dyzenhaus, *Legality and Legitimacy: Carl Schmitt, Hans Kelsen and Hermann Heller in Weimar* (1997); D. Dyzenhaus, 'The Difference Law Makes' (1997) 60 *Modern Law Rev.* 866.

66 id. See, also, D. Dyzenhaus, 'Hermann Heller and the Legitimacy of Legality' (1996) 16 *Oxford J. of Legal Studies* 641. Compare C. Sypnowich, 'Social Justice and Legal Form' (1994) 7 *Ratio Juris* 72: she argues that Dyzenhaus is too attached to liberal understandings of law but that he is correct about its emancipatory potential.

67 B. de Sousa Santos, 'Oppositional Postmodernism and Globalization' (1998) 23 *Law and Social Inquiry* 121, at 122.

3. *The contested nature of democratic law*

Before an adequate democratic understanding of law can emerge, core elements of this model must be questioned. As already indicated, in the face of societal complexity and the diversity within legal scholarship, it is unsurprising that the procedural paradigm of law and democracy is advanced as the self-understanding for our times. Habermas is only the latest to have laid emphasis on proceduralization.[68] The most persistent criticism of proceduralism is that it is ultimately impossible to divorce procedure from substance. Critics argue that there are unacknowledged substantive value commitments underpinning this work. In constructing the model, values have been imported but not acknowledged. Another criticism attaches to universalism. Is it appropriate to leave this century behind with a model of constitutionalism anchored in universalism? Attempts to reach understanding in democratic societies may well have a context-transcending character but many are concerned about the practical implications. The model can encourage a level of abstraction that is both dangerous and difficult to apply. 'Application' can fail to account for the historical context of a particular society. But this is to neglect the fact that the principles which Habermas offers are purely formal in character. This is a procedure which provides the basis for debate within local contexts. It claims to supply a procedure for argumentation when required. A democratic conception of law which attaches legitimacy to the value of self-government anchored in a concept of equality must be one that is content to remain wedded to contestation and argumentation within democratic societies. This contestation increasingly draws on transnational legal discourses but the political struggle must be understood in its local and historical context. This introduces an element of caution with respect to Habermas's schema.

Whether one agrees or disagrees with the variety of models of law and democracy presently on offer, one thing is clear. There has been a reinvigoration of the democratic tradition in legal scholarship underpinned by explanatory and critical theories which focus on conversations in a variety of institutional contexts. This trend is of the utmost significance for those seeking to understand not only specific developments in Northern Ireland but also the new devolutionary context in the United Kingdom. It is a particularly apt time to draw on neo-republican understandings in order to counter any upsurge in naïve legal liberalism. The conversational model offers an appropriate template for examining modern trends in constitutionalism. Much of the emerging literature is similar to a version of republicanism popular in the United States constitutional context. References to Michelman are particularly evident in *Between Facts and Norms*. This is unsurprising given the influence of Habermasian thinking on Michelman.[69]

68 See Teubner, op. cit., n. 51.
69 F. Michelman, 'Family Quarrel' (1996) 17 *Cardozo Law Rev.* 1163.

Habermas departs from republicanism in his preference for a deliberative concept of democracy which is not tied to a shared ethical-cultural consciousness. The ethnically-based aspects of republicanism trouble him. But is this critique of republicanism fair given the attachment to pluralism and diversity which is so evident in, for example, the work of Michelman? To what extent is Habermas's model of deliberative democracy in reality a form of sophisticated neo-republicanism? Republicanism involves what Michelman has described as 'normative tinkering' in the sense that dialogic constitutionalism stresses the revisionary and contestable nature of political and legal practices.[70] In other words, for republicans like Michelman, plurality is the primary virtue in his paradigmatic understanding and the dominant legal form is indeterminacy.[71]

It is not unfair to classify much of the argumentation discussed here as neo-republican. What is most interesting about this perspective is that it casts fresh light on the debate in Northern Ireland and Britain.[72] For the focus is on the actions of those who enter the conversation and disrupt it from the margins and thus not exclusively on the formal institutions of the state. For neo-republicans, legal discourse is best viewed, as Minow argues, as a form of 'communal language which is inherently attached to its social context'.[73] What is interesting is that it directs our gaze away from formal institutions towards informal arenas of dialogue. One will struggle to gain a comprehensive understanding of developments in Northern Ireland in the last five years without such a model. As both Minow and Michelman argue, transformative dialogue takes place primarily outside of formal settings.[74] The reconstructive approach evident in neo-republican legal scholarship is important precisely because it does not see law as merely a 'game' or view the desire for legitimacy and truth as simple nostalgia. The

70 F. Michelman, 'Law's Republic' (1988) 97 *Yale Law J.* 1493, at 1495. It is apparent that Habermas is in agreement with much of what Michelman has to say about law, see J. Habermas, 'Reply to Symposium Participants' (1996) 17 *Cardozo Law Rev.* 1477, at 1485: 'It is no accident that Frank Michelman is one of the three or four contemporary authors whom I have cited most frequently. Michelman's works have taught me the most about deliberative politics . . .' Compare D. Bell and P. Bansal, 'The Republican Revival and Racial Politics' (1988) 97 *Yale Law J.* 1609; they are sympathetic but suggest that the problems which surrounds the 'we' in this constitutional conversation run much deeper than Michelman thinks. They are sceptical also of the idea of the voices of the excluded being heard and included in the conversation.

71 Michelman, id., pp. 1528–9.

72 In the United States context, see C.R. Sunstein, 'Beyond the Republican Revival' (1988) 97 *Yale Law J.* 1539, at 1576: he notes that you cannot simply apply republican thought to public law issues but that many controversies look rather different if viewed through this lens. On concrete application, the task is to move beyond the republican revival 'by integrating aspects of traditional republican thought with the rise of the modern regulatory state, emerging theories of social subordination of various groups, and the need for intermediate organizations, public and private, to satisfy republican goals' (p. 1589).

73 M. Minow, 'Interpreting Rights: An Essay for Robert Cover' (1987) 96 *Yale Law J.* 1860.

74 Michelman, op cit., n. 70, p. 1531; Minow, id., p. 1862.

progressive heart of this neo-republicanism remains emancipation.[75] One should not however underestimate the severe difficulties of nurturing neo-republicanism in a United Kingdom context where the Crown has a continuing constitutional role.

I will briefly summarize the key points from the argument thus far. I have defended the importance of neo-republican scholarship. If it is to remain relevant, neo-republicanism must be recast to reflect more sophisticated dialogic understandings of legal discourse. Legal discourse is a contested terrain which is rooted in the local but which has context-transcending moments which point beyond the parochial. The dialogic model aids in understanding not only the struggles over law in national contexts but also the globalization and europeanization of conversations about legal discourse. I argue that it provides a vital insight into constitutionalism in Northern Ireland.

RECONSTRUCTING CONSTITUTIONALISM IN NORTHERN IRELAND

In order to demonstrate the explanatory and critical potential of the model advanced I will use a case-study of constitutional change in Northern Ireland. The problems with the Westminster model, when applied to the Northern Ireland context, have (with some notable exceptions) been neglected in the literature.[76] One would have presumed that it would have drawn more critical attention from legal scholars than it did. The neglect of constitutionalism in Northern Ireland is even more surprising when one considers legal and political developments in the last decade. Now the Northern Ireland settlement presents a formidable challenge to the orthodox model of British constitutionalism which surely will not go unanswered. My specific argument is that it is difficult to understand events without the more expansive canvas provided by the conversational model defended above. As to the substantive building blocks of the settlement, the centrality accorded to the concept of equality is best explained by a commitment to the values of participation and deliberation which underpin this model. I propose to explore these issues in five stages: the historical and constitutional context; the Agreement and beyond; equality; human rights; and democracy. What is revealing about the settlement is its explicit basis in normative principle. This is something of a departure from traditional versions of British constitutionalism. In other words, the Agreement represents a straightforward

75 On this, see B. de Sousa Santos, *Toward a New Common Sense: Law, Science and Politics in the Paradigmatic Transition* (1995); E. Darian-Smith, 'Power in Paradise: The Political Implications of Santos's Utopia' (1998) 23 *Law and Social Inquiry* 81.

76 For a notable exception, see J. Morison and S. Livingstone, *Reshaping Public Power: Northern Ireland and the British Constitutional Crisis* (1995).

rejection of what has been called ‘pragmatic empiricism’.[77] This rejection is of interest beyond the Northern Ireland context.

1. *Contested constitutional histories*

The time-scale selected for analysing any problem of law is in itself revealing. For what one chooses to omit may say as much as what one includes. The past three decades of political violence represent only the latest manifestation of a serious crisis of legitimacy which has existed since the creation of Northern Ireland.[78] The process of detachment from the rest of Ireland did not bode well for future stability. For it was the threat of violent opposition in the north to proposed Home Rule for the whole of Ireland that was to cement the process of partition. The blurred lines between constitutionalism and violence were thus evident from the formation of the ‘state’. From its creation until 1972, Northern Ireland had devolution within the traditional model of British constitutionalism. There was some novelty, however, with provision for proportional representation and what was in effect a written constitution. But, as McCrudden has noted, these arrangements rested on ‘the authority and experience of British experience and British practice and not on explicit normative principles or institutional arrangements designed to cope with local conditions [footnotes omitted]’.[79] The Northern Ireland context was particularly unsuited to the form of governance bestowed on it. A monolithic Unionist Party dominated the political scene and presided over systematic discrimination against the minority Catholic population. In practice the Catholic minority was constructed as the ‘enemy within’, a view which reinforced its ‘second-class status’.[80] More disturbing was the fact that calls for reform and protection from discrimination were constructed as subversive of the dominant legal order rather than as reasonable demands for recognition. The level of neglect from Westminster ensured that this devolutionary settlement remained in place until developments in Northern Ireland made passivity on the part of the British government impossible.[81] The civil rights movement gave a voice to calls for serious reform to which the British government responded.[82] To the majority Unionist community these demands raised the spectre of an insurrection to overthrow the ‘state’. Communal

77 C. McCrudden, ‘Northern Ireland and the British Constitution’ in *The Changing Constitution*, eds. J. Jowell and D. Oliver (3rd edn., 1994) 323.

78 See J.J. Lee, *Ireland 1912–1985* (1989) 411–57; R. Foster, *Modern Ireland 1600–1972* (1988) 582–92.

79 McCrudden, op. cit., n. 77, at pp. 330–1.

80 See K. McEvoy and C. White, ‘Security Vetting in Northern Ireland: Loyalty, Redress and Citizenship’ (1998) 61 *Modern Law Rev.* 341.

81 See Foster, op. cit., n. 78.

82 On the historical context, see N. Ó Dochartaigh, *From Civil Rights to Armalites: Derry and the Birth of the Irish Troubles* (1997).

tensions rose with violent consequences. The British Army was dispatched as a protective force to secure order but in a series of incidents it solidified suspicion amongst the minority population. From this background violent nationalism re-emerged to insist on the unification of Ireland as the primary solution to the problem.[83] As Foster argues, the eventual imposition of direct rule was one of the most decisive acts that the British government ever took in Northern Ireland to that point.[84] Direct rule has remained the dominant mode of governance since then.

Two key themes have emerged since the early 1970s. First, there were a series of political initiatives to try to secure agreement between the main political parties on a suitable form of power-sharing.[85] From the Sunningdale Agreement to the Assembly in the early 1980s through to the Anglo-Irish Agreement[86] and beyond, each such attempt has failed. As politicians tried to secure political agreement, Northern Ireland was subjected to appalling levels of political violence.[87] The second key theme was the gradual securitization of society in an attempt to marginalize and eradicate paramilitary violence. The basic idea was to marginalize paramilitaries and attempt to gain enough consensus amongst the established political parties. Emergency law was put to use to further this purpose. The human rights violations committed within the framework of this law served only to heighten the problem by provoking further political violence.[88] Although ostensibly aimed at isolating and eliminating the use of political violence it is now clear that various British governments were in contact with representatives of republicanism from the early stages of the conflict.[89] A resolution remained unobtainable and for much of the conflict the legal and policy response appeared to settle into a rut of conflict management and containment.

As has been suggested, the 'changing and volatile political milieu at the macro level deflect attention from a system of public service administration characterized by serious problems of accountability'.[90] There is a certain irony in the fact that the persistent abuse of power by local authorities in Northern Ireland resulted in the imposition of a system that has eroded local democracy even further.[91] Of course, in the wider United Kingdom

83 For an analysis, see H. Patterson, *The Politics of Illusion: A Political History of the IRA* (new edn., 1997).

84 Foster, op. cit., n. 78.

85 B. Hadfield, *The Constitution of Northern Ireland* (1989) 125–233.

86 *Anglo-Irish Agreement* (1985; Cmnd. 9657).

87 On victims see report of the Northern Ireland Victims Commissioner, *We Will Remember Them* (1998).

88 The human rights violations are well documented: see Amnesty International, *Political Killings in Northern Ireland* (1994); Liberty, *Broken Covenants: Violations of International Law in Northern Ireland* (1993).

89 See E. Mallie and D. McKittrick, *The Fight for Peace: The Secret Story Behind the Irish Peace Process* (1996).

90 J. Hughes et al., *Partnership Governance in Northern Ireland: The Path to Peace* (1998) 6.

91 id., p. 7.

context, this erosion of local democracy is not novel.[92] But what is the basic structure for governing Northern Ireland at present? Although the new arrangements propose restructuring of the system, direct rule was the dominant principle of governance. This system was consistently criticized for the lack of accountability which it fostered. The key figure in this structure was the Secretary of State for Northern Ireland who had control over the Northern Ireland departments[93] and was answerable to Parliament for their activities. He or she operated through the Northern Ireland Office (NIO) with the assistance of two Ministers of State and two Parliamentary Under Secretaries. The establishment of the Northern Ireland Affairs Select Committee in 1994 did not alter the accountability deficit significantly. Northern Ireland has experienced the same changes to public management as Britain with the increased use of contractual arrangements, the creation of Next Steps agencies, privatization, and competitive tendering.[94] The system has attracted severe criticism, often for reasons not unique to Northern Ireland. Many of the problems of accountability in Britain are simply exacerbated in Northern Ireland. The familiar response to calls for serious reform in this, as in a number of other areas, was that it would have to await a final constitutional settlement.

2. *The Agreement and beyond: mapping the law and politics of engagement*

The political process has involved a painstakingly slow period of engagement between previously antagonistic sections of the political community in Northern Ireland.[95] The Agreement adopted in April 1998 has now been incorporated into law in the form of the Northern Ireland Act 1998 (NIA 1998) and is intended to transform the governance structures in a radical fashion. The NIA 1998, if ever fully implemented, would in effect be a new constitution for Northern Ireland. The Agreement is the culmination of many years of negotiations. It is difficult to identify a precise starting date for the current peace process. The Anglo-Irish Agreement 1985 might be taken as an appropriate place to begin given its inclusion of an Irish dimension. But it is with the Hume-Adams initiative in the 1990s that some of the main protagonists commenced the process of disengagement from conflict. This process was predicated on inclusive dialogue among all participants and departed from the previous attempts to marginalize the paramilitaries. The political process is constructed on the basis of bringing those engaged

92 See M. Loughlin, *Legality and Locality: The Role of Law in Central and Local Government Relations* (1996).

93 Agriculture, economic development, environment, education, health and social services, and finance and personnel.

94 Hughes, op. cit., n. 90, p. 15.

95 This has been characterized as 'an historic effort at removing the Irish from British politics', see Morison, op. cit., n. 1, p. 511.

in paramilitary activities and their political representatives within an agreed version of constitutionalism. Inclusivity is the key term here with the emphasis on facilitating participants in reaching agreement on a new constitutional structure.

Throughout the process, the British and Irish governments have repeatedly provided the impetus for the political parties. The Downing Street Declaration 1993 signalled close inter-governmental co-operation but the paramilitary cease-fires of 1994 were a clear indication that the ground was shifting. The Framework Document 1995 gave impetus to the process but more importantly provided concrete proposals. In late 1997 the parties entered the final negotiations that would lead to the adoption of the Agreement. In referendums in the north and south of Ireland the Agreement gained overwhelming support.[96] While the support for the Agreement was substantial it has remained unclear to what precisely people had given their consent. As we will see, many aspects of the Agreement have been operationalized but there is still disagreement over what precisely full implementation means. The main problems have surrounded the Assembly and what precisely the Agreement requires. Here the problem is familiar. In order to reach agreement at the time, a measure of ambiguity was permitted to develop. This had the benefit of allowing participants to attempt to 'sell' it to their various constituencies. But to what extent is the Agreement ambiguous on the relationship between devolution and decommissioning? On any reasonable reading of the text there is no connection between executive formation and decommissioning.[97] To return to the conversational model, this particular situation raises interesting questions. For here we effectively see one party to a process of constitution-building attempting to renegotiate the text of the previously reached agreement during the period of implementation. This raises in stark terms the issue of closure. The need for some form of closure seems sensible in this context but how does this relate to the previous emphasis on contestation? If one is to adopt a neo-pragmatic model which privileges contestation then this attempt at reopening the debate is legitimate. One might argue that all elements of the Agreement should remain constantly negotiable. But how problematic is this position for a society that is emerging from conflict? This is a real challenge for advocates of deliberative democracy and the issue does raise troubling practical questions for those who want to keep the basic rules of constitutionalism

96 In Northern Ireland 71.12 per cent voted yes and 28.88 per cent voted no. In the Republic of Ireland 94.4 per cent voted yes and 5.6 per cent voted no to the Agreement and to changes in the constitution.

97 The Agreement, Decommissioning, para. 3: 'All participants accordingly reaffirm their commitment to the total disarmament of all paramilitary organisations. They also confirm their intention to continue to work constructively and in good faith with the Independent Commission, and to use any influence they may have, to achieve the decommissioning of all paramilitary arms within two years following endorsement in referendums North and South of the agreement in the context of implementation of the overall settlement'.

constantly on the agenda of discussion. What is to be done about those elements in society which either do not see constitutionalism as a contested conversation within which violence is ruled out or which seek to undermine the settlement because their dominant position will be undermined?

Since the adoption of the Agreement several attempts have been made to try to reach a compromise position in order to ensure that an executive was formed in line with devolutionary schemes elsewhere. The first legislative target was 10 March 1999. Although this was not met, both governments were making steady progress on drafting the inter-governmental instruments.[98] The next deadline did not advance things significantly although it did result in the publication of both governments' thoughts on the best way forward. The Hillsborough Declaration was a clear attempt to sell the idea of decommissioning to Republicans as part of a more general process of reconciliation. Having failed with this deadline the government decided it was time to impose a new one. The 30 June 1999 deadline was intended to draw parallels with the devolutionary schemes in Scotland and Wales. After five days of discussion, the government published the *Way Forward* document. The proposal was to bring about devolution by triggering the d'Hondt mechanism for executive formation on 15 July 1999. Central to this document were three principles agreed by the political parties on 25 June 1999: an inclusive executive to exercise devolved powers; decommissioning of all paramilitary arms by May 2000; and decommissioning to be carried out in a manner determined by the Independent Commission. As is now well know, the d'Hondt mechanism was triggered on 15 July 1999 but the Ulster Unionist Party (UUP), along with others, refused to nominate ministers and, in line with last minute alterations to the initial standing orders, the executive was not validly constituted. The decision to bring forward a 'failsafe' mechanism was not enough to convince the UUP.[99] The Assembly was suspended and a review process announced.

3. *Structuring deliberative democracy: the building blocks of the settlement in Northern Ireland*

(a) Equality

Respect for autonomy implies not only that the state refrains from interfering in the lives of citizens but also that the conditions of its realization are created. A commitment to democratic law includes making autonomy

98 See *Agreement Between the Government of the United Kingdom of Great Britain and Northern Ireland and the Government of Ireland Establishing A British-Irish Council* (March 1999); *Agreement Between the Government of the United Kingdom of Great Britain and Northern Ireland and the Government of Ireland Agreement Establishing a British-Irish Intergovernmental Conference* (March 1999); *Agreement Between the Government of the United Kingdom of Great Britain and Northern Ireland and the Government of Ireland Establishing a North/South Ministerial Council* (March 1999).

99 Northern Ireland Act 1999.

possible not only by anti-discrimination measures but with positive and proactive support for equality. Equality underpins any dialogic model of constitutionalism, for the existence of inequality has distorting effects. The commitment to participation and deliberation leads to a principle of inclusivity which yields a vital moment for critique. For those conditions which do not accord with the presuppositions of communicative action always permit agreement reached to be questioned. This may give rise to problems when seeking to conclude decisively that an arrangement is legitimate but the regulative ideal provides an increasingly useful critical standard. If there is a core value which underpins the Agreement, it is equality. The concept structures almost every aspect of the settlement and its implementation.[100] What is meant by equality differs depending on the context but its value continues to be recognized. If we take a conversational model as our starting point then any constitutional settlement must be able to clear impediments to inclusive dialogue. This commitment has been accepted at the formal level and the end result is the acceptance of the necessity of 'mainstreaming equality in the governance of Northern Ireland'[101] There are, however, different shades of equality. Representiveness underpins all major institutions yet it is equality in a narrow and specific sense. It is a notion of equality that reflects the bi-national nature of the conflict. The statutory duty on equality is, as we will see, more expansive that this.

The emergence and response to the equality agenda provides a useful case-study on the practical implications of some old questions in legal scholarship. Take, for example, the debate on formalism and informalism. In the specific context of enforcing equality what we see is a rejection of informalism in favour of structured institutional processes and practices. Affected groups in Northern Ireland have not been convinced of the benefits of informalism in the equality context. This argument applies to the specific context of enforcement of equality norms and the expressed desire for guaranteed structures. Informalism may well be appropriate in other contexts. But experience in Northern Ireland has shown that informalism allows equality to be sidelined in the process of public administration. The result is an institutional design with clear value commitments connected to a specific historical context. During the long debate on equality affected groups have shown a preference for structured processes that ensure full enforcement of normative commitments. The demand for equality has underpinned critical assessments of the 'state in Northern Ireland' since the civil rights movement gave voice to this concern in the 1960s. The response was the creation of a body of fair employment legislation to enforce anti-discrimination measures.[102] Anti-discrimination measures are not confined to fair employment or to discrimination on the ground of religion or political opinion. On the wider

100 NIA 1998 ss. 6(2)(d) and (e); 24(1)(b),(c) and (d); 73–76; sch. 8 and 9.

101 The term is borrowed from the title of C. McCrudden, 'Mainstreaming Equality in the Governance of Northern Ireland' (1999) 22 *Fordham International Law J.* 1696.

102 See Fair Employment and Treatment (NI) Order 1998.

equality agenda, Northern Ireland has benefited from anti-discrimination measures in EC and United Kingdom law and practice. The prohibition on racial discrimination came rather late in the day to Northern Ireland, only being extended in 1997.[103] Northern Ireland also had its own versions of the Equal Opportunities Commission and the Commission for Racial Equality in addition to the Fair Employment Commission. It is important to stress that the debate on equality has had a life of its own and concrete attempts were made to legislate against discrimination.

Another lesson from the Northern Ireland context is that anti-discrimination law, while essential, is not enough on its own. Affected groups voiced concern that the law was not impacting sufficiently on real-world contexts. What emerged in the 1990s was a serious debate about translating normative commitments into meaningful practice within institutional contexts. This debate can be traced to the 1980s when the British government started a process of re-examining the issue of discrimination in Northern Ireland. The Standing Advisory Commission on Human Rights (SACHR) was commissioned to investigate the effectiveness of the Fair Employment Act 1976. The result of this process was an influential report which eventually led to the enactment of the Fair Employment Act 1989. In 1990 a government circular was issued relating to discrimination on grounds of religious affiliation, political opinion, and gender. The measure was criticized for its narrow focus and in 1993 it was renamed and published as the Policy Appraisal and Fair Treatment (PAFT) guidelines.[104] PAFT came into operation on 1 January 1994. The publication of PAFT provided space for a more intense debate on flawed practice which included the input of affected groups. The work conducted on the practical impact of PAFT was not encouraging. What PAFT did achieve was to create a definite focus for an ongoing debate on how equality might find it ways into institutional contexts and thus have a practical impact on the lives of affected groups. It was at this stage that the language of 'mainstreaming' entered the debate.[105] Mainstreaming has been defined as:

> the reorganization, improvement, development and evaluation of policy processes, so that a gender equality perspective is incorporated in all policies at all levels and at all stages, by the actors normally involved in policy-making.[106]

103 See Race Relations (NI) Order 1997.

104 Central Secretariat Circular 5/93: *Policy Appraisal and Fair Treatment* (December 1993). See Morison and Livingstone, op. cit., n. 76, p. 157: 'At a rhetorical level PAFT is a powerful commitment to the idea that the value of equality constrains government decision-making. Though not a legal commitment it has the potential to be a significant *constitutional* principle in the organisation of government in Northern Ireland . . .'.

105 See C. McCrudden, *Mainstreaming Fairness? A Discussion Paper on 'Policy Appraisal and Fair Treatment'* (November 1996); C. McCrudden, *Benchmarks for Change: Mainstreaming Fairness in the Governance of Northern Ireland* (February 1998).

106 Council of Europe, Rapporteur Group on Equality Between Men and Women, *Gender Mainstreaming*, GR-EG (98) 1, 26 March 1998 at 6.

The term mainstreaming is unfortunate and raises interesting issues for oppositional movements that do not wish to lose their critical edge. But it has gained a powerful foothold in the equality debate. With mainstreaming, the gaze shifts to institutional contexts and the practical impediments to the realization of equality. This implies a more proactive response which requires action to eradicate actively the root causes of discrimination and also to ensure that equality is not sidelined in public administration. In distinguishing mainstreaming from traditional anti-discrimination measures, McCrudden states:

> [I]t concentrates attention on government decision-making, it concentrates on government proactively taking equality into account, and it does not concentrate primarily on discrimination as the problem to be resolved. Mainstreaming approaches are intended to be anticipatory (rather than essentially retrospective, or relatively late insertions into the policy-making process), to be extensively participatory (rather than limited to small groups of the knowledgeable . . .), and to be integrated into the policy-making of those primarily involved (rather than external add-ons perceived to be external by policy makers).[107]

This initially emerged in the context of mainstreaming a gender perspective but has become more expansive since. This thinking was fed into the debate in Northern Ireland and the result was a focused assessment of the practical impact of PAFT.[108] The signs were not encouraging.[109] Dissatisfaction led to calls for PAFT to be placed on a statutory footing. It is at this point that the ongoing equality debate merged with the election of a Labour government and developments in the political process. For this was a government more attuned to the language of equality and a context where some participants in the political process expressed interest in the equality agenda. The White Paper, *Partnership for Equality*, published in March 1998, was the Labour government's response to the report of SACHR from the previous year.[110] It was suggested that a new unified Equality Commission should be established to discharge the functions of the existing commissions.[111] This proposal was severely criticized in the responses to the White Paper yet the government was determined to push ahead. One fear that emerged clearly in the responses was that a hierarchy of discrimination might emerge with religious and political discrimination assuming a dominant position. While generally dismissive of arguments against a unified commission, the government was more responsive to calls to place PAFT on a statutory footing.

107 McCrudden, op. cit., n. 101, p. 11.

108 See T. Hadden, B. Rainey, and G. McGreevy, *Equal But Not Separate: Communal Policy Appraisal* (1998).

109 id.

110 SACHR, *Employment Equality: Building for the Future* (1997; Cm. 3684).

111 Para. 4.12: 'The most rational organisational solution would be the creation of a unified Equality Commission . . . This would not imply a downgrading of the priority attached to the work of any body. Indeed, the main purpose of such amalgamation would be to enable their work to be greatly extended into a new area, a positive engagement with the public sector to promote equality of opportunity in a broad sense.'

The equality agenda featured prominently in the political process and is reflected throughout the Agreement. The British government pledged itself to make 'rapid progress' with measures:

> covering the extension and strengthening of anti-discrimination legislation, a review of the national security aspects of the present fair employment legislation . . . a new more focused Targeting Social Need initiative and a range of measures aimed at combating unemployment and progressively eliminating the differential in unemployment rates between the two communities by targeting objective need.

The concept of equality structures almost every aspect of the Agreement and now the NIA 1998. For example, the legislative competence of the Assembly does not extend to provisions which discriminate on the ground of religious belief or political opinion.[112] The prohibition applies to subordinate legislation or any act which discriminates on the same ground.[113] The Assembly could have chosen to establish a new Department of Equality but it preferred to opt for an Equality Unit attached to the offices of the First and Deputy First Ministers. The translation of the equality guarantees into law was not a smooth one but as with the human rights guarantees they have found their place there.

A new unified Equality Commission is now a reality and it began its operations on 1 October 1999. It has a Chief Commissioner and a Deputy Chief Commissioner and eighteen commissioners. The Equality Commission is charged with exercising the functions previously exercised by: the Fair Employment Commission (NI); Equal Opportunities Commission (NI); Commission for Racial Equality (NI); and the Northern Ireland Disability Council. While there is a unified commission, there is no unified body of anti-discrimination law. This may become a problem. In exercising its functions the Commission must aim to secure an 'appropriate division of resources' between the functions previously exercised by the listed bodies.[114] As outlined in the White Paper, *Partnership for Equality*, the Equality Commission operates on the basis of separate directorates. It will also have regard to advice offered by consultative councils selected by the Commission to advise it in relation to these issues. One of its most important functions will be to 'police' the new statutory equality duty.[115] Public authorities must have 'due regard to the need for promote equality of opportunity' between the following groups:

- persons of different religious belief, political opinion, racial group, age, marital status or sexual orientation
- men and women
- persons with a disability and persons without
- persons with dependents and persons without

112 NIA 1998, s. 6(2)(e).
113 NIA 1998, s. 24(1)(c).
114 NIA 1998, s. 74(3)(b).
115 NIA 1998, s. 75.

The public authority must also have regard to the 'desirability of promoting good relations between persons of different religious belief, political opinion or racial group'.[116] The specific inclusion of sexual orientation is a notable expansion of the equality agenda in Northern Ireland. The commission is charged with keeping the effectiveness of the duties imposed by s. 75 under review[117] as well as advising public authorities and others of their duties.[118] In its annual report, it must report on steps taken by it and other public authorities to promote the equality duty.[119]

In order to ensure the effective implementation of the equality duty the legislation requires public authorities to submit equality schemes.[120] The new duties take effect from 1 January 2000 and the first equality schemes are due by 30 June 2000. The scheme must show how the authority proposes to fulfil the equality duty. The legislation establishes clear duties on public authorities on, for example, consultation with and the participation of affected groups.[121] Provision is also made for impact assessments,[122] compliance mechanisms, and public access to information.[123] Draft guidelines were issued for consultation by the Equality Commission on 22 October 1999.[124] The draft guidelines explain what mainstreaming is and why it is important as well as describing in an accessible way what is required of public authorities.

The aim of bringing equality to the heart of governance is plain in these detailed requirements. Much will depend on the effectiveness of the Commission in enforcing these provisions properly. Here the institutional dynamics of the Commission will be particularly interesting. In these measures we see a shift away from constructing individuals as passive recipients of legal protection to active participants in a process of mainstreaming equality. This dialogic emphasis conjoins public and private autonomy in its attempt to transmit the voices of affected groups into processes of public decision-making. This is a good practical example of how the law and politics of equality is linked to the model of deliberative democracy defended above.

The formalization of the equality agenda is the clearest practical example of one implication of the model of constitutionalism defended here. Proposals advanced by affected groups have emphasized the need for structured processes to achieve substantive results. The debate has shifted from anti-discrimination to the substantive goal of equality. The focus is now much more tightly directed at the institutional context and how mechanisms

116 NIA 1998, s. 75(2).
117 NIA 1998, schedule 9, para. 1(a).
118 NIA 1998, schedule 9, para. 1(b).
119 NIA 1998, schedule 8, para. 5.
120 NIA 1998, schedule 9, para. 2.
121 NIA 1998, schedule 9, para. 4(2)(a) and (b).
122 NIA 1998, schedule 9, para. 4(2)(c).
123 NIA 1998, schedule 9, para. 4(2)(f).
124 The guidelines were originally published in March 1999 in the report of the Equality Commission Working Group (1999).

can be created to achieve previously agreed value commitments. Affected groups were involved in all stages of this process of reform. Thus input was secured on both the substantive values to be promoted through legal regulation and the means to achieve this end. The progress of the debate involved many actors yet important levels of steering of the process came from the non-governmental sector. We can reconstruct from this the normative presuppositions of these practices. We would, I believe, end up with a model very similar to that sketched earlier in this paper. What is important is that the challenge of showing how these value commitments can be translated into precise institutional mechanisms has been taken on in the Northern Ireland context. This at least goes some way to provide empirical evidence for the claims made for deliberative democracy.

The equality debate has lead the way in innovative thinking about how change is to be achieved in practice. The clear implication for the argument advanced in this paper is the recognition that inequality seriously distorts the process of dialogue in a democratic polity. What it also demonstrates is that dialogic models must have 'critical bite'. In other words, too many discussions of participation and deliberation fail to show how policies and institutions might be redesigned to achieve substantive goals. Consultation can be a paper exercise regarded by government as no more than a troublesome mechanism that must be endured. The Northern Ireland provisions indicate how we might move beyond this in the sphere of equality by building learning processes into public decision-making and policy formation. This is most evident in the equality field where public authorities will be required to construct institutional mechanisms to evaluate and respond to the impact of their work on equality. The success or failure of this experiment in Northern Ireland will provide valuable lessons for elsewhere.

(b) Human rights

Rights guarantees are an integral aspect of the democratic understanding of law. They are inherently connected to democratization and do not necessarily conflict with it. While equality underpins deliberative democracy, it is also supported by human rights protections. The human rights movement could however learn lessons from the equality debate, certainly in its precision and in the hard thinking about institutional contexts. The politics of rights discourse has been one of the more intriguing aspects of post-Agreement political life in Northern Ireland. Human rights discourse flows throughout the Agreement and has been a prominent aspect of political life since its adoption. All participants in the political process and beyond have tried to capture the discourse of rights for their own political struggles. This is an understandable reaction given the moral force that rights claims possess. Rights-talk lends itself to this level of contestation precisely because of its ambiguous nature. The discourse is malleable even though a certain level of determinacy has been achieved through existing processes of adjudication. It also disguises political commitments and its imperial ambitions can silence other values that deserve full public debate. What is interesting in Northern Ireland is the political uses of rights discourse (for this is certainly an area where strategic thinking dominates) and the rights-based arguments which work and the ones which fail.

Things were not always like this. Human rights discourse, like equality, was treated with suspicion in official circles in the past. In these circles it was both peripheral to the goal of seeking a political settlement and in practice the preserve of one section of the community and thus potentially subversive.[125] This attitude contributed to a general failure to grasp the impact that human rights abuses had on fuelling the conflict. A markedly different approach is taken in the Agreement. To borrow a phrase in vogue, human rights discourse has moved from the margins to the mainstream.[126] Human rights language can be found throughout the Agreement.[127] Developments in Northern Ireland signify a sharp departure from the traditional incrementalism of British constitutionalism in this sphere. Although the traditional British approach to rights may have altered with the enactment of the Human Rights Act 1998, the Northern Ireland settlement gives human rights a significantly strengthened role.

As with the other progressive elements of the Agreement, there was concern that human rights commitments would be eroded in the process of translation into legislation. That this did not occur is due to the efforts of dedicated individuals and groups. Human rights discourse will figure prominently in the future governance of Northern Ireland, and as I have indicated, there are already signs of increasing deployment of rights discourse by a range of groups. Here we will see familiar debates emerge and a real test for the future will be the ability of decision-makers to adjudicate rationally between competing rights claims. Another test will be to combine the equality and human rights agendas in compatible ways. A tension may begin to emerge between the equality duty and human rights commitments. In particular, equality may come into conflict with the traditionally more individualistic aspects of human rights discourse. Resolving these questions will require hard thinking which goes beyond mere assertion. There is no escaping substantive commitments for they will always reappear in processes of justification and application.

One of the most important formal expressions of the commitment to human rights is the establishment of the Northern Ireland Human Rights Commission (NIHRC). The Commission is not the first such body with a human rights remit. SACHR made a useful contribution to the debate on human rights protection although it suffered from an insufficiently substantive mandate and many of its recommendations were not implemented by

125 McCrudden, op. cit., n. 101, p. 1697.

126 See P. Mageean and M. O'Brien, 'From the Margins to the Mainstream: Human Rights and the Good Friday Agreement' (1999) 22 *Fordham International Law J.* 1389.

127 See C. Harvey and S. Livingstone, 'Human Rights and the Northern Ireland Peace Process' [1999] *European Human Rights Law Rev.* 162.

government.[128] The NIHRC differs in significant respects but it is important not to lose sight of what went before. The Agreement makes provision for:

> A new Northern Ireland Human Rights Commission, with membership from Northern Ireland reflecting the community balance, will be established by Westminster legislation, independent of Government, with an extended and enhanced role beyond that currently exercised by the Standing Advisory Commission on Human Rights, to include keeping under review the adequacy and effectiveness of laws and practices, making recommendations to Government as necessary; providing information and promoting awareness of human rights; considering draft legislation referred to them by the new Assembly; and in appropriate cases, bringing court proceedings or providing assistance to individuals doing so.

The NIA 1998 established the NIHRC along these lines. Its functions include: keeping under review the adequacy and effectiveness of law and practice relating to human rights,[129] advising the Secretary of State and the executive Committee of the Assembly on whether a Bill is compatible with human rights.[130] It may give assistance to individuals and bring proceedings involving law or practice relating to human rights[131] and is charged with promoting awareness and understanding of human rights.[132] The NIHRC may also conduct investigations, although it has not been granted sufficient powers to make any such investigation effective.[133] On 30 September 1999 the commission published a draft strategy document to encourage the submission of views on the approach that it should adopt.[134] It has also issued briefing papers on proposed legislation. The NIHRC has indicated that priority will be given to drafting a Bill of Rights for Northern Ireland.

Given that one of its functions is to raise awareness, the continuing work of the NIHRC will ensure that the debate over human rights protection has only begun. The competing positions will surface most explicitly in the Bill of Rights debate. The Commission is responsible for advising the Secretary of State on a Bill of Rights for Northern Ireland. The Agreement refers to rights supplementary to the European Convention on Human Rights 1950 (ECHR) 'to reflect the particular circumstances of Northern Ireland, drawing as appropriate on international instruments and experience'. The NIHRC has indicated that it intends to initiate an inclusive consultative process and has proposed a draft timetable.[135] The consultation around a possible Bill of Rights could fulfil several useful functions. The first is to raise awareness of human rights throughout Northern Ireland and the

128 See S. Livingstone, 'The Northern Ireland Human Rights Commission' (1999) 22 *Fordham International Law J.* 1465.

129 NIA 1998, s. 69(1).

130 NIA 1998, ss. 69(1) and (2).

131 NIA 1998, ss. 69(5)(a) and 70.

132 NIA 1998, s. 69(6).

133 NIA 1998, s. 69(8).

134 See Northern Ireland Human Rights Commission, *Draft Strategic Plan 1999–2002* (September 1999). See, also, http//www.nihrc.org

135 id., pp. 15–16.

second is to test precisely what people wish to see included in the instrument. Although controversy over the role of the judiciary has been a aspect of public debate in many states, in Northern Ireland there has been surprisingly little discussion of the judicial role on this precise issue.[136]

Another feature of these provisions worth noting is the expansive definition of human rights which the NIHRC functions with. The NIA 1998 states that human rights 'includes Convention rights'.[137] The NIHRC therefore has the authority to draw on the full range of international standards. It is, for example, notable that it is not confined to making use of human rights 'law'.

The model of governance contains a series of checks on majoritarianism related directly to the principles of equality and human rights. For a start the HRA 1998 is effectively entrenched in the new constitution of Northern Ireland. The work of the Assembly, the executive, and the new departments will all be subject to specific human rights provisions in the NIA 1998. This is in addition to duties with respect to the work of the NIHRC. The legislative competence of the Assembly is, for example, tied to, among other things, compatibility with 'Convention rights'.[138] The same prohibition applies to the power to make, confirm or approve subordinate legislation or which is incompatible with 'Convention rights'.[139] The Secretary of State may have a role here too. For if he or she considers that any proposed action is incompatible with international obligations, he or she may order it not to be taken.[140] Alternatively if he or she considers that an action to give effect to international obligations is not being taken then he or she may direct that it be taken.[141] The provisions thus contain specific safeguards against potential abuse.

As with equality, the human rights provisions of the Agreement are impressive. They are, however, somewhat limited in their scope with no explicit reference to fundamental economic and social rights. This may be remedied in a future Bill of Rights and by the inclusive approach that the NIHRC intends to take. The challenge in the coming years will be to promote a more expansive rights agenda which goes beyond the 'two communities' model. There are a number of groups in Northern Ireland which have been effectively silenced by the dominant societal narratives. Ensuring that these voices are brought to the fore will require tactical awareness of the potential and limitations of rights discourse.

136 It has not been entirely absent. The public consultations undertaken by the Criminal Justice Review involved some discussion of the issue. See Criminal Justice Review Group, *Review of the Criminal Justice System in Northern Ireland: A Consultation Paper* (1998); Criminal Justice Review Group, *Review of the Criminal Justice System in Northern Ireland: A Progress Report* (1999).
137 NIA 1998, s. 69(11)(b).
138 NIA 1998, s. 6(2)(c).
139 NIA 1998, s. 24(1)(a).
140 NIA 1998, s. 26(1).
141 NIA 1998, s. 26(2).

(c) Locality, democracy, and multi-layered governance

Participation is a core aspect of the concept of deliberative democracy. Its importance has already been mentioned with reference to the equality duty. The commitment to participation is also evident in the formal institutional structures of governance. Equality and participation are, however, more carefully circumscribed. Here we are presented with a problem which relates directly to the model's heritage in consociational thinking. For the Agreement has helped to institutionalize a 'two-communities' model of governance which contrasts markedly with the expansive nature of the equality agenda. There are at least two ways of viewing this. First, the model is accepted as reflective of the harsh political realities of Northern Ireland and the fact that it ensures trust on the part of the minority community that its needs and interests will not be neglected. Thus, the consociational arrangements spring from a 'realistic' assessment of current developments. The second, critical view, is that this represents a narrowing of the equality agenda to a story of two dominant groups which does not reflect a commitment to multiculturalism and does not respect difference within the dominant blocks. This argument, which draws at times from the development of forms of postnationalism in Europe, warns that the maps that we make now will project themselves onto our collective futures. As we will see, while the institutional structures guarantee participation on the part of the dominant communities they give no recognition to either structural inequalities within the communities or the importance of pluralism to deliberative democracy. The structures may simply prevent what is a more fluid picture from emerging fully in the political public sphere.

If the Agreement is implemented in its entirety, then Northern Ireland will form part of a complex web of legal relations. Supranationalism is already a reality in the EU but the new governance structures go much further along the path of complex multi-layered arrangement. There are three essential elements of this examined in this section of the paper: the internal dimension; north-south relations; and east-west relations. It is evident that the model is intended to dissolve traditional absolutist arguments surrounding sovereignty by stressing multiplicity. The 'we' for the purpose of this deliberative model is a divided community which is permitted, within these structures and subject to continuing consent, to express diversity and pluralism in practice.

(i) *Structuring an internal dimension*

A key element of the settlement is the proposed return of devolution in the form of a new Assembly. Although there are significant differences, this aspect can be located within a general devolutionary trend in the United Kingdom. Northern Ireland has been left somewhat behind in this process of devolution. On the major constitutional question of precise status, the choice is left to the people of Northern Ireland and thus has not significantly altered.[142] A mechanism is in place, however, if a majority of people in Northern Ireland wish to cease to be part of the United Kingdom.[143] Although the complex relations designed in the Agreement seek to move beyond traditional versions of sovereignty, a mechanism exists for a definite decision on status to be made.

Strand one of the Agreement provides for democratic institutions in Northern Ireland. This has proven to be the most troublesome aspect of the settlement. A dispute emerged between two of the participants, the UUP and Sinn Féin, over the issue of decommissioning of paramilitary arms and formation of the executive.[144] Despite the best efforts of both governments no solution to this problem could be found. The attempts to force the issue resulted in an unsuccessful meeting of the Assembly in July 1999 which was boycotted by the UUP. Elections to the Assembly were held in June 1998 and it has met in shadow form.[145] At its first meeting in July 1998 the First and Deputy First Minister designate were elected jointly. The latter however decided that resignation from this post was an appropriate response to events in July 1999. Since its first meeting in 1998 some useful work has been done by the Assembly. At the time of writing, a review of the implementation of the Agreement was underway and the executive had not been formed.

Despite the current problems in the process, an examination of this institution is still justified even though continuing direct rule is the reality for now. The Assembly's composition and operation is structured by rules on cross-community support and a general concern with proportionality. This can be found in almost every aspect of the proposed internal structures, from the composition of the executive committee to the adoption or amendment of standing orders. The Agreement provides for the establishment of an 108-member Assembly elected by proportional representation with primary authority in all devolved matters.[146] The Assembly will have authority to enact primary legislation for Northern Ireland in devolved areas. Note, however, that this authority is not unlimited for there are safeguards relating to, for example, human rights. In other words, the primary law-making function will be subject to rights and other guarantees.[147] When, and if, a Bill of Rights is enacted, then law-making will be subject to compliance with it also.

The Assembly will exercise full legislative and executive powers in those areas presently covered by the six Northern Ireland departments. Given the historical context, it is unsurprising that structuring rules for proportionality have been adopted. In the Agreement the emphasis is on safeguards that

142 NIA 1998, s. 1(1).
143 NIA 1998, s. 1(2).
144 In making this connection, the unionist community has pointed to a letter written by the Prime Minister in May 1998 appearing to confirm its position.
145 Northern Ireland Elections Act 1998.
146 NIA 1998, ss. 5–51, schedules, 2, 3, 5, 6, and 10.
147 There is specific reference to entrenched enactments, see NIA 1998, s. 7.

will ensure that 'all sections of the community can participate and work together successfully in the operation of the institutions'. In other words, the safeguards have the explicit purpose of guaranteeing full participation of 'both communities' in the democratic polity. The safeguards include:

- proportional allocation of committee chairs, ministers, and committee membership
- human rights guarantees (discussed above)
- proofing of key decisions against ECHR and a future Bill of Rights
- cross-community voting rules
- equality guarantees (discussed above)

Ministers will also have to affirm the Pledge of Office which includes the duty:

> to serve all the people of Northern Ireland equally, and to act in accordance with the general obligations on government to promote equality and prevent discrimination.[148]

There is in addition a Ministerial Code of Conduct which includes the requirement that they:

> be accountable to users of services, the community and, through the Assembly, for the activities within their responsibilities, their stewardship of public funds and the extent to which key performance targets and objectives are met.[149]

In order to operate the cross-community voting rules members of the Assembly must register a designation of identity as: nationalist, unionist, or other. The 'equality rules' here have a much more context-specific focus than the broader equality agenda. There has been criticism that the rules 'institutionalize sectarianism' and many find such a process instinctively distasteful. This takes us back to the argument above and the limitations of consociational settlements.

The executive committee will be the key institution within the new structures. The committee will consist of the First and Deputy First Ministers and the ten ministers with departmental responsibilities and will discharge the executive responsibilities of the Assembly. Agreement has been reached on the new departments. These will cover: finance and personnel; enterprise, trade and investment; regional development; agriculture and rural development; higher and further education; education; health, social services and public safety; social development; culture, arts and leisure; and environment. Within the Assembly there will be committees for each of the departments with membership again allocated proportionally. The Agreement provides that these committees are to have a 'scrutiny, policy development and consultation role'. The Secretary of State for Northern Ireland will continue to have a role in the new arrangements. His or her main responsibility will be for those areas not devolved to the Assembly

148 NIA 1998, schedule 4.
149 id.

although as the legislation makes clear he or she will continue to have important functions in several areas.[150]

(ii) *North-south relations*

The bi-national nature of the conflict has resulted in a settlement with substantial all-Ireland dimensions. In the area of human rights the Irish government is committed by the terms of the Agreement to taking comparable steps to strengthen the protection of human rights. In particular, it is stated that this will involve increased constitutional protection which will draw upon the ECHR and other international legal instruments. It also pledged itself to look further at the issue of incorporation of the ECHR. The overall aim is to ensure 'at least an equivalent level of protection of human rights as pertain in Northern Ireland'. Specifically it committed itself to: establishing a human rights commission; ratifying the Framework Convention on National Minorities; implementing enhanced employment equality legislation; introducing equal status legislation, and taking further steps to demonstrate respect for the different traditions on the island of Ireland. Provision is made for institutional linkages with the suggestion that there be a joint committee of representatives between the two Human Rights Commissions as a mechanism for considering human rights protection on the island of Ireland. The NIHRC has stated that it will do all that it can to create the proposed joint committee.[151] The committee is invited to consider the possible adoption of a charter to endorse agreed standards for everyone on the island of Ireland. It is evident from these provisions that there is a clear north-south dimension in the human rights field. This makes considerable sense. Resting the legitimacy of the present arrangements on consent means that rights protections should be equivalent in both jurisdictions. This is in effect a form of pendulum theory which attempts to ensure equivalent protection in whichever jurisdiction individuals find themselves in. Since the adoption of the Agreement some progress has been made on advancing the human rights agenda.[152]

The structured internal dimension contains direct links with the rest of Ireland. Thus provision is made for a north-south Ministerial Council consisting of those with executive responsibility to develop consultation, co-operation, and action on 'matters of mutual interest'. Given the political context, structuring rules were necessary to try to ensure full participation of the executive. It is a ministerial responsibility for a minister or junior

150 For example, on the equality schemes where one is referred she or he has the power to approve it, request that a revised scheme be made or make a scheme for that public authority, NIA 1998, schedule 9, para. 7(1).

151 NIHRC, op. cit., n. 134, p. 42.

152 See Joint Committee on Justice, Equality and Women's Rights, *Report of the Committee on Proposals for Legislation by the Minister for Justice, Equality and Law Reform for Human Rights Commission Bill* (1999).

minister to participate.[153] The Pledge of Office contains an obligation to 'discharge in good faith all the duties of office'.[154] A minister would clearly not be in compliance with this obligation if he or she refused to co-operate in the north-south Ministerial Council. The Agreement states that participation in the council is 'one of the essential responsibilities attaching to relevant posts'. Where someone refuses to participate, the Taoiseach and the First and Deputy First Ministers are to make alternative arrangements.

The Council is to meet twice a year in plenary format with more regular meetings in sectoral format. There will be a joint secretariat consisting of civil servants from the north and south. The Council will use its best endeavours to reach agreement on the adoption of common policies. There is a clear attempt to link the Council's operation to the Assembly and the Agreement provides for the mutual interdependence of both institutions.

The Irish government has also committed itself to amending Articles 2 and 3 of the Irish Constitution. They are to be replaced by provisions more compatible with contemporary notions of belonging.

The Agreement has fed into an ongoing debate in Ireland on constitutional reform. The principles which underpin it are thus having an all-Ireland impact which differs from the influence that Northern Ireland developments have on the rest of the United Kingdom. It is a clear recognition of the need for a strong 'Irish dimension' in the governance of Northern Ireland.

(iii) *East-west relations*

The interlocking nature of each strand of the Agreement is no more evident than in the proposals for new east-west relations. The primary east-west dimension, for now at least, is Northern Ireland's continuing role within the United Kingdom. In recognition of the new devolutionary context the settlement includes arrangements to 'promote the harmonious and mutually beneficial development of the totality of relationships among the peoples of these islands'. This is an attempt to give institutional recognition to the importance of co-operation and friendly relations between the new, and not so new, entities.

Provision has been made for the establishment of a British-Irish Council (BIC) to comprise, among others, representatives from the British and Irish governments and the devolved institutions in Northern Ireland, Scotland and Wales. Notable amongst its powers is the provision for members to develop bilateral or multilateral arrangements between them. These arrangements would not require the approval of the BIC and would operate independently from it. While republicans will see obvious potential in

153 NIA 1998, s. 52(2).
154 NIA 1998, schedule 4.

the all-Ireland aspects of the Agreement, unionists are likely to view the BIC as a mechanism to promote links with Scotland and/or Wales. The result will be a local Assembly in Northern Ireland that will be moving in a number of directions that transcend the purely parochial. This may all come harmoniously together but one suspects that it will be rather cluttered and create much 'noise' in the system. To return to the theme of this paper it will, as with the north-south dimension, promote dialogue across jurisdictional divides.

In addition to the BIC, a new British-Irish inter-governmental conference is planned. The sensible aim, given the arrangements mapped out above, is to promote dialogue between the two governments on matters of mutual interest. The special nature of the Irish government's interest in Northern Ireland is recognized in the Agreement and there is a mechanism for it to put forward views on non-devolved matters. Members of the Northern Ireland administration will be involved in the meetings of the conference.

These arrangements have the potential to set in motion intriguing encounters between the devolved entities. If they become operational it is difficult to predict whether this will promote the notion of a 'union state' or facilitate its disintegration.

(d) *The demise of the Westminster model of governance*

The constitutional settlement in Northern Ireland raises serious issues for constitutional lawyers in the United Kingdom. For a start, it cannot be easily absorbed into Britain's pragmatic constitutionalism. It is a significant departure from this model and its distinctiveness must be accorded due recognition. Constitutional lawyers should pay close attention in particular to the centrality of equality to the new constitutional arrangements. Also of fundamental significance is the fact that the constitutional settlement was endorsed in referenda in the north and south of Ireland. This element of democratic legitimacy gives the Agreement a foundational status. But as the Agreement and developments that have followed it confirm the process of adoption and enactment is only the beginning for a model which places weight on continuing dialogue and participation.

The complex structures sketched above are a clear attempt to defuse traditional arguments about sovereignty by creating mechanisms that transcend tired dualisms. By promoting a complex set of conversations which cross borders, the potential is there for a form of postnationalism to take root. This is, of course, an optimistic reading of arrangements which might never be operationalized. There is an inordinate amount of space within these structures for severe tensions to emerge. For the structure points in several different directions at once and there is no guarantee that serious collisions can be avoided.

But there are more fundamental implications of the settlement. The Agreement's explicit basis in normative principle combined with the numerous safeguards and guarantees on, for example, equality and human rights marks a significant departure from the traditional model of British constitutionalism. The concept of an executive with effectively unlimited authority has been rejected in this context. The Agreement grounds democracy on rules of equality, human rights, and effective participation. Perhaps most interestingly, the settlement includes precise rules on how all of these might be 'mainstreamed' within the structures of governance. The settlement marks the translation of some highly abstract value commitments into rules intended to structure a precise form of governance. The innovative nature of the system should be noted for it provides an interesting practical example of how a deliberative model might be constructed. There are severe problems with the way this has been achieved. But a progressive critique of the arrangements will have to reveal its own normative commitments and thus confront the neo-republican model of deliberative democracy advanced here.

CONCLUSION

This is an important time to be engaging in a debate on constitutionalism. Reform in the United Kingdom occurs in the midst of the globalization and europeanization of law. Confusion and anxiety are understandable reactions to these processes. In this paper I suggest that the debate in constitutional law should be informed by neo-republican thinking on the nature of law and democracy. If there is only one reason for this it is to counter the misguided wave of euphoria that has greeted the enactment of the Human Rights Act 1998. The voice of the legal profession defending its 'professional faith' is particularly piercing in this debate. Neo-republicanism is important precisely because it wishes to know who wants the last word in our social conversation and why this is the case. This critical perspective will gain in importance in the coming years.

In this paper I combine a framework of democratic law with a case-study of constitutional change in Northern Ireland. I argue that the revival of democratic thought in public law scholarship offers a useful lens through which to view these developments. Central aspects of the complex arrangements that have emerged will not receive the attention they deserve without this more inclusive frame of legal reference. The Northern Ireland settlement may unravel and the constitutional vision it contains never operate in practice. Even if this is the outcome there are clear lessons from this experiment in restructuring a democratic polity from which others can learn. Perhaps the most enduring lesson is that any democratic settlement worth the name must be underpinned by solid safeguards which ensure that the continuing conversation about the norms and practices that structure the process of governance can be conducted in an inclusive way. There are serious flaws in the Northern Ireland model but at the very least it has brought into the public sphere hard questions about what a modern constitutional settlement might look like. In other words, participants have had to translate their normative commitments into precise and detailed legal mechanisms aimed at achieving meaningful change.

JOURNAL OF LAW AND SOCIETY
VOLUME 27, NUMBER 1, MARCH 2000
ISSN: 0263–323X, pp. 98–132

The Government-Voluntary Sector Compacts: Governance, Governmentality, and Civil Society

JOHN MORISON*

In 1998 government and the main representatives of the voluntary sector in each of the four countries in the United Kingdom published 'compacts' on relations between government and the voluntary sector. These were joint documents, carrying forward ideas expressed by the Labour Party when in opposition, and directed at developing a new relationship for partnership with those 'not-for-profit organizations' that are involved primarily in the areas of policy and service delivery. This article seeks to use an examination of the compacts, and the processes that produced them and that they have now set in train, to explore some of the wider issues about the changing role of government and its developing relationships with civil society. In particular, it argues that the new partnership builds upon a movement from welfarism to economism which is being developed further through the compact process. Drawing upon a governmentality approach, and illustrating the account with interview material obtained from some of those involved in compact issues from within both government and those umbrella groups which represent the voluntary sector, an argument is made that this overall process represents the beginning of a new reconfiguration of the state that is of considerable constitutional significance.

* *School of Law, The Queen's University, Belfast BT7 INN, Northern Ireland*

I am grateful to all those who spoke to me and sent me material from the Compact Development Office in the National Council for Voluntary Organisations and the Home Office Voluntary and Community Unit in London, the Voluntary Information Unit of the Scottish Office and the Scottish Council for Voluntary Organisations, the National Assembly for Wales and the Wales Council for Voluntary Action, the Voluntary Activity Unit in Belfast and the Northern Ireland Council for Voluntary Action, and a number of individual voluntary and community organizations. I am particularly grateful to Paul Berasi, Neil Bradley, and Seamus McAleavey. I am also happy to acknowledge a small grant towards travel costs given by SLS Legal Publications (NI).

I. INTRODUCTION

In an earlier contribution to this journal this author argued that the constitutional reform agenda was focused too exclusively on the traditional institutions of big government and thus was missing an opportunity to engage with a wider project of renewing and invigorating democracy in those new structures and relationships that make up a wider process of governance[1]. This wider idea of governance marks a move from the modern state to an idea of 'cosmopolitan governance'[2] and, as such, involves complex relationships at regional, national, and global levels and across political institutions, agencies, networks, and associations in the economy and in civil society at each level. It is at these levels and towards these processes and inter-relationships that a project for democratizing the operation of governance as it actually occurs should be directed.

This account attempts to look at a particular exercise of power taking place outside the formal constitution and at how it is structured by wider processes. It provides an examination of the four compact documents drawn up by government and representatives from the voluntary sectors in England, Scotland, Wales, and Northern Ireland. These seek to structure a new partnership relation between the formal state and those parts of the voluntary sector which are particularly open to moving from a traditional welfarist ethos towards a more managerial or economist one as they perform functions that at one time were considered the direct responsibility of government bureaucracy. In part one the general context of changing structures of governance is reviewed before consideration is given to the formal development of civil society that is encouraged within the third way approach that characterizes some aspects of government policy. Changing patterns within the voluntary sector are examined before the account focuses in part two on how the compact documents emerge as a point from which the details of a new relationship between government and the sector can be cultivated further in a continuing process. Drawing upon governmentality literature, it is argued in part three that this new relationship must be seen as a particular exercise of power where new frameworks for thought and action are being developed in a process of exchange and dialogue. Part four offers the conclusion that there are now and increasingly spaces beyond the formal constitution, even reaching into civil society, where the realities of contemporary public power escape the notice of much current constitutional scholarship and elude the reach of any formal constitutional control.

1 J. Morison, 'The Case Against Constitutional Reform?' (1998) 25 *J. of Law and Society* 510.

2 D. Held, *Democracy and the Global Order: From the Modern State to Cosmopolitan Governance* (1995).

1. *Changing structures of governance*

Although the scope of what is meant by *governance* is now widening to different levels and across various relationships, the whole project of *government* is becoming now reduced as there is a loss of decision-making power and accountability to bodies beyond the traditional state. This general process ought to be becoming more and more familiar to constitutional lawyers who now increasingly must struggle to make the traditional categories of public law fit the new processes of governance. Of course much of this has to do with what might be termed the de-nationalization of government. Another important feature is the emergence some years ago of a belief in market forces as the basis for the efficient allocation of resources and the revival of contract as the foremost organizing mechanism for organizing a range of relationships in ways that blur further the boundary between public and private spheres. The old battle between market and state may not be entirely over and won but even now, with a Labour administration, the main question is less likely to be about the nature of the good society than, more prosaically, about how government can secure services on behalf of consumers through contracts with quality assured providers.[3] This is the situation with medical services, university education, and even legal services. The Labour government has inherited a complex set of markets and quasi-markets where contracting out and outsourcing exists alongside contracting in regimes where competitive in-house agencies operate at a distance from the parent operation.[4] Overall, it seems set to continue with this. There has not been any significant shift back to large-scale, direct-service provision by local or central government such as existed before the public sector reforms of the 1980s and early 1990s. The joint public sector and private sector ventures are to continue through the Private Finance Initiative for public infrastructure projects and in the encouragement of private investment in local services infrastructure through the Public Private Partnerships Programme. The move from Compulsory Competitive Tendering (CCT) to the Best Value framework as outlined in the Department of the Environment, Transport and the Regions document *Modernising Local government: Improving Local Services through Best Value* (1998) provides only a change in emphasis rather than a counter-revolution.[5] There are even radical proposals for public service plcs

3 Of course public service contracting in this context means something very different from traditional ideas of regular commercial contracts. As P. Vincent-Jones puts it, 'only at the margins of the investigation do we encounter what lawyers would recognize as "contracts" operating within what economists would recognize as "markets"' ('Public Sector Contracting and Quasi-Markets' in *Contract, Co-operation, and Competition*, eds. S. Deakin and J. Michie (1997) at 144). Contracts in the public sector environment are better regarded as a species of policy implementation and control.

4 See, further, W. Bartlett, J. Roberts, and J. Le Grand (eds.), *Quasi-Market Reform in the 1990s: A Revolution in Social Policy* (1998).

5 See P. Vincent-Jones, 'Competition and Contracting in the Transition from CCT to Best Value: Towards a More Reflexive Regulation?' (1999) 77 *Public Administration* 273.

to bring together in a new form of company both investors and partners from the public and private sectors with certain local authority duties permanently vested in them and an ability to engage in certain other entrepreneurial activities.[6]

Acceptance of the main thrust of changing patterns of governance has not been accompanied by the development of any new mechanisms for constraining and democratizing the new forms of public power. Regrettably, as was argued previously, the reform programme of the Labour government has remained firmly focused on traditional reforms to the traditional constitution. This has meant that new structures, processes, and relationships have been subject largely only to the inadequate control of existing mechanisms. Conventional bureaucratic and legal control mechanisms involving legislation and courts, discretions and budgets – even when they are operated by a variety of regulatory agencies and bodies dispersed beyond the state – increasingly only show up deficits in both public and private law mechanisms in protecting the rights of consumers, purchasers, and providers (not to mention the public interest) in the new circumstances.[7] Of course, the new circumstances introduce a variety of new mechanisms including standard setting, monitoring and enforcement, inspection and oversight, adjudication of complaints and grievances, performance pay, indicators and targets, licensing and franchising, and benchmarking and audit. It is now perhaps these, rather than the traditional mechanisms, that provide what measure of control and accountability that exists.[8] However, it must be remembered that such regulatory devices are directed less towards ensuring the application of the democratic values of participation and accountability than towards ensuring a rather distorted idea of market efficiency in a public sector context.[9] The new techniques of regulation can be criticized for their democratic insufficiency or for failing to meet the standards of a more reflexive approach as outlined by Teubner and

6 See Local Government Information Unit, *The Abolition of CCT and the achievement of Best Value* (1997) and Vincent-Jones, op. cit., n. 5.

7 See, further, P. Vincent-Jones, 'The Regulation of Contractualisation in Quasi-markets for Public Services' (1999) *Public Law* 303.

8 See, further, for example, C. Scott 'The 'New Public Law'' in *Public Sector Reform and the Citizen's Charter*, ed. C. Willet (1996) 51 for discussion of the difficulties of making 'the traditional hierarchical model of control and accountability in the public sector' fit the new organizational culture and the need for public lawyers to examine the effectiveness of 'new forms of control and accountability' rather than ponder the inability of old mechanisms to capture fugitive power.

9 However, as Hood and Scott argue within the context of the New Public Management, while the rhetoric may stress market values, a loosening of control towards freeing managers and introducing market values, there is in fact a mirror image of control whereby the contractualization process becomes 're-regulated'. See C. Hood and C. Scott, 'Bureaucratic Regulation and the New Public Management in the United Kingdom' (1996) 23 *J. of Law and Society* 321.

others.[10] In particular, the accounting dominated paradigm of juridified, regulatory law may occasion criticism.[11] However, the point remains that such structures and mechanisms continue to make up the reality of government under a Labour regime and it is on this ground that battles over legitimacy, democratic sufficiency or reflexivity should be fought, rather than in the high constitutionalism of Westminster, Whitehall, and the local council chamber.

The case for now looking at constitutional law in this way has already been made – even if it is not completely accepted everywhere. The changes to the nature of public power are becoming familiar and it seems certain that the general direction of change under Labour will not alter radically. But there is, however, one significant and arguably novel aspect to the revolution in governance as it continues under the stewardship of the Labour administration. This relates to the role of the voluntary sector. Here, it will be argued, is a genuinely new space within the constitution, or at least a space which now is being subject to a new process of organization and management. Part of this may be explained by government overtly attempting to develop a new partnership approach in discharging its basic functions. However, a fuller story, it will be argued, can only be obtained by looking at wider processes of governmentality and the changes in the nature of the state whereby stark differences between public and private become more fluid and uncertain as power is dispersed through networks of action that traverse the legal-constitutional boundaries that supposedly separate state and civil society. This is a complex and developing process, involving, on the one hand, a paradigmatic shift from welfarism to economic rationality and, on the other, an idea of non-state actors developing autonomy or resistance to control in a complex engagement between actors from the formal state and those from within informal networks of power beyond the state.

This dynamic relationship can be seen in operation by looking at the compact documents drawn up by government and voluntary sector umbrella groups within each of the jurisdictions within the United Kingdom. The various compacts are essentially guides to good practice in the relationship between government and voluntary organizations. As shall be argued, they represent the formal tip of a very much larger iceberg of changing relationships between government and civil society.

10 See Vincent-Jones, op. cit., n. 7, p. 321, who asks important and difficult questions about the degree of 'reflexivity' of the regulatory regimes and wonders if 'it may be that social democratic objectives different from those pursued by the Conservatives can be achieved by retaining quasi-markets and contractualisation, but under a more reflexive and less prescriptive regulatory umbrella'.

11 See, further, for example, R. Laughlin and J. Broadbent, 'Accounting and Law: Partners in the Juridification of the Public Sector in the United Kingdom? (1993) 4 *Critical Perspectives in Accounting* 337.

2. *Civil society and the third way*

Civil society is an idea whose time seems to have come (again). There are a number of reasons for this. Originally the idea of civil society as expounded by Adam Ferguson in the late eighteenth century and Tocqueville and Hegel in the early nineteenth century suggested a network of independent self-sustaining groups and networks which exist as a counterpart to the state and as a means of countering or at least limiting its influence.[12] Although this conception remains, and has gained additional currency from the experience of the struggle against authoritarian regimes in eastern Europe,[13] a major attraction of the concept of civil society seems now to lie with its possibilities as an alternative to the tired old state-market dichotomy. Market solutions may have not entirely run out of steam but there is undoubtedly a search for something to moderate them and a renewed interest in ways to accommodate the existence of power beyond the formal state. As Cohen and Arato see it, 'the recent re-emergence of the 'discourse of civil society' is at the heart of a sea change in contemporary political culture'.[14] Some of this would seem to relate to the connections that can be made between civil society and ideas of citizenship[15] and social inclusion[16] as well as wider notions of civility.[17] Other aspects perhaps connect with the idea of civil society acting as a tonic for democracy. Certainly there has long been a view that, as Putnam argues, everywhere 'democratic government is strengthened not weakened, when it faces vigorous civil society'.[18] Often this means that civil society is given the job of both generating

12 See, for example, C. Taylor, 'Civil Society and the Western Tradition' in *The Nation of Tolerance and Human Rights: Essays in Honour of Raymond Klibansky*, eds. E. Groffier and M. Parradis (1991) 117, and K. Kumar, 'Civil Society: an inquiry into the usefulness of an historical term' 44 *British J. of Sociology* (1993) 375. (Of course early conceptions of civil society as developed by Aristotle or even Kant do not involve such a distinction between social and political life. See, further, M. Reiedel, *Between Tradition and Revolution: The Hegelian Transformation of Political Philosophy* (1984), and E. Gellner, 'The Civil and the Sacred' in *The Tanner Lectures on Human Values*, vol. 12, ed. G. B. Peterson (1991).

13 See J. Keane, *Civil Society and the State: New European Perspectives* (1988) and *Democracy and Civil Society* (rev. edn., 1998). See, also, J. Hall (ed.), *Civil Society: Theory, History, Comparison* (1995), and C. Hann and E. Dunn (eds.), *Civil Society: Challenging Western Models* (1996) for other applications of the concept in a variety of circumstances.

14 J.L. Cohen and A. Arato, *Civil Society and Political Theory* (1992) at 3.

15 See, for example, A. MacIntyre, *Whose Justice? Whose Rationality?* (1988); M. Sandel, *Democracy's Discontent* (1996); M. Walzer, 'The Idea of a Civil Society', *Dissent* (1993) 293.

16 See, for example, R. Lister, *The Exclusive Society: Citizenship and the Poor* (1990), and M. Bersford and S. Croft, 'It's our problem too! Challenging the exclusion of poor people from poverty discourse' (1995) 15 (2/3) *Critical Social Policy* 75–93.

17 E. Shills, for instance, suggests that this involves 'civil manners' and argues that 'civility is an attribute and pattern of conduct [that] . . . is solicitous of the well-being of the whole, and of the larger interest' ('The Virtue of Civil Society' (1991) 26 *Government and Opposition* (1991) 3, at 12–3). For a more recent working of this idea see, further, S. Carter, *Civility: Manners, Morals and the Etiquette of Democracy* (1998).

18 R. Putnam, *Making Democracy Work: Civic Traditions in Modern Italy* (1993) at 182.

solidarity and protecting freedom beyond the reach of the state, as well as articulating choice.[19] Advocacy of the value of civil society may be combined with a belief in participatory democracy to suggest ways of transcending the limits of traditional, liberal, aggregative democracy.[20] At another level the concept has even been used by bodies such as the World Bank and the Organisation for Economic Co-operation and Development (OECD) to stress ideas of accountability and transparency in government activity within an idea of governance designed to foster an environment where a market economy can flourish.[21]

Certainly there is an element of definitional elasticity with the basic term civil society. Fierlbeck indeed concludes that 'the concept of 'civil society' is overused, overrated, and analytically insubstantial'.[22] However, notwithstanding this, civil society emerges as a key notion in so-called Third Way thinking which is trying to chart a new social democratic agenda beyond the politics of both left and right. While traditional liberalism involves regarding civil society as an independent, self-governing sphere generally resistant to outside interference, the Third Way approach is willing to engage with the concept more closely in efforts to develop an alternative to market and state. As Giddens stresses, 'the fostering of an active civil society is a basic part of the politics of the third way'.[23] This involves generally renewing civic culture by developing partnership between government and civil society, harnessing local initiative to promote social entrepreneurship

19 Cohen and Arato, op. cit., n. 14, for example, see civil society as comprising 'self-limiting democratizing movements seeking to expand and protect spaces for both negative liberty and positive freedom and to recreate egalitarian forms of solidarity' (p. 17). For them, civil society has two components: civil society as 'the space of social experimentation for the development of new forms of life, new types of solidarity', and political society which is 'the space in which the autonomy of groups and the articulation of conflict among them are defended and discussion and debate of collective choice occur' (p. 38).

20 See Morison, op. cit., n. 1, pp. 528–35 for an overview of some of approaches advocating participatory forms of democratic engagement. See S. Verba, K. Schlozman, and H. Brady, *Voice and Equality: Civic Voluntarism in American Politics* (1995) for a more sceptical approach. This draws upon a large empirical study of the American public's engagement with the political process to argue that it is a complex and uneven process whereby the public participate in a civic voluntarism model. Resources of time and money and civic skills contribute to a hierarchy of effectiveness and, in reality, there is a very unequal voice given to poor and racial minorities. See also, J. Mansbridge, *Beyond Adversarial Politics* (1980) for a small-scale example.

21 World Bank, *Governance and Development* (1992) and, especially, *Governance: The World Bank's Experience* (1994). See, also, OECD, *Participatory Development and Good Governance* (1995) and *Our Global Neighbourhood* (1995).

22 K. Fierlbeck, *Globalizing Democracy: Power, Legitimacy and the interpretation of Democratic Ideas* (1998) 172.

23 A. Giddens, *The Third Way: The Renewal of Social Democracy* (1998) at 78. It is interesting to notice the origins of some of this in the related communitarian approach. Etzioni, for example, maintains that 'a person who is completely private is lost to civic life . . . [and that] the exclusive pursuit of one's self-interest is not even a good prescription for conduct in the marketplace'. A. Etzioni, *The Sprit of Community: Rights, Responsibilities and the Communitarian Agenda* (1995) at 259.

in the social and material refurbishment of society. It requires the protection and development of the local public sphere, including the physical public space of streets and parks, and the development of community infrastructure to encourage bottom-up decision making and local autonomy. Crucially, it involves the third sector as the organized vanguard of civil society but, significantly, Giddens maintains that the state should reserve to itself the role of 'protect(ing) individuals from the conflicts of interest always present in civil society'.[24]

The Labour government too sees particular value in civil society and the third sector. In part this must be due to the extent of the sector and its ubiquity in a whole range of areas. Estimates of the size and value of the voluntary sector vary, not least according to how it is defined. The voluntary sector may, however, account for up to one in twenty-five full-time paid jobs in the United Kingdom and one in ten service jobs while the total contribution to the economy is estimated at £25 billion per annum.[25]

Despite the fact that some commentators suggest that one of the main characteristics of the new wave of voluntary organizations is an emphasis on support rather than service provision,[26] there has been an increasing and significant involvement by the sector in delivering a whole range of services. Perhaps this has much to do also with a realization that the apparatus of central and local government has been so depleted by privatization, contracting out, and so on that it no longer has the capacity to deliver services in an old Labour way. The voluntary sector, and the voluntary sector in partnership with business and government, now perhaps provides the only possible solution to a range of problems, particularly relating to social exclusion, which are outside the reach of state bureaucracy and beyond the interests of the private sector.

24 Giddens, id., pp. 85–6. Again there is an echo with communitarianism where Etzioni maintains that 'many social goals . . . require partnership between public and private groups. Though government should not seek to replace local communities, it may need to empower them by strategies of support . . . there is a great need for study and experimentation with creative use of the structures of civil society and public-private co-operation, especially where the delivery of health, educational and social services are concerned'. Etzioni, id., at p. 260.

25 M. Taylor, *The Best of Both Worlds: the Voluntary Sector and Local Government* (1998). The Commission on the Voluntary Sector established by National Council for Voluntary Organisations (the Deakin report) suggests that there are about a quarter of a million voluntary bodies within a narrow definition (which does not include those sports clubs, trade unions, and business associations which do not deliver some public benefit) and about 1.3 million bodies of all kinds. There may be as many as 21 million people volunteering with up to four million adults giving time in the previous month. (*Meeting the Challenge of Change: Voluntary Action into the 21st Century* (1996)). The *United Kingdom Voluntary Sector Almanac 1998–99* contains more modest estimates suggesting a figure of £12.8 billion per annum as the contribution of the sector to GDP and a level of about 3 million volunteers. (See, further, <http://www.ncvo-vol.org.uk/main/gateway/almanac.html>.)

26 G. Mulgan and C. Landry, *The Other Invisible Hand: Remaking Charity for the 21st Century* (1995).

These new circumstances are reflected in the most basic aspects of Labour Party politics. Even the most casual student of Labour Party politics in the United Kingdom will have noticed that the famous Clause IV of the Labour Constitution,[27] for so long a talisman of the Left, has been subject to the modernization of New Labour. Not everyone, however, will immediately be able to recall to mind what has replaced it. In fact, the new Clause IV specifically contains a commitment to partnership and co-operation with voluntary organizations. It refers among other things to 'a dynamic economy, serving the public interest, in which the enterprise of the market and the rigour of competition are joined with the forces of partnership and co-operation'.[28]

This theme of the voluntary sector mediating between state and market is developed within the details of particular government programmes too. An important document, written just before coming to government and setting out Labour's policies for the voluntary sector, echoes the idea of finding an alternative to straightforward state or market. It claimed that 'in rejecting the old arid split between "public" and "private", Labour has recognized the richness and diversity of independent organizations and their potential'.[29] This potential is to be realized in a range of major policy initiatives from *Sure Start* and *Better Government for Older People* to *New Deal for Communities* and *Health Action Zones* and *Education Action Zones* which are all dominated by the language of partnership.[30] To some extent these develop existing structures such as the National Health Service and Community Care Act 1990 which, in refocusing care from institution-based to home-based provision has cast local authorities as enablers rather than providers who must now, in assessing need, consult and plan with the voluntary sector who themselves are increasingly encouraged into service provision.[31] This sort of approach is continued and developed through aspects

27 Clause Four, with its origins in *Labour and the New Social Order* (1918) written by Fabian leaders Beatrice and Sidney Webb, committed successive Labour governments to a policy of nationalization.

28 See clause IV, para. 2 as reproduced in Labour Party, *Labour and the Voluntary Sector: Setting the Agenda for Partnership in Government. A Consultative Document* (1996)

29 Labour Party, *Building the Future Together: Labour's Policies for Partnership between Government and the Voluntary Sector* (1997) at 1. The same document connects civil society, the voluntary sector, and the stakeholder society by claiming that 'creating a stakeholder society is about recreating a civic society in which "the rights we enjoy reflect the duties we owe"' (p. 3).

30 More general ideas about developing social capital which are appearing increasingly in policy rhetoric also draw upon the voluntary sector. See, further, M. Wann, *Building Social Capital: Self-help in the Twenty-First Century Welfare State* (1995).

31 See, further, C. Bemrose and J. MacKeith, *Partnerships for Progress: Good Practice in the relationship between local government and voluntary organizations* (1996). This was certainly the analysis of Labour when in opposition when they complained that 'relationships between local government and the voluntary sector have changed, largely as "contracting" has made some authorities view the voluntary and private sectors as synonymous' (see Labour Party, op. cit., n. 28, p. 18).

of the local commissioning arrangements in health service reforms.[32] It is present too in the Best Value programme where the voluntary sector may be involved not only in competition to provide services but with the consultation process that determines what best value actually is in a given situation, and in the drawing up of performance indicators and efficiency measures which assess if it has in fact been delivered.[33]

What is maybe increasingly becoming true for service delivery has, arguably, been the case for some longer time in relation to policy formation.[34] The literature here suggests that for some time 'the appropriate unit of analysis for studies of policy formation is not the state understood in the institutional sense, but the state as a collection of policy arenas incorporating both government and private actors'.[35] The state here is involved in a series of complex relationships with policy communities and policy networks and, as with other aspects of the process of hollowing out the state, this has both national, regional, and international dimensions.[36] Clearly though the voluntary sector is present throughout and at every level

32 See DHSS Northern Ireland, *Fit for the Future: A consultation document on the government's proposals for the future of the Health and Personal Social Services in Northern Ireland* (1998). (<http://www.dhssni.gov.uk/the_department/publications/fitforthefuture/fulldoc.html>) which is the latest development of the White Paper, *The New NHS – Modern and Dependable* (1997; Cm. 3807) setting out the future for the Health Service in England, the Scottish Office Department of Health, *Designed to Care – Renewing the National Health Service in Scotland* (1997; Cm. 3811), and Department of Health, *NHS Wales: Putting Patients First* (1998; Cm. 3841).

33 See, further, Department of Transport and the Regions, *Modern Local Government In Touch with the People* (1998), especially chapter 7 which sets out how Best Value differs from Compulsory Competitive Tendering by widening what quality means and adding consultation with local users in both setting objectives and measuring performance to existing values of efficiency and economy. The scale and importance of this policy can be seen from the fact that it will eventually apply across all local government which accounts for approximately 25 per cent of all public expenditure, some £80.3 billion. (Figures quoted in Select Committee on Environment, Transport and Regional Affairs, *Eleventh Report* 1998 <www.parliament.the-stationery-off.co.uk/PA/cm199798/cmselect/cmenvtra/705/70502.htm>.

34 Carroll and Carroll discuss the importance of permitting popular participation in the policy process through 'civic networks' in order to foster legitimacy for the state. (See B.W. Carroll and T. Carroll, 'Civic Networks, Legitimacy and the Policy Process' (1999) 12 *Governance* 1–23.)

35 E. Laumann and D. Knoke, *The Organizational State* (1987) at 9. For a general overview of the literature, see M. Atkinson and W. Coleman, 'Policy Networks, Policy Communities and the Problems of Governance' (1992) 5 *Governance* 154, and R. Rhodes, *Understanding Governance: Policy Networks, Governance, Reflexivity and Accountability* (1997).

36 In an introduction to a special edition of *Governance* (vol. 2, 1989) on policy networks and policy communities in an international context, Walker identifies the development of 'parabureaucratic communities of policy specialists based within and without the formal institutions of government' and the need to map 'the sources of creativity in society, and try to trace the channels through which the ideas of those with specialized knowledge filter into the policy-making process and eventually become the basis for reform' ('Introduction: Policy Communities as a Global Phenomena', at p. 2).

pursuing what is one of their most basic roles – that of campaigning and advocating change on behalf of particular interests. This role is something that Labour have been anxious to endorse from an early stage in their policies towards the sector.

Overall, it is apparent the New Labour project has a special place assigned to the voluntary sector. Mr Blair, writing while in opposition in 1996, referred to how:

> we want to restore a proper respect for the independence of the voluntary sector. I do not favour simply a contract relationship with the voluntary sector, I favour something more profound: working together to pursue common objectives in the public interest.[37]

This is to extend to a policy role too. A subsequent document talks of the need for a government that 'respects the creativity and independence of the voluntary sector and nurtures its power to change Society for the better' as well as of how 'an independent and creative voluntary sector, committed to voluntary activity as an expression of citizenship . . . is central to our vision of a stakeholder society'.[38] In government the desire to pursue this relationship has been expressed in the development of the compacts.

3. *The changing voluntary sector: welfarism to economism?*

Labour Party interest in developing the relationship with the voluntary sector has been matched by interest within parts of the voluntary sector in moving forward ideas of partnership with government.

Of course the term voluntary sector – defined widely here to cover organizations that are not for profit and independent of government – covers a very diverse range of organizations. Essentially, however, voluntary organizations fall in five categories, with considerable overlap.[39] There are service providers which may depend on voluntary contributions or government grants. There are those concerned with research and advocacy and these may be large and nationally or internationally organized such as Child Poverty Action or Greenpeace or very small and local. There are self-help groups which offer support and assistance. There are interest groups which often are oriented around leisure or sporting activity and, finally, there are intermediary bodies, like the councils for voluntary service, which exist to assist and advise. These different types of groups will be involved in three broad types of voluntary activity: mutual support, service delivery, and campaigning. Within this very general picture there are important

37 Labour Party, op. cit., n. 28, at p. 2.
38 Labour Party, op. cit., n. 29, at p. 3.
39 See, further, C. Handy, *Understanding Voluntary Organizations* (1988) 9–18 for some basic definitions. It is important to note particularly that the voluntary sector across the United Kingdom is wider that the charitable sector.

distinctions and fault lines between, for example, consumers of the activities of an association and members of the association.[40]

There is a particular and very significant tension between a professionalized, managerial approach and a more traditional, volunteering ethos. Certainly all those interviewed by the author for this study, on both the government and voluntary sector side, acknowledge a division in the sector and the emergence of a new breed of professionalized, well-funded, and well-organized voluntary organizations.[41] The term economism is used here to denote the general development towards an idea of economic rationality that has occurred at the expense of more traditional ideas of welfare professionalism.[42] It refers to the tendency generally to use the language of risk and reward, choice, economic rationality, targeting, and output as the governing concepts in preference to more traditional welfare ideas such as client need or professional values. The move to managerialism, with its emphasis on efficiency, business practices, and top-down management structures, has been identified with the growth of the contract culture but it has been growing in importance for some time.[43] One critic predicted that the use of contracts would favour large and well-organized groups with expertise and professional knowledge where 'opportunities for volunteers,

40 See, further, J. Landsley, 'Member involvement in non-welfare voluntary bodies: some comments and forecasts' in Commission on the Future of the Voluntary Sector, *Meeting the Challenge of Change: Voluntary Action into the 21st Century. Summary of Evidence and Selected Papers* (1996) 74–81. See, also, M. Taylor, 'The Future of User Involvement in the Voluntary Sector: A Contribution to the Debate', id., at p. 56. There are also interesting distinctions between organizations which emphasize existing social values, such as the National Trust and those that promote new values, such as Friends of the Earth. See, further, for example, P. Lowe and J.Goyder, *Environmental Groups in Politics* (1983).

41 For example, from the government side it was said:

> The sector is divided. There are extremes . . . the more professional, well-funded, well-established . . . organizations such as NCVO and at the other end of the scale, there are smaller, volunteer-led, self help, community groups. . . . We would want to see the more established voluntary sector delivering services effectively and efficiently and being business-like in the way it conducts itself . . . introduction of quality standards is important . . ..

From the other side of the equation, a member of an umbrella group representing a large part of the sector suggested that:

> The sector has always been split. . . . Main division is large-scale, professionalised organizations and smaller, community based ones . . . but also a big urban-rural divide. There are big divisions about language, policy etc. . . . There are still some smaller organizations . . . dinosaurs . . . [that are] . . . so PC [Politically Correct] . . . on New Deal, the Lottery or whatever . . . and for them the 'felt position' is the only thing . . . it is even more important than the facts.

42 For an good overview of this general process within social welfare, see J. Clarke and J. Newman, *The Managerial State* (1997).

43 See, further, for example, M. Taylor, *New Times, New Challenges: Voluntary Organisations Facing 1990* (1990), J. Lewis, 'Developing the mixed economy of care: emerging issues for voluntary organizations' 22 *J. of Social Policy* (1993) 173, and J. Charlesworth et al., 'Tangled Webs? Managing local mixed economies of care' 74 *Public Administration* (1996) 67.

both on management committees and in service provision may be severely restricted'.[44] This has proved to be true – at least to some extent.[45] The influence of managerialism, and all the cultural and structural changes that it brings,[46] has been absorbed by at least parts of the voluntary sector. For the larger organizations in particular, it is increasingly routine to use managers from the private sector, management consultants, professional fund raisers, and lobbyists. Indeed, the whole panoply of private sector management values and techniques are being brought into the voluntary sector in much the same way as they entered the lexicon of public sector management a little while earlier.[47]

Not only is there a trend for larger bodies to organize themselves in ways that emphasize the managerial rather than the professional or bureaucratic, but there is also an associated re-invention of the public that they serve and support. As Clarke and Newman see it, this involves identifying the community as a mobilizing focus for collective action in a way that links 'the sturdy "self-reliance" of the past' (drawing upon nostalgia for traditional working-class communities) with the '"active citizenry" of community action in the present' (which draws upon Blairite ideas of "social-ism" and communitarianism as a political ideology).[48] This in turn links to what Clarke and Newman describe as 'the increasing visibility of the voluntary sector in shaping a welfare pluralism alongside state and market forms, assisting in welfare provision, sustaining a diversity of needs and playing a role in community regeneration'.[49] Much of this finds expression in terms of the development of partnerships – at levels ranging from the local to the international and involving business, voluntary and community organizations, and all aspects of the state – as *the* most appropriate mechanism for recruiting stakeholders and bringing them together in new forms of

44 B. Waine, 'The voluntary sector – the Thatcher years' in *Social Policy Review* 4, eds. N. Manning and R. Page (1992) at 86.

45 *UK Voluntary Sector Almanac*, op. cit., n. 25 reports that although the overall number of general charities continues to increase at a rate of 3,000 per year, 88 per cent of gross income is accounted for by less than 10 per cent of organizations. A consultation document (on the compact Code of Practice on Funding) issued in autumn 1999 by the Working Group on Government Relations Secretariat (see <http://www.ncvo-vol.org.uk>) suggests that around 30 per cent (£4 billion) of the sector's income comes from government with just under half being grants and just over half being purchasing, including contracts.

46 See, generally, Clarke and Newman, op. cit., n. 42, and M. Power, *The Audit Society* (1994).

47 See. further, for example, C. Foster and F. Plowden, *The State Under Stress* (1996).

48 Clarke and Newman, op. cit., n. 42, at p. 131–2.

49 id. This can be further connected to 'community empowerment' models which aim to construct participatory structures and processes in local communities to augment traditional, representative local government. See, further, J. Stewart, 'A future for local authorities as community government' in *The Future of Local Government*, eds. J. Stewart and G. Stoker (1989) and S. Ranson and J. Stewart, *Management for the Public Domain: Enabling the Learning Society* (1994).

collaborative action to build civic culture.[50] Whether this impacts upon the voluntary sector to encourage genuinely new forms of interaction[51] or, more narrowly, to encourage a 'grant-grabbing' culture,[52] the overall effect is to encourage further the professionalized, organized voluntary sector.

This overall change in ethos and management within the voluntary and community sector is a very important development. Part of this (but only part) reflects the more general move from welfarism to economism that is observable across many of the caring professions and that can be plotted in a more or less developed form in, for example, the emergence of powerful ideas such as clinical governance which has come to dominate the organizational culture of National Health Service provision.[53] However, there is an element of shared vision here too. As shall be developed in the next section where the origins of the compacts are explored, there are parts of the voluntary sector that share the values of Labour's Third-Way approach – or at least see a legitimate opportunity there. It is this that has provided the basis for developing the compacts which in turn has given impetus to further reconfigure how the sector operates.

II. THE DEVELOPMENT OF GOVERNMENT-VOLUNTARY SECTOR COMPACTS

In the previous section it was argued that there has been a fundamental readjustment of the role of the state and the subaltern polities that are involved in carrying out the business of government. Traditional liberal models saw civil society existing as a counter to the state and as something to be tolerated rather than embraced. Government either provided services directly or organized them through statutory agencies. The role of voluntary organizations in discharging the business of government was restricted to that of innovators and pathfinders. Just as that model was altered by a rolling back of the state and an experimentation with markets, so too is there now the beginnings of yet another new configuration – perhaps

50 This, of course, is not a uniquely British phenomenon. (See, further, Organisation for Economic Co-operation and Development in Europe, *Partnerships for Rural Development* (1990); M. Murray and L. Dunn, *Revitalising Rural America: A Perspective on Collaboration and Community* (1996)). Indeed, there is even a history of application in the United Kingdom outside the New Labour project in the rather special circumstances of Northern Ireland. See, further, J. Hughes et al., *Partnership Governance in Northern Ireland* (1998).

51 See, for example, D. Chrislip, *Transforming Politics* (1995) or K. Bassett, 'Partnerships, Business Elites and Urban Politics: New Forms of Governance in an English City?' (1996) 33 *Urban Studies* 539.

52 See M. Jones and K. Ward, 'Grabbing Grants: The Role of Coalitions in Urban Economic Development' *Local Economy* (May 1998) 28.

53 See, further, G. Scally and J. Donaldson, 'Clinical Governance and the drive for quality improvement in the new NHS in England' (1998) 317 *British Medical J.* 61 for a brief overview of this process.

a third way. This sees civil society as a *resource* for the state, a reserve army of potential. Government may now be willing to accept a wider responsibility but, as it can not discharge this with the now depleted apparatus of the state or rely completely on the market, it must seek a new partner. This is where the voluntary sector emerges as important. In many ways it is well placed to respond. The sector generally has remained a repository for social democratic values during the culture shifts of the past two decades. It is growing in size and parts of it have become more professionalized and are themselves seeking an enhanced role. Beyond this there is undeniably a degree of common cause between parts of the sector and the government, particularly over social exclusion and community development. As the development of the compacts is considered it will be argued that the process must be seen in light of this fundamental reconfiguration of the state and in terms of a tension between the traditional welfarism of the sector and an economism that might be required in a new partnership relationship.

It is the more organized part of the voluntary sector that in each of the four jurisdictions within the United Kingdom has responded to overtures from the Labour Party. There is an argument that there is an important earlier phase to the new relationship between government and the voluntary sector[54] but undoubtedly the origins of the compact can be traced to Labour initiatives which began in 1994 when Tony Blair launched the Leader's review of the relationship between government and the voluntary sector. Following the adoption of a new statement of aims in Clause IV in 1995,[55] there were consultation processes in England, Scotland, Wales, and Northern Ireland and a consultation paper was issued early in 1996.[56] Meanwhile the sector itself has been debating similar issues through the Deakin commission in England and various initiatives in all the home countries.[57] The Labour Party document *Building the Future Together*[58] advanced

54 In 1989–90 the Thatcher government, suffering some annoyance from Shelter and other campaigning groups, instituted an efficiency scrutiny of the voluntary sector. Paradoxically, this identified shortcomings with government's strategy and argued for a more coherent approach there. Other than in the somewhat special circumstances of Northern Ireland where a Voluntary Activity Unit was set up and strategy document produced in 1993 (see, further, J. Morison 'Democracy, Governance and the Voluntary Sector in the New Northern Ireland' in *Human Rights, Equality and Democratic Renewal in Northern Ireland*, ed. C. Harvey (2000, forthcoming)), there was little formal action taken.

55 See n. 27 above.

56 Labour Party, op. cit., n. 28.

57 The Deakin commission, op. cit., n. 25 was set up the National Council of Voluntary Organisations and part funded by the Rowntree Foundation. Its proposals for a 'concordat' of basic principles to govern relations between government and the voluntary sector provided a model for the compacts. In Wales, the Wales Council for Voluntary Action published proposals and in Scotland too there was the commission on the future of the voluntary sector in Scotland (the Kemp report) which produced *Head and Heart* (1997). In Northern Ireland, where for various reasons the voluntary sector has been engaged closely in government (see, further, J. Morison and S. Livingstone, *Reshaping Public Power: Northern Ireland the British Constitutional Crisis* (1996) especially pp. 143–7) there was

the idea of a compact, underpinned by a series of principles, as necessary to provide the basis for a partnership between government and the sector. On coming to power the Labour government, with the various national councils acting as umbrella groups to represent the voluntary sector, initiated a series of consultation processes across the United Kingdom which resulted in the publication in November and December 1998 of separate compact documents in England, Scotland, Wales, and Northern Ireland.[59]

1. *The 'detail' of the compacts*

To the lawyer approaching them for the first time, the compacts may appear as genuinely baffling documents. They seem to be made up mainly of warm words, platitudes, and generalities. The compacts are joint documents from government and the four voluntary sector councils in the United Kingdom. They represent an important statement about a new relationship. In England the compact applies to the voluntary and community sector and to central government departments, including government offices for the regions, and all relevant 'Next Steps' agencies. In Scotland, the Scottish Parliament has debated the compact and will be invited to endorse it before it rolls out to take effect with the executive and all central government agencies.[60] In Wales, the Assembly has endorsed the compact

already since 1993 a developed *Strategy for the Support of the Voluntary Sector and for Community Development in Northern Ireland.* The continuing existence of this, and a widespread feeling that it was due for updating, provided a focus for both government and the sector to monitor their relationship. For development of the compact, the Voluntary Activity Unit within Government in conjunction with the Northern Ireland Council on Voluntary Action (NICVA) organized a working group to consult with the sector and circulate a draft to the 5,000 organizations on the NICVA database. See, further, Morison, op. cit., n. 54.

58 Labour Party, op. cit. n. 29.

59 *Getting it Right Together: Compact on Relations between Government and the Voluntary and Community Sector in England* (1998; Cm. 4100); *The Scottish Compact: The Principles Underpinning the relationship between Government and the Voluntary Sector in Scotland* (1998; Cm. 4083); *A Shared Vision: Compact between the Government and the Voluntary Sector in Wales* (1998; Cm. 4107); and *Building Real Partnership: Compact between Government and the Voluntary and Community Sector in Northern Ireland* (1998; Cm. 4167). Originally, as the author was informed by a member of one the voluntary sector councils, there was to be an overarching United Kingdom compact:

> There was to be a statement of commitment from Big Government . . . we wrote that off . . . at a meeting when the four councils were present . . . and the Home Office civil servants were present . . . What would we put in it? The four compacts were different but we couldn't find anything for the big one that was more than about a page so we agreed then, and it was coming from our side . . . that we would just have a foreword from the PM in each compact to give it some sort of central authority.

60 See *Scottish Parliament Official Report* vol. 2, no. 8, 23 September 1999, at col. 769–806, and *Scottish Parliament Social Inclusion, Housing and Voluntary Sector Committee Official Report*, meeting 4, 29 September 1999, at col. 101.

as its initial framework for dealing with the voluntary and community sector[61] but in Northern Ireland the late arrival of devolution has meant that there the compact, while activated already with regard to the structures of continuing direct rule, awaits endorsement from the Assembly. The idea of all four compacts is that eventually they will provide the basis for the relationship between all voluntary and community bodies that come into direct contact with government and all those aspects of government and emanations of the state in all the home nations that deal with sector.

The status of the compacts is unusual. They certainly are not contracts – even in the rather loose sense given to this term in the public services context. There is certainly nothing to make either party adhere to the very general aspirations that the documents set out. The English compact, for example, talks of it being a 'memorandum concerning the relations between the government and the voluntary and community sector' which is not 'a legally binding document' but one whose authority 'is derived from its endorsement by government and by the voluntary and community sector itself through its consultation process'.[62] There is also the fact that the content of the compacts, at least as viewed from the outside, is extremely vague and general – almost trite – while the general exhortations to 'take into account', 'to respect', and 'work towards' seem incontestable.

While each is slightly different, they all contain an identical 'message from the Prime Minister'[63] as well as various forewords from the Secretaries of State and the chairs of bodies representing the voluntary sector organizations. The emphasis here, and indeed generally in the short documents, is on acknowledging the validity and significance of the sector. The language throughout is that of *recognition*.

Each compact offers confirmation of the scope and extent of the voluntary sector and recognizes the validity of its role. The Scottish compact, for example, acknowledges that both government and the voluntary sector 'have their own spheres of actions with different roles, responsibilities and resources' and that 'not all voluntary organizations will have an interest in seeking partnership with government' and some, indeed, 'may find themselves more often in opposition to the government than in partnership'.[64] The Northern Ireland compact defines the proper roles of each partner – which includes a government obligation to work for the good health and continued growth of the sector and a sector obligation to 'advocate and

61 See *The National Assembly for Wales: The Official Record*, 21 July 1999, at 58–86.

62 Cm. 4100, op. cit., n. 59, at para. 1. In fact the English compact is the most developed in terms of mechanisms for resolution of disagreements. In addition to the possibilities flowing from the obligation to make an annual report to Parliament, there is a three-stage approach for disputes about the applicability of the compact moving from mutual resolution through mediation to a referral to the Parliamentary Commissioner in cases of possible maladministration (see para. 14). The enforcement mechanisms for the other compacts are to be worked out at later stages of their development. See further below.

63 See n. 59 above.

64 Cm. 4083, id., p. 1.

seek change' – and describes these as 'complementary, interdependent and mutually supportive'.[65] In the Welsh compact there is even some idea of the sector being more or less formally involved in representation where it states that the 'government recognizes that voluntary organizations have an obligation to represent the interests of their constituents and the people and communities they work with'.[66]

Each compact refers to and recognizes the sector's independence. This was seen as particularly important by the sector representatives in the councils in rendering the compact palatable to their wider constituency and government was willing to accept this. The English compact, for instance, goes so far as to contain an 'undertaking' by government 'to recognize and support the independence of the sector, including its right within the law, to campaign, to comment on government policy, and to challenge that policy, irrespective of any funding relationship that might exist'.[67] In the Welsh compact, government refer warmly to the contribution that the sector makes to the economic, social, environmental, and cultural life of Wales and 'the role they play in formulating and delivering public policy' while acknowledging that 'voluntary and community organizations are independent organizations which determine their own priorities and manage their own affairs'.[68]

This language of recognition generally seems to involve government acknowledging the sector and endorsing its validity rather than recognition in the other direction. In the Welsh and Scottish compacts the commitments of each partner are aligned into two columns in a balance sheet and the asymmetrical nature of this shows clearly that government is not only offering more quantitatively but also qualitatively.[69] This continues to be obvious, particularly where the various compacts set out 'shared visions and values' and 'shared principles'. Again these are expressed at a high level of generality. The English compact, for example, refers to a shared vision of voluntary and community activity being 'fundamental to the development of a democratic, socially inclusive society'.[70] The document goes on to detail how within this

65 Cm. 4167, id., p. 10.
66 Cm. 4107, id., p. 10.
67 Cm. 4100, id., at para. 9.1.
68 Cm. 4017, id., at p. 8.
69 For example, within the Welsh compact there is a two page section with a sub-heading of 'Recognition' (pp. 8–9). Government recognizes variously the scope of the sector, its diversity, independence, and representative role and makes commitments to designate a minister with appropriate responsibility who will be charged with drawing up policies on measures to support working with the sector and promote volunteering and community development. The sector meanwhile is required only to recognize the very obvious fact that the government has an important role in the development of public policy and services, that government works within a legal and financial framework and that the sector itself should have 'clearly defined procedures and structures' to promote accountability – although these remain undefined. Despite having their obligations in a larger typeface, the column containing the voluntary sector's commitments fails to make it across to the corresponding second page of the government's obligations.
70 Cm. 4100, n. 59, at para. 5.

vision, voluntary and community organizations 'act as pathfinders for the involvement of users in the design and delivery of services and often act as advocates for those who otherwise have no voice'. In doing so, it continues, 'they promote both equality and diversity . . . help to alleviate poverty, improve the quality of life and involve the socially excluded . . . [and] make an important direct economic contribution to the nation'.[71]

These are very fine words indeed. Their general tenor is continued across all the compacts as they describe the 'Shared Values' as including (to take the list provided in the Scottish compact,) 'democratic society, active citizenship, pluralism, equality of opportunity, quality services, cross-sectoral working and sustainable development'.[72] The 'Shared Principles' are expressed at a similar level of generality to include (using the list given in the Northern Ireland compact) 'Accountability, Active Citizenship, Community, Democracy, Equality, Partnership, Pluralism and Social Justice'.[73]

It is only as the compacts move towards addressing the development of partnership relations and, particularly, as regards resources, that the documents begin to speak with any degree of specificity. Even here, however, the language is characteristically vague and non-specific. On partnership relations generally, the compacts carry government promises to meet and consult with the sector while the sector agrees to respect confidentiality and ensure that a full range of interests are represented in any consultations. The documents are, as might be expected, non-committal on the level of resources but there are important references made here to accounting mechanisms and to quality assurance systems. For example, in the Scottish compact, government refers to 'best practice in monitoring publicly funded work' and the sector undertakes to 'champion the importance of good management . . . [and] maintain agreed monitoring, performance evaluation and report-back systems to secure effectiveness in the use of resources'.[74] The English compact is even less specific, referring only to an undertaking 'to develop quality standards appropriate to the organization'.[75] However, when further action on developing the process started by the compacts is mentioned then the language becomes more specific and detailed. At this point. arguably, it becomes just possible to discern that these documents may in fact be concerned with radically changing the configuration between the state and the sector.

2. *Future development of the compacts*

Throughout the documents it is emphasized they are a starting point only. Indeed, there is elaborate machinery to take this all forward. The compacts

71 id., at para. 6.
72 Cm. 4083, id., at p. 2.
73 Cm. 4167, id., at pp. 12–13.
74 Cm. 4083, id., at p. 4.
75 Cm. 4100, id., at para. 10.3.

themselves generally give indications of what is to come. For instance, the English compact refers to the ministerial group, chaired by the Home Secretary and containing representation from across relevant sections of government that is to oversee and monitor the implementation of the compact as well as the voluntary and community sector working group on government relations, and associated reference group which contains representation from across the sector and is charged with liaising with government. Codes of good practice are to be prepared in five key areas: funding, consultation and policy appraisal, volunteering, community groups, and black and minority ethnic organizations.[76] In addition, and in recognition of the activity that is carried out locally, there are to be a number of pilot projects organized with the Local Government Association to develop local compacts.[77]

In Scotland, the compact contains promises from the Scottish Office to set up a dedicated unit within the Scottish Office, designate a minister and a senior person in relevant non-departmental public bodies and agencies as having responsibility for compact issues, and set up reporting and review mechanisms.[78] As mentioned above the Parliament has recognized the compact and a relaunch is expected as a further move towards rolling out the compact across central and local government. Draft codes of good practice are being drawn up by the Scottish executive with input from lead voluntary sector bodies on funding, community development, policy proofing and appraisal, partnership, and cross-departmental working. In addition, the Scottish Unit has undertaken to provide a protocol for those government bodies that work across the United Kingdom and therefore potentially across more than one compact.

In Wales the Welsh Office voluntary sector forum, made up of officials and a minister from the Welsh Office and the voluntary sector, has set up working groups to produce five papers (also called compacts) on volunteering, consultation procedures, community development, working in partnerships, and guidance on voluntary sector grants. With the exception of the paper on community development these were produced before transfer of functions to the Assembly in June 1999. They have now become part of an overall process to discharge the statutory duty imposed by s. 144 of the Government of Wales Act. This requires that a scheme be devised by the Assembly in consultation with the sector, to promote the interests of relevant voluntary organizations and explain how the Assembly intends to

76 See, further, Cm. 4100, n. 59, paras. 15–17 and annex A and National Council for Voluntary Organisation, *Guide to the Compact* (1999) at <http://www.ncvo-vol.org.uk/main/gateway/compact.html>.

77 See, further, the study by G. Craig et al., *Developing Local Compacts: Relationships between Local Public Sector Bodies and the Voluntary and Community Sectors* (1999).

78 Cm. 4083, n. 59, pp. 4–5. It was suggested to the author in an interview that the fact that the Voluntary Issues Unit which has responsibility for compact has now been re-located to the executive secretariat (roughly equivalent to the Cabinet Office) indicated the importance of the whole process, particularly in relation to making the New Deal programme work in Scotland.

exercise those functions affecting the voluntary sector. The Assembly must further explain how it intends to consult the sector, provide financial assistance, and monitor that assistance. In a sense, the process of constructing this amounts to taking the compact apart to draw up the five papers and then re-assembling it to make up the Assembly scheme. It is envisaged that overall this process will put considerably more flesh on the skeleton that is the Welsh compact.

In Northern Ireland the development of the compact has been hindered by the fact that devolution did not occur in the summer of 1999 as anticipated. Indeed, during interviews with the author officials from the long-standing Voluntary Activity Unit (VAU) within government expressed a degree of envy of those systems which have devolved and where compact issues can be developed. It was felt that it was inappropriate to issue documents with a clear local emphasis in the absence of an Assembly. Nevertheless the VAU has set up a joint forum which contains representation from all departments and from ten members of the sector. Presently it is concerned with developing a document containing various codes as an update of its *Strategy* from 1993.[79] This document is to support the compact and, like those in the others countries, will be more detailed in spelling out the commitment of government and its agencies to the compact. Also, and this too follows the approach in the other countries, it is not to be issued jointly with the sector – although there has been consultation. As an official in the VAU put it in an interview with the author, 'it will be a *stronger* document . . . requiring government to go along with it if it is not a joint document. We want a document that will spell things out in support of the compact. It will be quite categorical on what government expects of itself . . . targets, action points . . .'. Following devolution, a new Department of Social Development has taken responsibility for the voluntary and community sector generally. In addition to this there are plans to constitute a civic forum where more formal representation from civil society generally can be factored in to the already complex blueprint for governance in the new Northern Ireland.[80]

It was suggested earlier that the compacts may appear as genuinely baffling documents, composed as they are mainly of warm words, platitudes, and generalities. Even when put into their immediate context they retain something of these traits. However, three important features do emerge. First, although the compacts are starting points only they do suggest a schedule requiring a gradual but inexorable move from the very general

79 See n. 57 above.

80 Para. 34 of strand one of the Belfast Agreement specifies that this will comprise representatives of the business, trade union, and voluntary sectors and is to act as a consultative mechanism on social, economic, and cultural issues. S. 56 of the Northern Ireland Act 1998 charges the First Minister and Deputy First Minister with making arrangements for obtaining the views of the forum, providing administrative support, and establishing guidelines for its selection to be approved by the Assembly.

and incontestable to the more specific and potentially problematic. Secondly, although it is the government who generally will be giving undertakings in the near future, there is a clear expectation that something from the sector will be expected in return: general ideas of 'good practice' within voluntary and community organizations will need to be articulated more fully. Thirdly, there is a sense that something bigger than the present exercise in simple recognition is going on here. The compacts are perhaps a first stage in a much wider process involving bigger changes in the state and a new configuration of the relationship of government and civil society. In the next section an attempt will be made to begin to look at the wider issues behind the processes whose start has been signalled by the development of the compacts.

III. GOVERNMENTALITY, CIVIL SOCIETY, AND CONSTITUTIONALISM

Clearly what the compacts represent is the beginning of a process of sustained dialogue between government and voluntary and community organizations and, at a deeper level, the opening up of a new space between the state and civil society. Within one reading it appears that a new relationship is being essayed here in the dialogue that the compacts represent. At another level it seems that a new political rationality is being developed by the state and articulated through governmental technologies of control and measurement that so far are only hinted at in the discourse but are being responded to by parts of the sector from its side of the dialogue.

In this section, an effort will be made to engage with this general process whereby relationships between state and civil society are being renegotiated. Drawing upon scholarship that builds on Foucault's later work on governmentality, the suggestion will be made that the process started by the development of the compacts can be best understood as an instance of 'degovernmentalization'. This is a process where new 'technologies' and 'rationalities' of power are being developed to stimulate agency while simultaneously reconfiguring (rather than removing) constraints upon the freedom of choice of the agent. This is 'governing through freedom'. Through the compacts process, the sector is being encouraged to exercise a 'responsibilized autonomy' and pursue its interests through a framework where the 'systems of thought' and 'systems of action' emphasize and reinforce an economic rationality alongside the more traditional welfare ethos. Of course it is not a one way process where the state by itself creates whole epistemologies and idioms of political power. The sector is an 'active subject' which not only collaborates in this exercise of government but also shapes and influences it.

In sketching out this process the account will be illustrated with material that the author obtained in interviews with personnel in both the voluntary councils who co-operated in drawing up the various compacts, and those in government who had similar responsibility. The aim here is not to represent this directly as government or voluntary-sector policy but to suggest the style of thinking that has accompanied the development of the compacts so far. Language here is not merely contemplative or justificatory, it is performative. As Rose and Miller, writing from within the governmentality perspective put it,

> An analysis of political discourse helps us to elucidate not only *the systems of thought* through which authorities have posed and specified the problems for government, but also the *systems of action* through which they have sought to give effect to government.[81]

1. *Governmentality and civic space*

The governmentality approach which many writers (including several of those contributing to this volume) now are finding useful in understanding how power is now deployed in changing circumstances, has its origins in the later writings of Michel Foucault and some subsequent criticism.[82] Foucault's earlier account of discipline, with its emphasis on 'docile bodies' as surfaces for the inscription of power,[83] was supplemented by later work which stressed the importance of the active subject as the entity through which and by means of which power is actually exercised. In the nearest to a definition that he approaches, Foucault suggests that by the term governmentality he refers, among other things, to:

> the ensemble formed by the institutions, procedures, analyses and reflections, the calculations and tactics that allow the exercise of this very specific albeit complex form of power, which has as its target population, as its principle form of knowledge political economy, and as its essential technical means apparatuses of security.[84]

While sovereignty and discipline are part of government, they are only a part, and one which must be augmented by understanding the 'development of a whole complex of *savoirs*'.[85] Rather than simply concentrating on

81 N. Rose and P. Miller, 'Political Power Beyond the State: Problematics of Government' 43 *Brit. J. of Sociology* (1992) at 177 (emphasis in original).

82 See, particularly, M. Foucault, 'Governmentality' in *The Foucault Effect: Studies in Governmentality*, eds. G. Burchell, C. Gordon, and P. Miller (1991) 87; L. Martin, H. Gutman, and P. Hutton (eds.), *Technologies of the Self: A Seminar with Michel Foucault* (1998). Important later work, developing these ideas from their largely historical immediate context, includes Rose and Miller, id., A. Barry, T. Osbourne, and N. Rose (eds.), *Foucault and Political Reason: Liberalism, Neo-Liberalism and Rationalities of Government*, (1996); D. Garland, '"Governmentality" and the Problem of Crime: Foucault, Criminology and Sociology' (1997) 1 *Theoretical Crim.* 173; N. Rose, *Powers of Freedom: Reframing Political Thought* (1999); and M. Dean, *Governmentality: Power and Rules in Modern Society* (1999).

83 M. Foucault, *Discipline and Punish* (1977).

84 Foucault, op. cit., n. 82, at p. 102.

85 id. This need to widen understanding of how power is exercised is captured well in Foucault's remark that two centuries after the political revolution that overthrew absolutist monarchies, in the field of political theory we have not yet cut off the King's head. M. Foucault, *The History of Sexuality Volume One: An Introduction* (1978) at 88–9.

how the state controls and disciplines the body, governance is now involved in two aspects: there are the forms of rule by which authorities govern populations and the 'technologies of the self' through which people shape their own subjectivity and 'make themselves up' as active subjects of power who can make choices . As Garland summarizes it, 'government is not, then, the suppression of individual subjectivity, but rather the cultivation of that subjectivity in specific forms, aligned to specific governmental aims'.[86]

If we see government as the process by which individuals are made to act and to align their particular wills with ends imposed on them through constraining and facilitating models of possible action, it can be seen that government both presupposes and requires the activity and freedom of the governed. As Rose and Miller argue, power is not so much about imposing constraints on individuals as about 'making up' citizens capable of bearing a sort of regulated freedom.[87] New structures are imposed and with them new forms of choosing and deciding. Of course this is not a new 'freedom to choose' as such, but rather a choice that is entangled in a whole new and pre-existing, complex chain of constraints, calculations of interests, patterns and habits, and obligations and fears.[88] The importance and value of the governance approach is that, as Burchell says, 'Foucault focuses on the connections between ways in which individuals are politically objectified and political techniques for integrating concrete aspects of their lives and activities into the pursuit of the state's objectives'.[89]

The ways in which this exercise of state power is organized around a series of rationalities rooted in very different objectives, techniques and 'ways of knowing' is examined by Foucault in the period between the sixteenth and eighteenth century as he offers a genealogy of the modern state. His argument is that from the sixteenth century onwards, Western states have been progressively 'governmentalized'. Garland summarizes this as the process whereby 'state authorities have increasingly understood their task as a matter of governing individuals and populations, civil society and

86 Garland, op. cit. n. 82, p. 175.

87 Rose and Miller, op. cit., n. 81, p. 174: 'Personal autonomy is not the antithesis of political power, but a key term in its exercise, the more so because most individuals are not merely the subjects of power but play a part in its operations'.

88 Garland (op. cit., n. 82, at p. 197) offers the example of the general practitioner who, in the context of the 1990s National Health Service reforms chooses to become a fund-holder and is thus faced with choices across a whole new set of incentives and disincentives. The doctor is now a purchaser in a health market and this requires much greater choice about selection, rationing, and expenditure. However, the imposition of a structure which requires agents to choose within a predetermined range of possibilities is not a 'freedom to choose'. (Indeed, the option that many doctors may prefer – adequate pubic funding for health or whatever – is denied them.) Even where these structures have been internalized, and choices have the experienced quality of being freely made, it must be clear that in fact they are the result of a complex range of technologies of the self and conceptions of personhood which have been acted on, with greater or lesser effect, by governing authorities.

89 G. Burchell, 'Civil Society and "the system of natural liberty"' in Burchell et al., op. cit. n. 82, at pp. 122–3.

economic life'. (This contrasts with earlier conceptions of rule which mainly involved the ruler securing and consolidating a hold over his territory where states were redefined from medieval 'states of justice' centred around the sovereign's power, into early modern 'administrative states' with an emphasis on police and discipline and then on into contemporary 'governmental states'.) As Foucault says, 'what is really important for our modernity – that is, for our present – is not so much the *étatisation* [state-domination] of society, as the "governmentalization" of the state'.[90]

Later work has detailed the many ways in which the state has been governmentalized and how, at the centre of many of the choices that people in society must make, and indeed in the very way that they think about how these choices are made, there is to be found governmental power dispersed throughout the social – which is now itself a realm of government.[91] For instance, as Donzelot[92] and others have demonstrated, there are whole networks of professional enclosures and agencies through which governmental power can flow and multiply through schools, hospitals, workplaces, courts, and social work centres. Each one of these becomes a concentration of professional power and a centre of governmental power. Censuses and statistics help to create conceptions of the population as entities with social dynamics and patterns.[93] This knowledge feeds into bio-political technologies which produce budgetary calculations, economic forecasts, actuarial tables, epidemiological studies, and demographic projections. These fuel institutions such as insurance and social security and, in turn, contribute to how people adjust their self-conception and behaviour to fit in with the 'normal' as produced by statistics.[94] Insurance, either state or private, is to be seen as a social means for the 'taming of chance'. It amounts to a liberal technology of governing in that it promotes and underwrites some of the risk-taking activity in individuals' lives relating to work, marriage, investment, and so on. The actuarial database that is generated by insurance also regularizes and orders what otherwise seems as accidental, negligent or wrongful and so it offers an element of control through anticipation and management of risk.

All of this suggests that power exists beyond the state: power is less about imposing sovereign will and more about engaging with the many networks and alliances that make up a chain or network which translates power from one locale to another. Rose and Miller[95] develop this idea of government

90 Foucault, op. cit., n. 82, at p. 103.

91 Garland, op. cit., n. 82, pp. 179–82 provides a useful overview of some of the ways in which governmentality has developed after Foucault.

92 J. Donzelot, *The Policing of Families* (1979) and 'The Mobilization of Society and Pleasure in Work' in Burchell et al., op. cit., n. 82, at pp. 169–80 and pp. 251–80.

93 See I. Hacking, *The Taming of Chance* (1990) and 'How Should We Do the History of Statistics?' in Burchell et al., id., at p. 181.

94 I. Hacking, 'Making Up People' in *Reconstructing Individualism*, eds. T. Heller, M. Sosna, and D. Wellbery (1986).

95 Rose and Miller, op. cit., n. 81.

being a domain of strategies, techniques, and procedures through which different forces and groups attempt to render their programme operable. The following analysis draws extensively on their framework. Instead of thinking about one, overarching, single web of social control, they argue that we should be considering the countless, often competing, value systems and their various methods of promulgation that exist across state and non-state institutions and centres of power and expertise. In particular there are 'enclosures', bounded areas of expertise within governmental networks, which exist as a result of esoteric knowledge, technical skill or command of crucial resources. Here power and authority is concentrated and defended. Linkages exist across the networks as the concerns of one sector or enclosure in the network (and its 'moralities, epistemologies and idioms of political power') are 'translated' from one space to another and along the chain.[96] In short, the centres of governmental power, like its objectives and its techniques, are multiple and differentiated. Furthermore, individuals relate to power not as simple coerced objects, but as autonomous subjects whose objectivity is shaped by their active engagement with the powers that govern them and by which they 'govern themselves'.

This means, according to this general approach, that the proper subject of an analysis of contemporary forms of government should be those networks and alliances which exercise 'government at a distance'. The space of government is thus extended far beyond the formal aspects of the state. In particular, civil society now appears not as an opposite of state but as a space where government can happen: it is a correlate of the political technology of the state.[97] Further, the problematics of government should be examined in terms of their 'governmental technologies' – in the words of Rose and Miller, through 'the complex of mundane programmes, calculations, techniques, apparatuses, documents and procedures through which authorities seek to embody and give effect to governmental ambitions'.[98]

If we see government as thus 'a domain of strategies, techniques and procedures through which different forces seek to render programmes operable',[99] then it can be agreed that the power of a government or any individual agency comes from the assemblage of forces by which particular objectives and injunctions can be activated to shape the actions and calculations of others. Some of these assemblages of power can be obvious: the payment or withholding of money, recognition or support. Some are deep-seated involving the inculcation of habits and the development and maintenance of specialist professions and vocabularies or systems of training.

96 'To the extent that actors have come to understand their situation according to a similar language and logic, to construe their goals and their fate as in some way inextricable, they are assembled into mobile and loosely affiliated networks' id., at p. 184.

97 See further discussion in B. Burchell, 'Peculiar Interests: Civil Society and Governing "The System of Natural Liberty"' in Burchell et al., op. cit., n. 82, at pp. 119–49.

98 Rose and Miller, op. cit., n. 81, at p. 175.

99 id., at p. 183.

Some of them appear as innate, as an intrinsic aspects of ordinary life, such as the design of buildings or architectural forms and the assemblage of professional and judgmental opinion through legal, financial, administrative, and medical expertise. Drawing upon Latour's account of power as the effect that comes when an actor or agency is able to enrol and mobilize all these diverse forces in pursuit of its goals, Rose and Miller maintain:

> we need to study the humble and mundane mechanisms by which authorities seek to instantiate government: techniques of notation, computation and calculation; procedures of examination and assessment: the invention of devices such as surveys and presentational forms such as tables . . . the list is heterogeneous and in principle unlimited.[100]

With this understanding of power we can turn to now look briefly at the compact process, and particularly the language in which it is actioned, as an expression of governmentality.

2. *Governmentality, the compacts, and the rationalities of power*

The governmentality perspective develops the essential Foucauldian insight that power as well as being concentrated in the state is dispersed throughout society. The formal limits between civil society and state are in reality traversed by networks which operate across constitutional boundaries. Indeed, the governmentality approach suggests that civil society as such does not exist – at least not as viewed within liberalism where it appears as a domain outside politics, somewhere where useful innovation may occur and be managed, but which ultimately has its autonomy preserved. The insights of the governmentality approach suggest a chain or network of enclosures where disparate technologies, drawing upon a whole range of resources and techniques, struggle to instantiate particular programmes of action. Of course formal government (in the sense of the institutions of the state) retains more of these resources and so remains the *most* powerful. However, others exist too. Although we should not simply discard any distinction between the formal state and informal networks, nevertheless we should understand how bodies beyond the state too have a role in the operation of government. The compact relationship, and the responsibilization strategy that is being initiated there, provides an excellent example of an exercise of constitutional power in a complex, multi-agency network that includes the state but goes beyond its formal limits.

(a) Translation – creating and developing a shared view

Rose and Miller refer to how a 'translatability between the moralities, epistemologies, and idioms of political power, and the government of a specific problem space, establishes a mutuality between what is desirable and what

100 id.

can be made possible through the calculated activities of political forces'.[101] There is no doubt that the fact of the existence of the compacts indicates the degree to which government and parts of the voluntary sector share a similar basic analysis while the process of further development indicates a continuing elaboration of a shared analysis, common vocabulary, and mutually agreed position on how to progress.

For example, as already discussed, the documents paving the way for the compacts, as well as the compacts themselves, are suffused with the language of affirmation and recognition. (The Welsh compact is even titled *A Shared Vision* while the others reflect a similar vocabulary.) The idea of a special relationship has been encouraged on both sides. The voluntary sector, particularly in Scotland and Wales, regarded itself in many ways as the effective opposition to Conservative government, and see these policies as belonging to them.[102] The political side of government has encouraged and reinforced this view.[103] Also from within the civil service there is a recognition of some idea that there is an appropriate new role for the sector.[104]

Overall, the compact process is built on and develops a view of a common interest and expresses this in the joint nature of the documents and the commonality of the language.[105] From the sector perspective, it was said:

> It is perceived as being of mutual advantage. Mutuality is very important. Somehow we have found common ground here . . . It really is an 'Us Thing' . . . never mind what is in the document, we have got this far and that is what's impressive.

101 id., at p. 182.

102 The comments in the Scottish Parliament of Mr George Reid, a Scottish National Party member, can illustrate this view. He declared 'During the long years when we had a government imposed on us for which we had not voted, the voluntary sector was a light in the darkness, pointing the way to a Scottish legislature that would do things differently'. *Scottish Parliament Official Report* vol. 2, no. 8 (23 September 1999) col. 790.

103 A member of one of the National Councils told the author of the effect that a speech to a conference of the National Council for Voluntary Organisation:

> Blair's speech to the NCVO . . . he actually talked about how government in the past treated the voluntary and community sector badly. Not just them – the Tories, but us. We forgot our own origins in the co-operative movement, in voluntary organizations . . . our own Labour Party past . . . I think there was a real notion within Labour that they were going to change and I don't think they wanted to write off the sector as 'the blue rinse brigade' . . . They were going to carry some of this through.

104 For example, a civil servant in one of the Voluntary Sector Units told the author that:

> Voluntary organizations get into areas where the public sector can't reach . . . is not geared up, doesn't have the expertise or knowledge . . . Often the private sector isn't interested. It doesn't see a profit in it or is mainly concerned with corporate image and this or that doesn't fit'. This is the Voluntary Sector's niche. It can provide services . . . in terms of actually delivering and in the consultation in a way that no one else can . . . That's the proper place for the sector.

105 Rose and Miller (op. cit., n. 81, at p. 179) are in no doubt about the importance of language. As they point out, 'political rationalities . . . are morally coloured, grounded upon knowledge and made thinkable through language'.

The Voluntary Issues Unit of one of the devolved administrations expressed the view that:

> these are *shared* aims and values . . . Yes, they are warm words, but it took a lot of work to get there. The language is so important. We had a different vocabulary and we had to make a new one . . . (but even now I'm not sure that everyone means the same thing).

Clearly there are times when there is noise and distortion and misunderstanding as the new vocabulary is developed. The author was told of many incidents in the drafting of the compacts, and some in relation to the drawing up of subsequent codes, when the shared language broke down:

> There is quite a broad view in the sector that 'should' is a sell-out – they're not going to do it.
>
> Where we [government] use 'as appropriate' it usually means that we don't accept it all – but will fight about it another day.

Sometimes disagreement will be as a result of mistranslation between different cultures.

> We said, 'government will have regard to'. They said, 'No chance' . . . a big argument ensued. 'Will you accept 'government will consider'? 'Yes, no problem with that'. . .. There is a symbolism to language which doesn't always translate to the other side . . . and anyway it's not about legal language here, it is about symbolism – what works for your constituency.

Sometimes there is an uneven interpretation for more strategic reasons. Variations in language may be simply about trying to maximize gains for one side or another, and this can be done without introducing bad faith. From the voluntary sector side it was said:

> what you do is try to get them to sign up to things. You don't always tell them the bad news, the problems it might cause them or the restrictions it might involve. That's politics . . . maybe it works that way from the other side too . . . people are pushing things through all the time by representing them in different ways to different people.

Sometimes the language was created to satisfy other audiences.

> We created the term 'community infrastructure' because that is what the European Commission were thinking about and it rang a bell for them.
>
> People, our people in the sector, kept saying it should be written in a language that we can all understand . . . It wasn't anti New Labour but anti jargon . . . (I think they really wanted us to use our jargon).

Overall the language does mean something and the meaning is largely shared – or at least accepted such that it can be employed by both government and the sector representatives (and later the sector more widely):

> Generality is the language of politics . . . this [a particular compact] is the sort of the stuff you need when you're making change . . . There are key things written in that are there just very matter of factly . . . like social partnership . . . it's in the introduction – the aims of the compact . . . 'the shared vision is to work in partnership etc.' This really does *mean* something.

Of course the meaning is not yet fixed and the process of translation, of persuading others of a particular way of seeing the world and responding to it, is continuing. This is envisaged, of course, by the different processes across the countries which will lead variously to the codes and the statutory scheme, and from there to local government and local community organizations.[106] From the government side the view was:

> Do bodies actually speak the language of the compact? Certainly the ones that we fund do. Those that are used to us do have the language but at the local level there is less understanding so far . . . it will evolve and develop from the high level framework underpinned by codes of practice . . . and change the way everybody works.

A view expressed from the voluntary sector side was that:

> There is no one voluntary sector view on how it should be used. It is available for every one of the organizations to interpret how they like . . . it is only something to go on.[107]
>
> This is essentially a political document, a persuasive document . . . in negotiation you can use it to say 'Well, you suggested this . . .' or (and this is really useful) 'You are outside "the spirit of the compact".'

Indeed, this idea of the 'spirit of the compact' along with a notion of its 'wave factor' (referring to how it can be brandished to support an given proposition) is very much part of its strength and appeal to those in voluntary sector who have encountered the compact.

Overall, as a member of one of the National Councils put it:

> The compact has been an exercise in confidence building. 'You are more trustworthy' says government. 'We are entitled', says the sector. It's been OK so far . . . everybody on best behaviour, trying to be helpful . . . But the conflict will eventually arrive . . . we don't all want quite the same thing, all the time'.[108]

Clearly the movement from the generality of the compacts to the more specific detail in codes for local government and smaller community organizations will bring increased conflict. However, the compact process provides a mechanism for facilitating translation between the moralities, epistemologies, and idioms of political power of the two broad groups, and the further development of the relationship.

106 See above.

107 The same member of one of the councils for voluntary organisations complained that:

> sometimes organizations will ring me up and say 'such and such a thing has happened to us and it's outside the compact . . . it's outrageous . . . I thought we had the compact to sort this sort of thing out . . .'. And I will say, 'Don't be so naïve. The compact doesn't work on autopilot. . . . Just because it exists doesn't mean everything changes. It only gives you a weapon but you have to use it'.

108 A view was expressed from another voluntary sector source that 'The compact is a test of how well we are doing and whether government should continue to draw upon the voluntary sector to deliver on various fronts . . . government has always said it is worth building a sustainable voluntary sector, but now it can be seen to'.

(b) Political rationalities – operationalizing partnership

Aside from the important processes by which the beginnings of a common language and a common approach are developed, there is also the notable development of a strategy to operationalize partnership in a form that is at least acceptable to all parts of both constituencies.[109] The voluntary sector concerns here are focused mostly on independence and the right to continue to criticize and campaign. As has been noted already, government is willing throughout the compact formally to recognize the sector and acknowledge its independence. Even informally there seems to be a realization that this is a most important element for the successful dissemination of the compact to a wider voluntary-sector world.[110] From the government side the emphasis is on the development of 'good practice' standards and this in turn has been recognized by the sector, or at least those who are open to the opportunities that a more professionalized approach might now bring.

This idea of good practice is very significant in terms of the development of a responsibilization strategy which can bring the sector into partnership with formal government. It is here that the individual and disparate efforts of all those diverse bodies in the voluntary sector can be calibrated and adjusted in relation to what is presented as an agreed best standard, as in the interests of everyone. It is here that the messy realms of practices and relations across a compromised reality can be subjected to consideration against an ideal framework where economism or the accounting paradigm can be realized and given expression as a powerful guiding tool.

The idea of good practice is mentioned in general terms in all the compacts. It is however the main subject for development in the subsequent codes. For example, the Welsh compact refers to 'acknowledged codes of practice on the use and administration of public funds appropriate to the scale of funding and operation' as well as 'effective and proportionate systems for the management, control, accountability, propriety and audit of finances'.[111] However, the *Manual of Guidance on Voluntary Sector Grants* (the first code to be developed by any of the countries) is more much more

109 It is important to realize that government, like the voluntary sector, is made up of different constituencies. Not only is there the division between central, devolved, and local government but there are a whole variety of cultures among different departments which in no way reflect the same approach The various voluntary sector units seem aware that they have the job of 'selling' the compact to appropriate departments.

110 The idea of the independence of the sector seems to have been scrupulously observed even in the process of developing the compacts. For example, in an interview with a member of a government compact team, the author was told:

> in the development of the compact there was a problem with one of the sector reps. who came from a big environmental group . . . There were stresses and strains within that world . . . It was not helpful for her to be seen cosying up to government. She distanced herself . . . to be able to carry the more vocal organizations in that sector . . . That is fine . . . quite acceptable to drop in and out of the compact generally as circumstances change.

111 Cm. 4107, op. cit., n. 59, at p. 12.

detailed.[112] The trend towards spelling out good practice is continued in the other Welsh codes. For example, the code on consultation procedures, although mainly concentrating on government undertakings, contains extremely detailed guidance on how, when a voluntary groups is involved in representing a particular group or cause to government, good practice involves 'defining and demonstrating how they represent their stated constituency'.[113] It is certain that the codes in other countries will follow suit.

This fits in very much with how government sees the compact process developing.

> We want to do business with them and, yes, it is easier for us if they are professionalised and know what they are doing and conform to certain procedures et cetera. But it's in their interests too. Funding . . . everything is made more simple . . . We don't want to tame them as such but this is the way it is going . . . a more professionalised sector is inevitable . . . it fits the moment.

There is clearly an ambition that these standards will develop even beyond the context of a direct funding relationship between government and the sector.

> Developing quality standards appropriate to the sector . . . is essential if we are to have confidence in how an organization handles money, not only public money in the sense of government money, but money raised by the public or from whatever source . . . if there is a mismanagement of other funds how could we expect them to manage government money?

There is also the view that good practice will stretch far beyond the funding relationship and into other issues:

> If they are in a funding relationship we can insist . . . in the grant offer letter . . . or in the annex there will be conditions, details of good practice . . . but in a partnership they are more equal. We cannot insist . . . In the new relationship it does need to be spelled out to the sector . . . Are user groups really consulted? Who, how, how many, how representative are they? . . . When they [voluntary organizations] are invited to meetings, they must turn up or send apologies . . . Keep records, do accounts, proper audits . . . proper business practice.

There are a whole range of monitoring devices, audit requirements, and measurements of output envisaged. Standards, guidelines, and reporting mechanisms together will transform the ways in which at least some of the voluntary sector think about themselves and exercise choices within a newly constructed framework that reinforces economic forms of reasoning. What may be presented as increased autonomy, a chance to govern oneself, is in fact a reconfiguration of rationalities so that the self-interest of (parts of) the sector aligns with the interest of a state seeking to mobilize a reserve

112 *Compact between the Government and the Voluntary Sector in Wales – Manual of Guidance on Voluntary Sector Grants* (1999). This document, which runs to 76 pages in both Welsh and English, contains extremely detailed checklists and flowcharts covering almost every aspect of what amounts to good practice in the funding relationship.

113 *Compact between the Government and the Voluntary Sector in Wales – Consultation Procedures* (1999) at p. 8.

army of support effectively and in its own terms. As a director of a medium-sized voluntary organization commented:

> 'Investors in People', Charter Marks, continuous improvement and measurement . . . It is the world we work in now . . . it is becoming accepted . . . [as normal] . . . [like] the contract culture when it first appeared . . . How the voluntary sector wins is by playing the game.

Part of the compact process is obviously economically driven: there is an idea of good practice which requires standardization across the sector so that it can be used effectively across government. Some of this is about saving money directly. As one government official speculating on future developments said, '[The compact] includes the possibility of better co-ordination . . . Shared premises and services . . . legal advice . . . there are clearly times when duplication is simply that . . .'. More than simple economy, however, the compacts are about changing and moulding the landscape and culture of the government – voluntary sector interaction. There are ideas about producing a single grant form for all voluntary and community groups to complete with appropriate information about finances, management structures, outputs, and methods of evaluation. This is presented as being in the interests of the sector and some of the more managerially minded there might even willingly accept this interpretation. Technology is being involved too in creating structures and frameworks within which the sector is to act and respond. In several of the home countries there are plans for internet developments to inform voluntary organizations on best practice both in organizing themselves and in discharging their consultation role.

> We are getting ready for a big jump . . . an internet site giving a complete managerial guide: how to run a group, how to act as an employer, how to recruit, how to deal with finance . . . It will also give links to any information site that the group may want access to . . . For example, any government documents that are put out for consultation are put on websites . . . they will link straight in . . .

Of course, this is about responsibilizing the sector and structuring choice. In general, as Rose and Miller point out, 'making people write things down, and the nature of the things people are made to write down, is itself a kind of government of them, urging them to think about and note certain aspects of their activities according to certain norms'.[114] The whole compacts process that has been set in train is a kind of government although not in the sense currently acknowledged in most constitutional accounts.

IV. CONCLUSIONS

In the earlier article[115] it was argued that the present agenda of constitutional reform was missing the point, and that the main constitutional action

114 Rose and Miller, op. cit., n. 81, at p. 200.
115 Morison, op. cit., n. 1.

has moved on from the big institutions of parliament and the formal constitution. In this essay the intention was to begin to follow power into just one of its newer manifestations through the increasingly blurred boundaries of public and private, and state and civil society. Although government in this new context of a government and voluntary sector partnership has escaped formal democracy, the processes that the compacts have marked the beginning of, and are now continuing, show that it is not uncontrolled. The compact process can be seen as part of an exercise of governmentality and subject to complex rationalities developing within the context of a newly emerging partnership relationship between formal government and some more managerially minded parts of the voluntary sector. Government, perhaps in pursuit of a third way, is seeking to operationalize a particular, ultimately more managerially driven programme by influencing, allying with, and co-opting the voluntary sector as a resource that they do not directly control. Parts of the sector, interested in developing opportunities for partnership with government, are responding to the processes that the compacts have started.

The compact process is concerned with establishing a new role for the sector (and indeed government), and with the way in which this role is to be discharged within constraints and controls provided by concepts of good practice that are being further developed in codes at increasingly local level. Indeed, the very idea of what is an appropriate target for government action is being restructured in the compact process and the boundaries between government and civil society are disappearing in this reconfiguration. This is not, of course, a simple one-way process with government controlling all the action. It does not involve tricking the sector or destroying their subjectivity but rather cultivating a specific form of subjectivity, aligned to a view of partnership. Not every voluntary organization need subscribe.[116] Civil society will invariably remain incompletely domesticated. However, for those voluntary and community organizations that want to work in the new partnership relationship, their world view is changed and is changing further. Indeed the sector, along with formal government at many levels, is contributing and will contribute to this reworking of the relationship. The compacts are joint documents. The exact content, scope, and range of the process that they have started is to be worked out by government at various levels and by the sector. The sector actors are not mere ciphers within the network or an empty space where government is occurring. The insights of the governmentality approach shows us that they are active subjects. They are contributing to the reconstruction of their world view by actively engaging with the powers that govern them and by which they govern themselves. As Foucault points out, 'power is exercised only

116 As the director of one of the councils put it, 'Voluntarism will always re-emerge. There's always going to be people who just do what they want: they see an issue and just get stuck in. That's what the voluntary sector is in the end – people just doing things, and you can't really hope to control that'.

over free subjects, and only insofar as they are free.[117] And of course the process works both ways: formal government too is being changed and governed as it seeks to operationalize its programme through the networks of civil society and responds to new priorities and rationalities. In short, there is a space here where issues of power are being worked out.

This account suggests that there is need for at least a recognition of this new constitutional space. Just as the importance of the formal constitutional arenas is declining so these new spaces are opening up. The issues here, relating to how the relationship between the formal state and civil society is being reconfigured in the partnership relationship, and how this might be promoting a managerialist or economist approach over more traditional welfare values, are producing not just sociological points about how power operates in society. They are raising important constitutional questions too. An understanding of how constitutional power now and increasingly exists well beyond the scope of the formal constitution, even in spaces such as civil society which are traditionally seen as separate, raises questions about the ability of traditional constitutionalism to accommodate, let alone seek to control, the realities of contemporary public power.

117 M. Foucault, 'The Subject and Power' in *Michel Foucault*, eds. H. Dreyfus and P. Rabinow (1982) 221.

JOURNAL OF LAW AND SOCIETY
VOLUME 27, NUMBER 1, MARCH 2000
ISSN: 0263–323X, pp. 133–50

The Devil and the Deep Blue Sea? A Critique of the Ability of Community Mediation to Suppress and Facilitate Participation in Civil Life

LINDA MULCAHY*

This article revisits debate between academics and practitioners about the potential of community mediation. While mediation evangelicals make bold claims about the possibility of mediation helping to rebuild communities, academic critics have been suspicious of such contentions and claimed instead that mediation has provided just another route through which the state can interfere in the life of its citizens. It is argued here that debate on the topic has been clouded by unduly high expectations of disputes as agents of social change. Their importance has been understood by reference to their ability to rebuild communities or their potential to become test cases. It is argued here that mediated disputes make much more modest challenges to state authority but that they can be aided in this by the intervention of mediators prepared to take a pragmatic approach to the unachievable ideal of neutrality. The article does not conceive of community mediation as an alternative of the state or its agent. Rather, it suggests that mediators can be embedded within both worlds and act as message-bearers between them.

INTRODUCTION

This article considers whether community mediation is capable of facilitating the increased participation of the disadvantaged in democratic society. A key test of the confidence of a democratic structure is its ability to accept challenges and react in an open minded way to criticism. Academic debates

* *Reader in Law, Birkbeck College, Malet Street, Bloomsbury, London WC1E 7HX, England*

My thanks go to Lee Summerfield, friend and colleague, who has supported me through the process of writing this article and been prepared to argue with me at every juncture. Any insights I have achieved are probably down to him. I would also like to thank the editors of this special edition who were extremely patient and supportive of an author who did not manage her time very well.

on the value of informal justice have tended to result in polarized positions about the ability of mediation to frame grievances and disputes in a way which challenges, rather than reinforces, dominant normative orders and state control. Viewed by some as a practice in search of a theory, community mediation has none the less provided social theorists with material through which to examine the nature of the relationship between the individual and the state. Proponents of mediation have seduced us with common sense notions of how disruptions in civil life might be avoided and calmed. They appeal to a utopian vision of society and human relations to which we all aspire. In contrast, left-wing critics have prompted a rude awakening to the harsh realities and injustices in society and argued convincingly that the production of calm could be dangerous when what was called for was the emergence of a collective consciousness about injustices in society.

Conflict between neighbours in inner city communities does much to reveal the tensions implicit in living in disadvantaged, over-crowded, poorly maintained social housing. They make explicit the ways in which notions of identity, ownership, belonging, ethnicity, and sexuality are constantly being challenged and renegotiated within, and between, communities. The study of disputes leads straight to key issues for socio-legal scholars: norms and ideology, power, rhetoric and oratory, personhood and agency, morality, meaning, and interpretation.[1] It allows us not only to see social relations in action but also to understand cultural systems and the relationship between social structure and formal state law.[2]

This article attempts to plot the various ways in which the development of academic critiques of informalism have moved on from a rejection of informalism as an instrument of state control towards a position where it can be seen to facilitate resistance to the state, albeit in much more modest ways than those identified by the proponents and evangelicals of community mediation. The issue is one which is relevant to contemporary debates about changing patterns of governance in which increased emphasis has been placed on compacts between the state and the voluntary sector. These are said to create a new space within the constitution and allow for the dispersal of power through networks which traverse the legal constitutional boundaries that appear to separate state and civil society.[3] It is argued here that community mediation agencies are one such network and the processes through which they resolve disputes admit of the possibility of increasing the ability of disadvantaged groups to participate in society.

The article is in four parts. The first section considers the ideological foundation of the community mediation 'movement' and arguments put forward in support of its growth. The second section considers criticisms of

1 P. Caplan, 'Anthropology and the Study of Disputes' in *Understanding Disputes: The Politics of Argument*, ed. P. Caplan (1995).

2 D. Trubek, 'Studying courts in context' (1980–81) 15 *Law and Society Rev.* 485–501.

3 See J. Morison, in this issue, pp. 98–132.

the community mediation 'movement' offered by academic writers. These first two sections make clear that there is a reasonably clear divide between those who advocate and those who oppose the development of community mediation. The third section considers whether there are ways in which the notions of community mediation can be theorized so as to admit of the possibility of it being able to engender independence and promote change within communities whilst also recognizing that it allows for expanding state control of the private sphere. The final section reflects on this debate and considers its implications for the future development of theory and empirical work in the field. The section draws on a two-year empirical study of community mediation which the author undertook with a colleague for the Nuffield Foundation. This paper does not present the data collected as the full report of that research will be reported elsewhere.[4] Instead, it seeks to address some of the problems posed by the data and issues raised.

THE PROMISE OF COMMUNITY MEDIATION

The first community mediation centres were set up in the early 1980s and there has been a significant increase in their number since then. Many of the early centres which were established were largely dependent on the vision of particular people or groups including professionals from the fields of probation work and psychology, and religious groups such as the Anglican Clergy and Quakers.[5] In the United States of America, community mediation has become the most pervasive form of mediation and the number of centres has also grown rapidly there.[6] In the United Kingdom the majority of schemes are concerned with neighbourhood conflict although many direct their attention to victim/offender work and to working with schools.[7] Community mediation centres are particularly prevalent within the inner cities where rates of conflict may be higher because of the high density living and general stresses in the urban environment.

There are a number of different models which fit under the rubric of community mediation but the term tends to denote an ideological rationality rather than single or homogenous identity.[8] A number of vague social and political ideals underlay the community mediation movement.[9] First,

4 L. Summerfield and L. Mulcahy, *Final Report to the Nuffield Foundation* (2000).

5 M. Liebmann, 'Community and Neighbourhood Mediation: A UK Perspective' in *Rethinking Disputes: The Mediation Alternative*, ed. J. MacFarlane (1997).

6 J. Murray, A. Rau, and E. Sherman, *Processes of Dispute Resolution: The Role of Lawyers* (1989).

7 id.

8 G. Pavlich, 'The power of community mediation: government and formation of self-identity' (1996) 30 *Law and Society Rev.* 707–34.

9 Murray et al., op. cit., n. 6.

emphasis has been placed on the empowerment of local residents and the desirability of having individuals voluntarily resolve their own disputes. Empowerment is achieved by allowing the parties to take control of the resolution process. Private ordering is given moral superiority and the parties do not have to face the ritual of formal adjudication. Instead they commonly find a community mediator who is dressed like them, sits with them round a table, talks like them or at least uses accessible language, and stresses help rather than threats.

Disputants are encouraged to provide a personal narrative detailing what it is that they want to achieve and to identify resolution options which are workable, achievable, and acceptable by them.[10] In this way, it is argued that mediation provides an opportunity for disputants to reject the intervention of the state and reclaim control over conflict resolution by choosing a settlement process which requires, rather than thwarts, their participation.[11] It is suggested that mediation allows people to resolve disputes according to frameworks which make sense to them rather than by reference to frameworks imposed by the state.

Secondly, emphasis is placed by proponents of community mediation on the importance of restoring peace and equilibrium to relationships. It has been suggested that instead of polarizing parties into two enemy camps, mediation encourages them to focus on the problem between them. Community mediators stress the importance of focusing on common ground between the parties, looking to the future, and accentuating the positive aspects of the disputants relationship.

A third ideal is that of a grass-roots approach to disputes and an opposition to formal law. This reflects a distrust of governmental agencies as tending to impose bureaucratic, short-term or 'outside' solutions on the community. It has been argued that disputes managed by state officials are often allowed to run on with no consistent policy being followed. Rather than facilitating resolution this can cause an escalation of the issues and an entrenchment of positions.[12] This distrust of government agencies also extends to the courts which are viewed as unresponsive to the needs and interests of disadvantaged groups. Legal rules are seen as inflexible and unpragmatic as opposed to mediation, which is responsive and flexible. Lawyers are viewed as élitist, expensive, and responsible for the intensification of disputes because they treat them through the adversarial forms prescribed by the legal order and remove them from their natural context.[13]

10 Liebmann, op. cit., n. 5.

11 Pavlich, op. cit., n. 8.

12 Tebay et al.'s research shows that most complaints about neighbours are handled by housing assistants who did not always find their working methods to be effective: S. Tebay, G. Cumberbatch, and N. Graham, *Disputes Between Neighbours* (1986).

13 R. Miller and A. Sarat, 'Grievances, claims, and disputes: assessing the adversary culture' (1980–81) 15 *Law and Society Rev.* 536–66.

By encouraging such ideologies, proponents of mediation argue that the process helps individuals to become involved citizens within functioning communities. In this way it can be seen to underpin the requirements of a democratic society that people operate as free individuals. Thus, community mediation is implicated in a quest to revitalize communities by nurturing individual freedom.[14] In the words of Brown and Marriot:

> Mediation schemes have been developing in Britain with the aim of bringing disputes arising within local communities under community control, thus avoiding the use of the legal system to deal with inter-personal or social agreements . . . Far from being a second class service, such volunteers can bring knowledge of the local community, its cultures facilities and problems, and evidence of living there, to their mediation and for most neighbourhood conflicts this is a very valuable asset. It enables them to speak 'on the same wavelength' as the disputants and understand the unspoken undertones of their arguments. It makes them more acceptable to clients as being 'one of us'.[15]

Shonholtz has argued that the suppression of conflict is destructive to the safety and vitality of communities and that community justice forums provide a ready vehicle for the early suppression and potential resolution of conflict.[16]

CRITIQUES OF COMMUNITY MEDIATION

Given the range of literature on mediation it is relatively rare to find critics of these movements. Delgado et al. have asserted that negative evaluations have been left to a small number of left-wing critics.[17] Whilst the aims of community mediation and governing ideology are laudable there has been much concern about the ability of mediation to achieve such goals. This section focuses on critiques of informalism and places particular emphasis on the ways in which it is said to expand the control of the state over its citizenry.

A major concern of academic commentators has been the over inflated claims that mediation can serve to heal community rifts. Partly this relates to the problem over what is being referred to. Critics have suggested that the ideological role played by community is overused and underdefined and that ironically it began to be utilized at exactly the time when the working class was fragmenting and communities ceased to be so consensual and harmonious.[18] Modern societies have high levels of mobility and cultural diversity and even where mobility is restricted, it can not be assumed that the

14 Pavlich, op. cit., n. 8.

15 H. Brown and A. Marriot, *ADR Principles and Practice* (1993) 218, 220.

16 R. Shonholtz, 'Neighbourhood Justice Systems: Work, Structure, and Guiding Principles' (1994) 5 *Mediation Q.* 13.

17 R. Delgado et al., 'Fairness and Formality: Minimising the Risk of Prejudice in Alternative Dispute Resolution' (1985) *Wisconsin Law Rev.* 1359–404.

18 R. Matthew, 'Reassessing Informal Justice' in *Informal Justice?*, ed. R. Matthew (1988).

fact that people are constrained to live together creates cohesive communities. Moreover communities exist in different places and have to be understood as existing along vertical and horizontal lines. Communities may be geographical locations, but there may also be communities of understanding founded on such notions as gender, ethnicity, class, occupation, lifestyle, and age. They may also be highly transient and this is especially the case in inner cities. If heterogeneity rather than homogeneity is the norm and the social structure is diffuse and population transient, it may be that the challenge of healing communities is too great for mediators to tackle on their own.[19]

This argument is reinforced by data on the extent to which mediation agencies engage with communities. Despite the increasing presence of community mediation organizations they are just one of a number of agencies dealing with neighbourhood disputes. Neighbours may also involve the police, the local housing office, environmental health and noise teams, legal and social services departments, citizens' advice bureaux, racial equality councils, local doctors, solicitors, and the courts. Moreover, many conflicts are likely to go unreported as people may prefer to deal with the matter informally or develop coping strategies. In their survey of 1062 householders, Karn et al. found that only 2 per cent of people with complaints about a neighbour would even threaten to report their neighbour to the local authority or police.[20] This could mean that looking at community problems through formal disputes can present a skewed picture of the importance of formal voicing. An approach to dissatisfaction which uses disputes and complaints as a prism through which to understand the emergence of dissatisfaction may miss the usual in its search for the beginnings of conflict or disagreement.

Other critiques have concentrated on macro-level concerns about community mediation. Particular concern has been expressed about claims that mediation removes the state from dispute resolution by giving control over disputes to the parties.[21] Abel has claimed that the relationship between the formal and informal sphere is not necessarily complementary with one contracting while the other expands.[22] Critics claim that there are a number of ways in which mediation can actually expand state control. Matthew summed up the position of critics thus:

19 S. Silbey and S. Merry, 'Mediator Settlement Strategies' (1986) 8 *Law and Policy* 114–32.

20 V. Karn, R. Lickiss, and D. Hughes, *Tenants' Complaints and the Reform of Housing Management* (1996); General Accident, 'Good neighbours survey' (1995), unpublished report discussed in J. Dignan, A. Sorsby, and J. Hibbert, *Neighbour disputes: Comparing the cost-effectiveness of mediation and alternative approaches* (1996).

21 Of this group, Richard Abel's various publications on the issue provide some of the most important and influential treatments of the subject. He has identified a number of issues which should remain at the forefront of evaluations by law and society scholars (see, in particular, R. Abel, 'The Contradictions of Informal Justice' in *The Politics of Informal Justice, Vol 1: The American Experience*, ed. R. Abel (1982) 169–70).

22 id.

> The proliferation of local agencies penetrating deep into the heat of society and personal life, ultimately responsible to an ever unaccountable state bureaucracy, fuelled popular fears and anxieties about the totally administered society and the advent of 1984. Behind the engaging rhetoric of informalism the critics saw sinister motives.[23]

According to this school of thought, mediation allows state dispute handlers to offload trivial cases whilst retaining some control over them. This is particularly likely where core funding for mediation agencies comes from the state and brings with it a responsibility to process its cases and account to it for the expenditure of funds and success of resolution. Harrington's study of a neighbourhood justice centre demonstrated the ways in which informal processes do not become alternatives to, but rather supplemental agencies of the state. She showed that 88 per cent of cases referred to it came from prosecutors, judges or police who would otherwise have had to process the dispute. In this way formal state institutions retain control over gatekeeping and funding whilst offloading the resolution of disputes to other agencies.[24]

A more serious concern of critics is that such expansion is made worse by the fact that many state agencies would be predisposed towards ignoring trivial cases. According to this view informalism increases the exposure of disputants to state interference in their disputes and expands state control by bringing more cases into the dispute resolution arena. Abel reminds us in his review of the American literature that informal institutions rarely reject a case.[25] Moreover, in his recent review of neighbourhood mediation services Dignan suggested various ways in which community mediation 'claws in' new cases and expends money on disputes which would otherwise not be the subject of protracted negotiations.[26]

It has also been argued that informalism encourages the further suppression of the disadvantaged and reinforces existing inequalities between disputants.[27] This is significant since proponents of mediation have used the rhetoric of egalitarianism to justify their more conciliatory approaches to disputes and argued that mediation promotes access to resolution services because of its informality. It is clear that informal approaches to the resolution of disputes have frequently been targeted at the disadvantaged – people with violent partners; divorcing women who have been carers and lack sufficient work experience to allow them to command a decent wage in the job market; lay members of society challenging experts; and disputants who have not invoked the law before.[28] In the United States and the United Kingdom,

23 Matthew, op. cit., n. 18, p. 9.

24 C. Harrington, *Shadow Justice? The Ideology and Institutionalization of Alternatives to Court* (1985).

25 Abel, op. cit., n. 21.

26 Dignan et al., op. cit., n. 20.

27 T. Grillo, 'The Mediation Alternative: Process Dangers for Women' (1991) 100 *Yale Law J.* 1545–610 (also in M. Freeman (ed.), *Alternative Dispute Resolution* (1995)).

28 Abel, op. cit., n. 21.

neighbourhood justice centres tend to be positioned in neighbourhoods with a disproportionate number of disadvantaged groups. Research in a United Kingdom setting has shown that disputes between neighbours are also more likely to come from disadvantaged groups such as council tenants, women about men, and from older people about younger people.[29]

These concerns are exacerbated by the fact that many forms of informal resolution, community mediation included, discourage legal representation. In their extensive review of the literature on informalism and racial prejudice Delgado et al. raise concerns that informalism increases the risk of unfair discrimination. Drawing on psychoanalytic theory and the socio-economic and political causes of prejudice, they argue that many people suffer from a moral dilemma which arises from a conflict between socially espoused precepts of equality and humanitarianism, and personal attributes and dispositions. The manner in which these conflicts are resolved depends largely on situational factors but certain settings tend to foster prejudiced behaviour while others encourage it. They contend that the rules and structures of formal justice tend to suppress bias and cite intra-neighbour disputes as particularly unsuitable for informal resolution because they touch on sensitive or intimate areas of life and so increase the risk of outcomes being coloured by prejudice.

Others have claimed that the appealing rhetoric of voluntarism, popular justice, and individual empowerment disguises coercion. For some this is a feature of the postmodern state. Foucault has argued that to the extent that modern power operates by constituting and disciplining bodies and minds, creating desires, and then naturalizing them as drives, this severely limits the possibility of protest. Technical, hidden, and individuated forms of power defy the possibilities of revolt or collective resistance because they are less visible.[30] In a similar vein, Hofrichter saw neighbourhood dispute resolution as being prompted by the need for changing projects to suppress working-class resistance.[31] Moreover, Silbey and Merry's study of a court-based and community-based mediation programmes suggest that mediators manipulate outcomes in subtle and covert ways by reinterpreting disputants' statements into euphemistic, morally neutral terms, selecting issues for discussion, 'concretizing' some issues and postponing others which may raise more fundamental concerns about power imbalances or injustices.[32]

In a United Kingdom context, important work by Greatbatch and Dingwall on divorce mediators suggests that the process of mediation can be used to press weaker parties into accepting less than they could have expected had their case gone through more adversarial channels. They argue that the influence of mediators goes beyond process and that disputants can be guided towards outcomes that the mediators find appropriate. They

29 Tebay et al., op. cit., n. 12.

30 M. Foucault, *Power/knowledge: Selected interviews and other writings (1972–1977)* (1980).

31 R. Hofrichter, 'Neighbourhood justice and the social control problems of American Capitalism: A Perspective' in Abel, op. cit., n. 21.

32 Silbey and Merry, op. cit., n. 19.

conclude that the idea that mediation is a purely neutral activity could not be sustained as a general proposition. Mediators in their empirical study were 'selective' facilitators. They regularly exerted pressure in favour of certain options over others, encouraged discussion in certain directions, and inhibited exploration of other issues.[33] Critics have maintained that such covert coercion is detrimental to the parties' interests because properly recognized coercion stimulates resistance and justifies the demand for the protection of formal due process. Viewed in this way, mediation substitutes the mystification of law and is more pernicious because its sources are less obvious and points of resistance concealed.

The libertarian vision of the reclamation of the private sphere promoted by mediation proponents does not appear to work so well in the context of social housing. In reality, the private space of tenants is limited. It has always been dependent on public legal forms for its creation, maintenance, and dissolution. Their identity as a tenant is legally constituted and their formal obligations and responsibilities are dictated by their tenancy agreement. Private ordering brings with it the possibility of the state's imposing a settlement which is grossly unfair when measured against an external standard of 'fairness'. The parties are also not equal in neighbour disputes because of the bargaining endowment conferred by legislation. The complainant can threaten to pursue their dispute and encourage the enforcement of the tenancy agreement, possession of equipment or eviction.

Recent research suggests that the threat of coercive action by the state remains a shadow in many neighbourhood mediation sessions. Mediation agreements are commonly not binding on the parties and do not exclude the local council from intervening in the future or pursuing the case further themselves. Housing officers commonly send a letter to the alleged perpetrator quoting the terms of their tenancy agreement and reciting their powers to evict them before they even consider referring a case to a mediation agency.[34] Not surprisingly, many disputes files are 'closed' at this stage as the behaviour complained about ceases fairly rapidly after. The threat of eviction has a significant impact on tenants as it can lead to a loss of home, livelihood, security, social networks, and schooling arrangements for children and makes clear that the relationship of tenants in social housing is bounded in a way not experienced by home owners or tenants in the private sector.

Finally, critics of mediation have expressed concern that community mediation can lead to the suppression of criticism about the state. Informal processes may work to get opposing parties to acknowledge shared values and resolve their dispute on the basis of those values.[35] Peace emerges from

33 D. Greatbatch and R. Dingwall, 'Who is in charge? Rhetoric and evidence in the study of mediation' (1993) 17 *J. of Social Welfare and Family Law* (199–206).

34 See, also, Karn, Lickiss, and Hughes, op. cit., no. 20; Tebay et al., op. cit., n. 12; K. Walsh and K. Spencer, *The Quality of Service in Housing Management* (1990).

35 Abel, op. cit., n. 21.

the literature as something of a moral imperative in the mediation process. Informal systems can operate to defuse the anger of those with grievances and forestall public sympathy by satisfying claims through handling them at a local level. It purports to offer solutions in which no one wins and no one loses. Anger is seen as destructive and there is a predisposition to compromise which may be unsuitable in a case ripe for the setting of precedent. Conflict is depicted as a failure of communication or a misunderstanding. Emphasis is put on the cathartic effect of mediation or expressive rather than instrumental functions.

Colson has argued that the expectation that disputes are resolved and lead to harmony is a Western construct derived from Christianity. She contends that this arouses expectations that processing of the dispute will lead to reconciliation and restoration of social harmony and that this is considered to be the ideal condition for human beings. These criticisms have not only been levelled at practitioners.[36] Cain and Kulcsar criticize academics for their assumptions of ideological functionalism or the reformist desire to eliminate disputes evident in many academic tracts on the issue.[37]

According to this line of argument, mediation serves to underplay the conflicts between powerful and less powerful groups in society such as social landlords and impoverished tenants. Disagreement about social and political values does not feature as a dominant issue. Informalism can have the effect of siphoning discontent from the courts and in doing so reduces the risk of political confrontation.[38] The result is the preservation of the stability of the social system. In these ways informalism can be seen to serve private interests at the expense of public ones and, unlike adjudication, can fail to further the substantive public goals that shape adjudication. Nader has put the case that it is unlikely that the force of law can be marshalled to address little injustices unless they are reconceptualized as collective harms. In a similar vein, Trubek has suggested that the growing interest in dealing with issues such as domestic violence out of the courts can be seen as a reaction against the successes of the women's movement in their use of courts.[39] Adler et al. argue that emphasis is placed on wholeness rather than fragmentation:

> There is nothing about rights and claims, about neighbourhoods fighting city hall in the name of justice, or about the ethnic lawyer rising out of (but still practising in) the old neighbourhood to fight the big boys downtown, or for that matter, to join the big boys down town and become a member of the successful political machine.[40]

The construction of 'neighbourhood' disputes also lays emphasis on the intra-community aspects of the dispute. The state emerges as the dispute

36 E. Colson, 'The contentiousness of disputes' in Caplan, op. cit., n. 1.

37 M. Cain and K. Kulcsar, 'Thinking disputes: an essay on the origins of the dispute industry' (1982) 16 *Law and Society Rev.* 375–402.

38 O.M. Fiss, 'Against settlement' (1984) 93 *Yale Law J.* 1073–90; Delgado, op. cit., n. 17.

39 D. Trubek, 'Turning away from law?' (1984) 82 *Michigan Law Rev.* 824–35.

40 O. Adler, K. Lovaas, and N. Milner, 'The ideologies of mediation – the movement's own story' (1988) 10 *Law and Policy* 317–39, at 325.

processor rather than as one of the parties. Yet research into community mediation has suggested that the state is often implicated in the cause of disputes. Liebmann draws attention to eight major factors which go some way to explaining the increased potential for conflict in inner cities, three of which directly implicate the state in disputes. These include a shortage of housing which means that residents from different generations and with different lifestyles are more frequently housed close by to each other; the right-to-buy policy of the Conservative administration which led to an increasingly mixed population, and less tolerance on the part of home owners about environmental noise and conditions. In addition the introduction of a care-in-the-community policy for mental health has led to many more vulnerable people being in the community, often inadequately supported.[41] By conceptualizing complaints about such problems as disputes between neighbours, the state avoids direct challenged about the quality of its social housing and social services.

These criticisms of mediation have posed a serious and important challenge to proponents of mediation. Have critics of mediation been overly zealous in their assertions about encroaching state control? Have they remained insensitive to the possibility of community mediation facilitating sites of resistance to the state by encouraging disputants to conceive of their dispute within frameworks which are different from those espoused by the state? In the final section of this article these questions will be considered in the context of the work of a new wave of scholars who have attempted to circumvent the pessimistic diagnosis of traditional critics of informalism. New informalists claim to have found a way to theorize about mediation so that the its constraining potential can be recognized alongside of its ability to instigate change, albeit at a different level from that anticipated by earlier critics.

THE PROMISE OF NEW INFORMALISM

It is clear that there is considerable concern that intellectual debate has reached something of a stalemate over the issue of informalism. It has frequently been suggested that the arguments for and against mediation have become too polarized and that there has been a failure to distinguish between types of informal justice in a theoretically adequate way. This is seen as precluding meaningful discussion of the political dimensions of mediation. Pavlich summed up this viewpoint when he suggested of traditional critics:

> They have, in short, narrowed the debate on community mediation to an exploration of the extent to which it expands and/or intensifies state control. In the process, sustained

41 Liebmann, op. cit., n. 5.

> analyses of community mediation as possibly harbouring elements that are not embedded in state control, or functional for the latter, are not placed on critical agendas.[42]

Cain has expressed similar concerns about the intellectual stalemate reached:

> Academic criticism and negative evaluation have created a growing chorus of despair, a feeling that the devil of formal justice may, after all, be better than his dangerously unfamiliar informal brother. This chorus is occasionally punctuated by a attenuated left-wing squeak of hope that by some dialectical feat 'genuinely' human and popular form of justice may emerge in spite of all from this newly identified diabolical situation.[43]

Although informalism may not work in the ways which proponents have claimed and has been a source of some disappointment, the courts do not, as has been suggested, provide a more attractive alternative to which we should automatically return. Focusing on rights has played an important part in the transformation of Western ideology from the 'harmony' ideal of feudal societies into the modern ideal of participatory democracies but whilst the creation and use of legal rights may have placed a brake on the tyranny of the majority, the extent to which it has achieved significant change is hotly contested. There is an increasing recognition that legal standards can not in themselves ensure an end to systemic inequalities, or a change in attitudes.[44]

There are several reasons for contemporary academics being disappointed by the rights-based approach. First, assumptions about the radiating effect of court decisions may have been overplayed. Secondly, access to the courts is so severely limited that it is not clear that representative samples of the injustices experienced by the underprivileged are ever adjudicated on. On the contrary, it has been argued that the bargaining endowment created by the courts is capable of manipulation by the advantaged and experienced users of the system.[45] Thirdly, the rights model assumes that the judiciary are capable of adjudicating on disputes in a fair and balanced way, an issue which has been intensively debated.[46] Finally, much doubt has been cast on the assertion that the courts are considered legitimate guardians of the collective interest and that there is a tacit agreement between the public and legal system about this. In fact the adjudicative system may be of only symbolic importance as a representative of stability and social cohesion.

There has also been concern about the ease with which it is possible to define what constitutes state control and the consequent ability of critics to identify an expansion or retraction of it. Matthew has argued that critiques of informalism have tended to equate social control, which is inevitable and pervasive, with state control which need not necessarily be. He suggests

42 Pavlich, op. cit., n. 8, p. 713.

43 M. Cain, 'Beyond Informal Justice' in Matthew, op. cit., n. 18, p. 51.

44 J. MacFarlane, 'The Mediation Alternative' in MacFarlane, op. cit., n. 5, pp. 1–21, at p. 9.

45 M. Galanter, 'Why the haves come out ahead: Speculations on the limits of legal change' (1974) 9 *Law and Society Rev.* 95–160.

46 See, for instance, V. Kerruish, *Jurisprudence as ideology* (1991).

that all alternatives to the state are equally capable of producing the effects complained of.[47] Such arguments reflect an understanding of power as more pervasive and complex than has traditionally been suggested.

Community mediation is not necessarily entirely autonomous from state legality or completely encompassed by it. Fitzpatrick claims that the two domains are mutually constitutive social fields that affect one another's historical identities. Thus, each depends on the presence of the other, and the difference between them, to formulate their identity. According to this line of thought community mediation can have embedded and unembedded elements, that latter of which constitutes the 'dark side' of liberal legality. Within the sphere of community mediation it is the power to transform the disputing self to a non-disputing self which makes the operation of power in the community sphere different from the operation of state power.[48]

Drawing on the works of Foucault, Pavlich argues that it is possible to identify ways in which community mediation can be conceived of as a form of governmental rationality that involves techniques of discipline and techniques of self and is able as a consequence to sway between stability and change. Foucault's governmentality concerns itself with the creation of specific self-identities that support a wider totality, the state. It is a related political development to the state which none the less had developed with a political rationality of its own. Through this analysis we are able to conceive of a form of governmentality fostered by such movements as community mediation which exists outside of, but draws on, the state. It is in this guise that community mediation allows for the possibility of popular justice.

The techniques of self referred to are those geared towards the creation of non-disputing self-identities which in turn support and strengthen the neo-liberal state. According to Pavlich, this permits that even if subjects are historically placed they do perform active work on themselves to shape their own self-identities under the pressures of particular social locations[49] such as community mediation. Mediated agreements are reached within the framework of pre-agreed ground rules about behaviour within an informal setting in which the parties are encouraged to give accounts of their perceptions of self, their aspirations and desired outcomes. These accounts are offered for scrutiny and discussion to the other party and the mediator and are probed and challenged by them. Pavlich argues that such sessions are a form of confession and secular atonement in which mediators counsel the wayward, admit their transgressions, and allow them back into the fold. But, significantly, the fact that mediation is not always successful in achieving agreement is given as evidence that this is an open-ended regulatory complex which remains partially unembedded within the ambit of the state.

47 Matthew, op. cit., n. 18.
48 P. Fitzpatrick, 'The rise and rise of informalism' in Matthew, id.
49 Pavlich, op. cit., n. 8.

Empirical studies by legal anthropologists are supportive of this vision of the identity work which forms an integral part of disputes. Although they seem to be out-of-the-ordinary events, disputes nevertheless mobilize support systems, highlight social cleavages and are argued in terms of general morality.[50] Disputants are dependent on others for support and are subject to the coercive power of public opinion, including their own cohort of supporters. For this reason its is important for arguments to be framed in such ways that they address general community standards. Public disputes can actually mobilize social units in a context which dramatizes their interdependence and the necessity of transcending individual interests to achieve group goals. In the words of Colson:

> [These] rituals inevitably stress the value of co-operation, common interests, and harmony that transcend, rather than underwrite the divergence that in fact organise human communities.[51]

But disputes can also prompt the re-thinking of normative frameworks. Consideration of a dispute may involve not only a question of rights, wrongs and culpability but an existential predicament: how else in those circumstances could that person have acted and what are the wider social directives and constraints which make sense or non-sense of the event.[52] Thus, the cultural norms of a group are not only referred to but can be renegotiated during the course of a dispute.[53] Disputes and their settlements act as normative referents which shape the interpretation of bargaining strategies and future conduct. They allow the parties, communities and the state to debate what is legitimate behaviour.

In this way it might be argued that conflicts within communities provide important contextual material which facilitate improvement and change. Thus, community mediation can be seen as a way of allowing for more effective participation in dispute resolution processes and democratic society. It has been argued that this is because, unlike state sanctioned adjudication, it does not avoid the discussion of a range of issues of importance to the parties and does not conceive of conflict as a manifestation of deviance or social illness.[54] It may not have the potential to deal with disputes *and* rebuild communities but it can change levels of consciousness and produce new frameworks within which to consider issues.[55] Arguing from a working-class perspective, Cain has provided a catalogue of success stories of informalism which have prompted significant changes for underprivileged groups and raised political consciousness. These include the Knights of Labour

50 Colson, op. cit., n. 36.
51 id.
52 D. Parkin, 'Disputing human passions among the Giriama of Kenya', in Caplan, op. cit., n. 1.
53 Delgado et al, op. cit., n. 17.
54 Shonholtz, op. cit., n. 16.
55 Liebmann, op. cit. n. 5.

trade union courts to the growth of radical lawyering in the community sphere and the development of law centres in the United Kingdom.[56]

More recently others have approached the debate from a more grounded perspective and in doing so addressed the concern that critics of informalism have failed to ground their contentions about encroaching state control and power in empirical reality.[57] Ewick and Silbey's compelling account of everyday narratives of justice argues that whilst scholars in the field have traditionally concentrated on more obvious collective forms of challenge to the state such as revolutions, rebellions, strikes, boycotts, petitions, and marches, there needs to be more emphasis on commonplace everyday acts of resistance which illustrate the ways in which relatively powerless people accommodate to power whilst simultaneously protecting their identities.[58] It is clear that much legal scholarship continues to focus on a top down approach to resistance, what Annandale and Hunt refer to as the strong end of disagreements. Most commentaries focus on mature disputes which have reached formal institutions.[59] While this reveals much about those who complain or make legal claims, it reveals nothing about those who do not or the normative frameworks, other than formal law, to which the aggrieved citizenry might appeal.

In response to such concerns, Ewick and Silbey identify three narratives of law which are common to the stories that people tell. One is based on the perception that law is magisterial and remote. Another views the law as a game with rules that can be manipulated to one's advantage. But it is the third that is most important in the context of this article. This narrative describes law as an arbitrary power that can be actively resisted. They detail a number of ways in which the 400 Americans they spoke to challenged the distribution of resources in society and cultural legitimacy.

Ewick and Silbey argue that even a small resistance to power is a way of experiencing autonomy and that socio-legal scholars should take more account of such phenomena. It does not matter that such action may not achieve its objective. Each resistance involves a consciousness of being less powerful and a positioning of self as being in opposition. It also requires a consciousness of opportunities for resistance which represent an awareness of both constraint and autonomy. Finally, 'small' resistant acts involve assessments that power has produced unfairness.[60] They admit that such small resistances are rarely motivated by the collective ideal of social justice and that they are practised to escape rather than change the structure of power. Moreover, their results are commonly temporary. But they do they

56 Cain, op. cit., n. 43.

57 Matthew, op. cit., n. 18.

58 P. Ewink and S. Silbey, *The Common Place Of Law, Stories From Everyday Life* (1998).

59 E. Annandale and K. Hunt, 'Accounts of Disagreements with Doctors' (1998) 1 *Social Science and Medicine* 119–29.

60 Ewink and Silbey, op. cit., n. 58.

provide temporary relief from insufferable situations and in doing so may insulate power from sustained and collective challenge. They contend:

> . . . to dismiss everyday forms of resistance on the grounds that they are individualistic, unprincipled and temporary is to foreclose questions about the relationship between power and resistance. Although resistance may be opportunistic and individualistic it is neither random nor idiosyncratic. The opportunities for resistance arise from the regular exercise of power . . . Through everyday practical engagements, individuals identify the cracks and vulnerabilities of organised power and institutions such as law.[61]

Most importantly they argue that a consciousness of the structures of power and an experience of its openings and lapses may be necessary, if not sufficient, precursor of political mobilization. Research on apparently mundane acts of resistance allows scholars to enquire whether they provoke more collective contests of power. In the next and final section, I consider some examples of resistance in a community mediation setting which suggest that, rather than dismissing mediators as agents of state power, it is possible to conceive of them as encouraging resistance in a way which challenges the state order and as acting as conduits between the empowered and disempowered.

EMPIRICAL EXPERIENCES

Recent empirical research into community mediation conducted by the author has posed a number of questions which it is difficult to resolve within the paradigms of debate set by traditional proponents and critics of community mediation.[62] At a purely intuitive level I became concerned that there was more to community mediation that was allowed for by critics and slightly less than was being contended by proponents. Moreover, working in disadvantaged communities with highly committed mediators makes one brutally aware of the responsibility of the researcher to remain open to participants' understandings rather than assuming a passivity and lack of consciousness on their part.

The mediators being shadowed for the research all lived the vicinity of the neighbourhoods in which they mediated disputes and lived in the same conditions as impoverished social tenants whose lives they seek to improve. Many of them had first-hand experience of the social problems with which the inner cities are associated and all stressed the importance of community mediators in their agency being 'street-wise'. Whilst all of them subscribed to a model of 'transformative mediation' which placed emphasis on non-interventionist techniques, they also admitted to being pragmatists who would do what was necessary to help repair the damage done by conflict

61 id., p. 187.
62 Summerfield and Mulcahy, op. cit., n. 4.

and social conditions. Participant observations revealed that in some situations they were prepared to 'step out of role' and give advice to disputants about the responsibilities of state agencies and other organizations which might be able to address their social problems.

The agency did not comply with the standard line adopted by the national community mediation umbrella group or local housing officers that certain types of disputes were only suitable for formal adjudication. Disputes in this category included domestic violence, conflicts about homophobic behaviour, and quarrels with a racial element where there was a fundamental disagreement between the parties about value systems. The justification for mediating such controversial subjects was that 'victims' in such disputes did not have sufficient confidence in agencies such as the police to ask for their dispute to be processed by them. In many instances the mediators shared these concerns and took such cases on because the victims might otherwise run the risk of receiving no assistance from the state.

Drawing on their understandings of the local community they also contended that such disputes constituted an integral part of life within the inner city. Mediators in the study did much to stress that they did not condone violence or racism, but that they could understand the context in which it became possible. This empathy made it possible to deal with a dispute in a way which was more likely to result in a change in attitude by the assailant.

It was also clear that the mediators acted as a vehicle through which collective grievances could be channelled. Individual disputes were dealt with as discrete episodes as far as the parties were concerned but mediators did keep a mental note of collective grievances and issues arising from disputes. A good example of this was provided by disputes about noise which were caused by poorly insulated accommodation. In these cases mediators commonly managed the conflict by attributing blame to the council. They depersonalized the dispute by suggesting to the parties that they were both in dispute through no fault of their own. This had the effect of facilitating compromise and raising consciousness about the responsibilities of the state. Moreover, although the details of individual disputes remained confidential, mediators would report collective concerns about poor insulation in blocks of flats and estates. In this way they acted as conduits for the collective voicing of dissatisfaction and challenged the priorities and strategies of housing officers.

It was also clear that the mediators actively sought to divert cases away from the courts and the use of more draconian powers. Although they were often the most complex of grievances by the time they reached mediation, the agency would encourage housing officers to refer cases even when every other avenue save the issuing of proceedings had been attempted. In this way the agency was able to deflect cases from the gaze of formal institutions and keep the issue within the community sphere.

These examples suggest that it is possible for mediators to remain embedded within communities while acting as agents of the state. They are best characterized as message-bearers between the state and local residents. Their function as conduits for state power is not denied but the legitimacy gained by the connection with state agencies can also act as a veil for resisting interference in residents' lives. Most importantly, the examples make clear that the generalizations of earlier critics are not adequate. They fail to take account of the potential for everyday resistance to state powers undertaken in small measures, and the occasional dominance of local normative frameworks for what constitutes acceptable behaviour.

CONCLUSION

This article has reviewed the treatment of community mediation by practitioners and academics. It has suggested that the claims of proponents of mediation remain attractive but that the possibility of them becoming reality have been undermined by debate about the nature of the relationship between the state, agencies, and individuals, formalism and informalism, the empowered and disempowered. These debates are of wide significance and have been the subject of much contemporary debate. But much of the debate allows only the impossibility of achieving popular justice and is suggestive of intellectual nihilism. At the same time even the most vocal critics of community mediation have found it hard to deny the plausibility of all aspects of the community mediation project.

More recent scholars, whilst remaining cautious of the inflated and often evangelical claims of proponents have rejected the impossibility argument. Their arguments are convincing because they make use of much more sophisticated concepts of power and resistance than was formally the case. A new generation of thought has brought with it a more incremental conception of challenge which suggests the possibility of a slower change in legal and political consciousness than was suggested by earlier generations of left-wing scholars who were hopeful of more rapid change. There are also suggestions of a closer alignment between the interests of socio-legal scholars and social theorists. Recent empirical work has indicated ways in which resistance to state encroachment in the private sphere can occur and has made possible a link between everyday narratives of resistance and grander projects for change. It has also suggested that rather than suppressing opposition to the state mediators are able to rephrase grievances in a way which stresses their collective appeal rather than undermines it.

JOURNAL OF LAW AND SOCIETY
VOLUME 27, NUMBER 1, MARCH 2000
ISSN: 0263–323X, pp. 151–77

Business, State, and Community: 'Responsible Risk Takers', New Labour, and the Governance of Corporate Business

GARY WILSON*

In December 1998, Peter Mandelson MP, one of the principal architects of the Labour Party's victory in the May 1997 general election, dramatically resigned as Secretary of State for Trade and Industry. Nevertheless, despite his relatively brief period in that office, Mr. Mandelson left his imprint on policy through the publication in November 1998 of a major White Paper, 'Our Competitive Future: Building the Knowledge Driven Economy'. *The White Paper sets out the New Labour analysis of the national political economy in a globalized world economy and is very much influenced by Mr. Mandelson's experience of the entrepreneurial spirit during his fact-finding visit to the United States of America. This article seeks to chart the relationship between New Labour's desire to foster the development of the corporate sector within a vibrant entrepreneurial culture and the need to ensure that the integrity of the market is preserved in an arena which is seen as inimicable to strong regulatory intervention by the state. As well as mapping New Labour's political rhetoric onto contemporary debates in corporate governance, the analysis will involve an examination of the interface between business practice and morality. In particular, the article will focus upon the role of the conception of company directors as 'responsible risk takers' and the upon the use of name-and-shame sanctions in the development of an entrepreneurial culture in which all corporate enterprises are seen as having a legitimate societal 'licence to operate'.*

INTRODUCTION

> The changes we face in the 21st century economy involve permanent economic revolution: continuous and rapid innovation that compels unprecedented flexibility and adaptability in skills and knowledge. Increasingly every good and every service will be

* *Department of Law, University of Leeds, Leeds LS2 9JT, England*

I wish to thank Michael Cardwell, Sarah Lowrie, Jo Shaw, and Sally Wheeler for their helpful comments and suggestions. This article is written as at 31 October 1999.

> exposed to relentless global competition. And to equip ourselves best to meet and master these challenges, we need a pro-enterprise, pro-opportunity Britain.[1]

This article seeks to examine some of the various dimensions of the governance of corporate business in modern Britain. In order to do this, it is proposed to sketch out an overview of New Labour's approach to the subject as informed by its analysis of the wider political economy. It should be noted that the primary objective of the article is to map this political rhetoric on to contemporary debates in corporate law and governance and that space does not permit an extensive critical analysis of the many contestable concepts involved therein.

The importance of the current political interest in corporate law and governance should not be underestimated. Whilst such interest is hardly novel, the communitarian approach of New Labour has the potential to transcend the Thatcherite neo-liberal dichotomy between the private world of the economic actor and the public world of the societal actor through the creation of new regulatory spaces and community-based discursive processes. It remains to be seen if such spaces or processes will emerge in actuality, as this will depend upon whether New Labour's particular communitarian mix proceeds by dialogue or edict.

There is no shortage of primary source material in relation to United Kingdom company law as there is at present a great deal of interest in the subject in a large part due to the very extensive technical review of the area being undertaken currently by the Department of Trade and Industry. The aim of the review is to evaluate critically and holisitically the structural basis of United Kingdom company law that was laid down in the nineteenth century (and which has only been revised incrementally during the present century), so as to address explicitly the regulatory issues arising in the contemporary global economy, and thereby to provide a modern facilitative framework of company law that will be effective in promoting and sustaining an entrepreneurial economy.

The article will, in particular, draw upon two crucial Department of Trade and Industry (DTI) consultation documents that have been issued in the course of the review.[2] In order to chart the political dimensions of the debate, it is also proposed to centre discussion around three key speeches by the present Secretary of State for Trade and Industry, Stephen Byers MP, namely, the speeches at the Lord Mayor's Trade and Industry Dinner at the Mansion House (2 February 1999), which first introduced the concept of the director as a responsible risk taker; at the Pensions Investment Research Consultants (PIRC) Annual Corporate Governance Conference (23 March 1999); and at the London Business School (21 July 1999).[3]

1 Extract from the speech of the Chancellor of the Exchequer, Gordon Brown MP, to the Newspaper Conference (22 July 1999).

2 DTI, *Modern Company Law for a Competitive Economy* (1998) and *Modern Company Law for a Competitive Economy: The Strategic Framework* (1999).

3 Hereafter, respectively, the 'Mansion House speech'; the 'PIRC speech'; and the 'LBS speech'.

The principal substantive focus of the article will be on the Blair government's perception of the inherent conceptual tension between the need for the state to promote the entrepreneurial flair required in order for the nation to prosper in the global knowledge economy, and the need to find an effective means of regulating the actors in that market-place. In order to examine this tension (which, although to some extent oppositional, is nevertheless not a paradox), it is necessary to consider the interface of morality with entrepreneurial culture. It will be argued that only by so doing can an appropriate balance between risk taking and fraudulent or immoral business failure be established. This interface thus provides the key to the maintenance of the integrity necessary for the market to function, thereby ensuring both its economic and wider societal legitimacy. The vital importance of cultural attitudes in attaining the optimum form of business governance for the welfare and prosperity of the nation, together with the magnitude of the task in hand and the need to involve all of the members of society in the debate, are clearly demonstrated by Stephen Byers in his LBS speech:

> Clearly, shifting British culture onto a more enterprising and less risk-averse track will take time. But we must all aspire to change the national mood if we are to create an outward looking, confident society, fit to take on the 21st century.

However, as will be demonstrated, New Labour does not perceive itself as having a free hand to engineer the desired broad regulatory framework. For, in the globalized economy, 'excessive' state regulation by traditional command and control techniques is rendered untenable, as inimicable and burdensome to the vital creative small and medium-sized enterprise (SME) sector and due to the possibility of larger companies engaging in forum shopping by way of capital flight to a more favourable regulatory regime. Given the constraints thus believed to be imposed by the processes of globalization, at a high level of abstraction the creation of the new governance regime is said, therefore, to require nothing less than '. . . a new coalition between government, business and society'.[4]

At a more concrete level, the political construction of a market morality depends upon a matrix of factors, one of the most important of which, since the legislative reforms of the Thatcher government, is the structure of the insolvency regime.[5] In contrast to company law, which is generally permissive and enabling in nature, insolvency law is by its very nature rather more interventionist. Accordingly, the state's interest and role in managing the orderly winding up and dissolution of companies is uncontentious. As such, the insolvency process provides an ideal mechanism for the state to undergird business values through the utilization of the examples of bad

4 See LBS speech, id.

5 See, further, T.C. Halliday and B.G. Carruthers, 'The Moral Regulation of Markets: Professions, Privatization and the English Insolvency Act 1986' (1996) 21 *Accounting, Organizations and Society* 371.

practice thereby gleaned in order to illuminate desirable business behaviour. A model of this practice in operation (which this article will focus upon by way of example) is the Blair government's policy of naming and shaming rogue and phoenix company directors.

Unfortunately, whilst such a governance mechanism is a potentially powerful weapon in the armoury of the modern regulatory state, it is in the present context a policy instrument that requires careful handling. Once more, this difficulty refers back to the pervasive interface of business practice with morality introduced above, as it is also the case that the government places a high priority on encouraging entrepreneurs in order to boost Britain's international competitiveness, and the stigma attaching to business failure is thought to be a powerful disincentive to such individuals. Indeed, such is the current weight that the government attaches to the stigma arising from business failure, that the Insolvency Service has been instructed to undertake a review into this subject on behalf of the DTI and a consultation paper is awaited at the time of writing.

It will be argued that the notion of the director as a responsible risk taker has gained substantial political and commercial currency (although it should be acknowledged that the concept has yet to receive significant attention from the judiciary or legal profession) as a way of balancing these opposing objectives, and that the concept also has the potential to unify certain otherwise disparate aspects of company law and insolvency law and public and private company governance.

In conclusion, it will be suggested that some form of value-based signalling in relation to the interface of business practice with morality is essential to the establishment and continuing development and maintenance of company directors as responsible risk takers. Further, it will be argued that this concept forms a vital element of the wider societal compact that is necessary to foster an entrepreneurial culture in which the full spectrum of companies, from the owner-managed private limited company to the public company with a full stock-exchange listing, are perceived by society as having a legitimate 'licence to operate'.[6]

NAMING AND SHAMING AND PHOENIX COMPANY DIRECTORS

On attaining office, the former Minister for Competition and Consumer Affairs, Nigel Griffiths MP, spearheaded a much publicized campaign against phoenix directors who abuse the privilege of limited liability by trading through successive limited companies which fail, leaving unsatisfied creditors in their wake. This is the general notion of the phoenix situation and the essential complaint is that traders are utilizing undercapitalized

6 See the Royal Society of Arts (RSA) report: *Tomorrow's Company* (1995).

limited liability companies as a means of insulating themselves from the financial repercussions of repeated business failure. Concern over this type of activity is by no means new and, indeed, was commented upon extensively in the Cork report:

> It has been made evident to us that there is a widespread dissatisfaction at the ease with which a person trading through the medium of one or more companies with limited liability can allow such a company to become insolvent, form a new company, and then carry on trading much as before, leaving behind him a trail of unpaid creditors, and often repeating the process several times. The dissatisfaction is greatest where the director of an insolvent company has set up business again, using a similar name for the new company, and trades with assets purchased at a discount from the liquidator of the old company.[7]

It should be noted that this oft-quoted paragraph refers not only to the general notion of the phoenix abuse, but also to the more specific and aggravated practice of setting up a new company and trading in the same business with a name similar to that of the insolvent company. In such a circumstance the controllers of the phoenix company have not only sheltered themselves from the full ramifications of the first business failure by the use of a limited company, but they have also transferred the value of the goodwill attaching to the name of the original business to the new phoenix company, thereby seeking to misrepresent the credit status of the new company in the eyes of its potential creditors. The complexity of the underlying policy issues is demonstrated by Parliament's response to the Cork committee's recommendations, which was to make the use of a similar company name for the phoenix company a criminal offence pursuant to s. 216 of the Insolvency Act 1986 and to leave the general phoenix scenario to fall within the factors to be taken into account by the courts in determining whether a director is unfit to act as such, thereby meriting disqualification under the Company Directors Disqualification Act 1986.

The case of J & L Ashworth (Hardware) Ltd[8] illustrates a typical use of publicity sanctions as part of the name and shame campaign. The decision is indicative of the wider usage of the phoenix term as the director had been found unfit to be a company director pursuant to s. 6 of the Company Directors Disqualification Act 1986 on the basis, among other things, that he had 'caused three companies to commence trading in a business which had failed previously'. Although the companies were all undertaking the same type of business, they were not utilizing prohibited names, and s. 216 of the Insolvency Act was thus irrelevant, as the companies were not therefore phoenix companies in the technical sense. To add to the confusion, it should

7 See *The Report of the Review Committee on Insolvency Law and Practice* (1982; Cmnd. 8558, chair Sir Kenneth Cork) para. 1813. The committee's recommendations formed the basis of the statutory reform of insolvency law in the mid-1980s. The phoenix problem was discussed in chs. 43 and 45 and the structural nature of the problem is clearly identified in para. 1815.

8 Unreported. For details, see DTI press release, 'Griffiths Double-Barrelled Attack on 'Phoenix' Directors' (18 March 1998), which is also available on the internet.

be noted that, even if a prohibited name had been used, there is nevertheless an automatic exemption for the phoenix company directors from the operation of s. 216 if full consideration is given for all the assets (including any goodwill attaching to the company name) transferred to the new company![9]

From the above, it can be seen that the phenomenon known as the phoenix company is not only a subject of much complexity, but is also is the subject of much contemporary interest, and not simply within the relatively narrow confines of either the legal academy or insolvency practitioner circles. As a consequence of the well publicized name-and-shame campaign orchestrated by the DTI, the phoenix problem has also been the focus of considerable attention in the political and commercial spheres as part of the government's campaign to create an actively hostile business environment for rogue directors.[10]

GLOBALIZATION, THE THIRD WAY, AND ECONOMIC GOVERNANCE

Such support for good market practice is unsurprising, as more generally the government has given a high profile to the vital importance of commercial enterprise to the United Kingdom, with particular reference to the need to be competitive and flexible in a post-Fordist global market-place with its emphasis on just-in-time delivery, short production runs, and product quality.[11] An elaboration of the policy consequences of post-Fordism forms a pervasive theme in the DTI White Paper, *Our Competitive Future: Building the Knowledge Driven Economy*.[12] Examples of the interrelationship of these points can also be found in many of the speeches of the Prime Minister, Tony Blair MP; see, for example, the speech at the Trades Union Congress (9 September 1997), where he says of the Third Way:

> . . . it starts from a recognition of certain realities about the modern world:
> (1) We live in a global economy, where financial irresponsibility by governments leads to immediate punishment from the markets.
> (2) There is a technological revolution transforming the workplace and production.

9 See Insolvency Rules 1986, S.I. no. 1925, r. 4.228.

10 For example, see DTI press releases: op. cit., n. 8; 'Crackdown on Unfit Directors' (23 July 1998); 'Kim Howells Delivers Warning to Directors' (9 December 1998); and 'Rogue Director "Hotline" Hits 1,200 Calls' (4 January 1999).

11 For a more extended discussion of post-Fordism, see C. Hay, *The Political Economy of New Labour* (1999) at 28–30, and M. Castells, *The Information Age: Economy, Society and Culture* (rev. edn. 1999, 3 vols.) vol. 1, ch. 3.

12 DTI, *Our Competitive Future: Building the Knowledge Driven Economy* (1998; Cm. 4176). For an analysis of some of the broader sociological and political themes arising, see S. Lash and J. Urry, *The End of Organized Capitalism* (1987); A. Giddens, *Beyond Left and Right* (1994); Castells, id.; P. Hirst, *Associative Democracy: New Forms of Economic and Social Governance* (1994); D. Held, *Models of Democracy* (2nd edn., 1996) part III; and C. Leadbeater, *Living on Thin Air: The New Economy* (1999).

(3) Consumer tastes have become varied, highly demanding, expecting very high standards of quality and service.
(4) The future of modern developed nations lies in the knowledge and information economy.
So, mass production is out. Go-it-alone microeconomics is out. Jobs for life are probably out. Quality is in. Skills are in. Prudent finance is in. We compete in a global economy that is spinning with change.[13]

The import of the these ideas has led to the recognition by the Blair government of various facets of the so-called 'competition state', which in contrast to the welfare state (which sought to remove certain economic activities from the market) pursues, as Cerny puts it, 'increased marketization in order to make economic activities located within the national territory . . . more competitive in international and transnational terms.'[14] However, whilst globalization is generally perceived as a multi-dimensional set of processes capable of both emptying and empowering states, New Labour has been accused of taking a significantly more absolutist 'hyper-globalist' stance. Following this analysis, the role of the state is conceived simply in terms of adapting individuals to the economic realities of the global market and government has little choice other than to adopt a minimal regulatory function consistent with the broad neo-liberal economic paradigm of the 1980s.[15] Indeed, this view has caused one commentator to lament that:

> New Labour now accepts that there is simply no alternative to neo-liberalism in an era of heightened capital mobility and financial liberalisation – in short in an era of globalisation.[16]

Accordingly, for New Labour, the new role of government is to facilitate the development of a 'knowledge driven economy'[17] (where ideas, know-how, and services rather than traditional manufacturing industries are the key to economic success) populated by 'serial entrepreneurs'[18] in order to

13 See, also, particularly, the speeches to the TUC (24 May 1999) and to the CBI (27 May 1998).

14 See, further, P.G. Cerny, 'Paradoxes of the Competition State: the Dynamics of Political Globalization' (1997) 32 *Government and Opposition* 251.

15 See, for example, D. Held, 'Globalisation: The Timid Tendency', and S. Hall, 'The Great Moving Nowhere Show', both in *Marxism Today* (1998). For a nuanced discussion rejecting both the hyper-globalist and the more sceptical European social market conceptions of globalization, see J. Gray, *False Dawn: The Delusions of Global Capitalism* (rev. edn., 1999) ch. 3 and postscript.

16 Hay, op. cit., n. 11, at p. 136.

17 See, further, T. Blair, *The Third Way: New Politics for the New Century* (1998) 8; Leadbeater, op. cit., n. 12; and *Our Competitive Future* (with particular reference to the associated analytical report). See, also, DTI, *Manufacturing in the Knowledge Driven Economy* (1999).

18 The terminology employed by the then Secretary of State for Trade and Industry, Peter Mandelson MP, in his speech to the British American Chamber of Commerce in New York (13 October 1998) (hereafter the 'New York speech'). His successor to that office, Stephen Byers, has developed the more balanced term of the 'responsible risk taker': see Mansion House speech.

maintain national prosperity. Indeed, it is in the light of this analysis that New Labour has sought to undertake an ambitious reconfiguration of the relationship between the state, the private sector, and the citizen by adopting a broadly communitarian approach to governance, citizenship, and regulation.[19] Whilst the precise nature of the project remains vague (perhaps unsurprisingly, given the oft-noted lack of clarity in the concept of community that underpins the broad church of communitarian theories),[20] the most comprehensive political statement to date (albeit expressed as work in progress) is to be found in Tony Blair's own book, *The Third Way*.[21] Although New Labour's central notion of community is undoubtedly in part indebted to the responsive communitarian movement in the United States of America,[22] it would seem that the distinctive influence of the domestic communitarian heritage and of the Labour Party's own political roots should not be overlooked.[23]

This project[24] is, in the words of the Chancellor of the Exchequer, Gordon Brown MP, to the News International Conference (17 July 1998), consciously conceived of as a 'new politics' designed to meet the needs of a 'national politics for the global marketplace'.[25] It is interesting to note that the first-order analysis in this speech is one of the economic position of the nation in the global economy and that the parameters for both domestic economic action and social policy are treated as being both exclusively established and severely constrained thereby. Criticisms have been made of the reality of globalization in reducing the effective powers of action of the nation state, and some movement towards greater state regulatory intervention, at least at an international level, seems to have been prompted by the South East Asian financial crisis. A good summary of the position is given in a subsequent speech by Gordon Brown to the Commonwealth Finance Ministers in Ottawa (30 September 1998) entitled,

19 The aspirational aspect of the project is well brought out in I. Hargreaves and I. Christie (eds.), *Tomorrow's Politics: The Third Way and Beyond* (1998) ch. 1, and M. Harris, 'New Labour: Government and Opposition' (1999) 70 *Political Q.* 52.

20 For a discussion of the political space thereby created, see S. Driver and L. Martell, 'New Labour's Communitarianisms' (1997) 17 *Critical Social Policy* 27.

21 Blair, op. cit., n. 17. For further early influences on the Blair revolution, see W. Hutton, *The State We're In* (1995) and *The State to Come* (1997); and D. Marquand, *The Unprincipled Society* (1988).

22 See, especially, A. Etzioni, *The Spirit of Community* (1993) and *The New Golden Rule* (1996).

23 See, respectively, H. Tam, *Communitarianism: A New Agenda for Politics and Citizenship* (1998) and K. Morgan, 'The Historical Roots of New Labour' (1998) 48(10) *History Today* 15.

24 For a critical overview of the creation of New Labour and of its current principal policies, see S. Driver and L. Martell, *New Labour: Politics After Thatcherism* (1998); the special November 1998 edition of *Marxism Today*; and Hay, op. cit., n. 11.

25 For a short summary of the arguments of W. Hutton and P. Hirst on this point, see K. Faulks, *Citizenship in Modern Britain* (1998) at 180–2. See, also, L. Weiss, *The Myth of the Powerless State* (1998).

'New Global Structures for a New Global Age'. The new measures proposed to regulate international finance (with a particular focus upon transparency and stability) and to provide for a code of good practice on social policy are of especial interest.[26]

Despite these potential international ramifications, the New Labour communitarian project seeks to present a new holistic vision of the individual and society that is very much premised upon the concept of the retrenched state in a globalized economy. The idea has been labelled the 'Third Way'[27] as it attempts to avoid, what are perceived by its advocates as, the pitfalls of both the corporatism of the old Left and the market-led neo-liberalism of the new Right.[28] Hence, the new politics is presented rhetorically as a synthesis of (or, as its progenitors are keen to stress its distinctive nature, at least by way of contrast with) what have been traditionally viewed as a series of binary oppositions.[29] For example, New Labour speeches are peppered with references to the good society and the good economy; enterprise and fairness; individualism and community, and it is always stressed that there is no inherent tension between the juxtaposed ideas but, rather, that they are strongly complementary. Rather unsurprisingly, the theory underlying this type of articulation has been subject to vigorous critique, particularly by members of the more traditional Left of the political spectrum such as Stuart Hall, who comments somewhat disparagingly that:

> The 'Third Way' speaks as if there are no longer any conflicting interests which cannot be reconciled. It therefore envisages a 'politics without adversaries'.[30]

In any event, the new ground that emerges (or which may be thought to be in the process of emerging as the modernizing project is explicitly described as one of 'permanent revisionism') is of a society of opportunity and responsibility which draws upon, and is informed by, not only traditional socialist ideas of social obligation and solidarity but also the core

26 For the effect of such international action on the powers of the nation state see Castells, op. cit., n. 11, vol. II, ch. 5, especially at pp. 266–9.

27 For the most recent pronouncements, see speeches of Tony Blair on the occasion of the Beveridge Lecture (18 March 1999) and at the TUC Partnership Conference (24 May 1999). A more sustained analysis is to be found in Blair, op. cit., n. 17; A. Giddens, *The Third Way* (1998) and Hargreaves and Christie, op. cit., n. 19.

28 For an analysis of this breakdown of the traditional political spectrum, see Giddens, op. cit. n. 12, introduction and chs. 1 and 2; Tam, op. cit. n. 23, ch. 2; Driver and Martell, op. cit. n. 24, ch. 6. Compare N. Bobbio, *Left and Right* (1996) and W. Hutton, 'The State We Should Be In' *Marxism Today* (1998) 34 who argue that the approach adopted to the notion of equality (especially in relation to some parity of outcome through redistributive policies rather than simply equality of opportunity) will always provide a meaningful political differentiation in the use of the terms Left and Right .

29 For a feminist critique of the dichotomized mode of thinking that pervades contemporary Western liberalism and communitarianism, see E. Frazer and N. Lacey, *The Politics of Community* (1993) ch. 6.

30 Hall, op. cit., n. 15, at p. 10.

Thatcherite motifs of economic opportunity and dynamism. And, as the following extract from the speech of Gordon Brown to the News International Conference (17 July 1998) amply demonstrates, New Labour has not been shy to emphasise the vital importance and desirability of the latter ideas:

> People say that Mrs Thatcher created an enterprising society. I say there is still not enough enterprise and we have to do better. I want Britain to be, in every area, a creative innovative and enterprising economy.

A prime example of this aim is to be found in 'Competitiveness UK', a concept launched by the then President of the Board of Trade, Margaret Beckett MP, on 4 June 1997. Mrs Beckett went on to outline her vision of United Kingdom industrial policy in a number of keynote speeches which denoted strong markets, modern companies, and an entrepreneurial culture as the three pillars which the state, in partnership with other interested groups, must foster in order to promote a competitive economy.[31] With the development of the idea of the knowledge economy by her successors at the Department of Trade and Industry, the recent policy emphasis has moved to capabilities, competition, and collaboration.[32]

In particular, as part of a series of policy initiatives centred around 'Competitiveness UK', the Blair government has proved keen both to stress the key role that small and medium-sized companies have to play in building an enterprising nation[33] and to undertake a comprehensive review of company law so as to provide a modern framework for a modern economy.[34] These two themes are of some importance in the phoenix company context for such companies are invariably small owner-managed enterprises. Hence, as the government encourages the growth of this sector,[35] by seeking

31 For example, see speech to the Engineering Council's Annual Conference (30 April 1998).

32 See, further, DTI, op. cit., n. 12, and Mansion House speech.

33 For example, 'A dynamic SME sector is fundamental to President of the Board of Trade Margaret Beckett's three pillars of competitiveness – strong markets, modern companies and an enterprising nation. The government is keen to work in partnership with SMEs in taking forward the Competitiveness UK initiative' (extract from speech of the then Small Firms Minister, Barbara Roche MP, to British Chambers of Commerce Conference, 16 June 1998). See, also, PIRC speech where small businesses were stated to be '. . . at the heart of job creation and the government's drive to promote competitiveness' and the 'think small first' principle (enunciated in DTI, op. cit. (1999), n. 2, para. 2.25), by which companies legislation would be made 'SME-centric', was roundly endorsed.

34 The framework of the review and its terms of reference are set out in DTI, op. cit. (1998), n. 2. See, further, DTI, op. cit. (1999), n. 2 which identifies the needs of small and closely held companies as a key issue within the review (see para. 2.19 and ch. 5.2) and indicates that the phoenix company issue will be pursued in depth in the next phase (see para. 5.2.12).

35 The latest business statistics indicate that at the beginning of 1998 there were 3.7 million active businesses in the United Kingdom (representing an increase of 1.3 million over the figure for 1980, being the first year for which statistics are available): DTI, *The Statistical Bulletin: Small and Medium Enterprise (SME) Statistics for the UK, 1998* (1999). Although over 99 per cent of businesses are small businesses (that is, with fewer than 50 employees), the majority are conducted by sole traders or partnerships rather than through companies.

to foster a culture[36] in which many more individuals view it as natural to aspire to become risk-taking entrepreneurs,[37] the phoenix scenario has the potential to affect fundamentally a very large and growing number of people whether as victims or as perpetrators.[38] It is thus important that the governing legislative provisions should articulate a clear policy which is both accessible and intelligible to this constituency.[39] Such transparency is of especial significance given the severity of the sanctions which apply to infractions of the complex statutory provisions relevant to the phoenix company, and this is all the more the case if the government chooses to maintain a policy of naming and shaming those responsible for such transgressions.[40]

THE GOVERNANCE OF CORPORATE BUSINESS: PUBLIC COMPANIES

The Labour government's early stress upon naming and shaming phoenix directors is indicative of the fact that the phoenix company problem squarely raises, in terms of both the appropriate regulatory mechanisms

36 Institutional manifestations of this desire can be seen in the creation of the Small Business Service, the Better Regulation Taskforce, the Better Payment Practice Group, and the Enterprise Zone internet information service; the Access Business and Export Explorer initiatives and the development of the Business Link Service. See, also, various initiatives set out in the implementation plan published by the DTI, 10 March 1999, in relation to the objectives set out in *Our Competitive Future*.

37 For example, '. . . we need a new approach in Britain to risk-taking that will increase the number of entrepreneurs and raise the growth and survival rate of small businesses': extract from speech by Gordon Brown at the Mansion House (11 June 1998). This theme was at the heart of virtually all of Peter Mandelson's speeches whilst Secretary of State at the DTI, but see, especially, his speech to the CBI Annual Conference (2 November 1998). It is also central to *Our Competitive Future* (see, in particular, ch. 2 discussing entrepreneurial culture) which was itself referred to as 'a manifesto for the DTI' in Stephen Byers's Mansion House speech.

38 At 31 March 1998 there were roughly 1.3 million British companies registered at Companies House of which approximately 1.2 million had either no issued share capital or an issued share capital of less than £5,000: DTI, *Companies in 1998–99* (1999).

39 This is one of the main priorities of Access Business and is also reflected in the DTI's stated aim that legislation should be 'drafted in clear, concise and unambiguous language which can be readily understood by those involved in business enterprise': DTI, op. cit (1998), n. 2, para. 5.2 (i)(c). The response of the Company Law Committee of the Law Society to the consultation document (Law Society Memorandum 360) expresses the view that such an aim is unrealistic in the legislative context given the complexities inherent in company law and that the transparency function would be better served through the production of explanatory memoranda. This submission is not at odds with the view stated in the main text as the emphasis remains on enabling the persons directly affected to be able to clearly discern the broad policies underlying the legislation. See, also, PIRC speech and DTI, op. cit. (1999), n. 2, para. 2.24 on the importance of this point.

40 For a detailed discussion of the legislative measures pertinent to the phoenix company scenario, see G. Wilson, 'Delinquent Directors and Company Names: the Role of Judicial Policy-Making in the Business Environment' (1996) 47 *Northern Ireland Legal Q.* 345.

and the substantive standards to be employed, the wider issue of the governance of corporate business. Whilst there has been considerable interest in this topic in recent years,[41] the traditional focus in the United Kingdom has been towards a more circumscribed notion of corporate governance conceived primarily in terms of determining the appropriate relationship between the board of directors and the shareholders[42] of a relatively small number of quoted public limited companies.[43] Given the tremendous power that many of these companies command, such a high level of interest is undoubtedly justified and even though this form of corporate governance (being principally addressed at the accountability of publicly traded companies[44]) is not directly relevant to the narrow phoenix company issue, there are certain aspects of the debate which are illustrative of the current relationship between the state, business sector, and wider community towards the governance of business in its broader sense.

In particular, it is acknowledged that the power of publicly traded companies arises not simply from the deficit in the level of accountability to their shareholders but because such companies are also in an increasingly autonomous position *vis-à-vis* the state due to the opportunities offered by information technology and open capital markets for global re-location.[45] In

41 There is now a considerable body of academic literature: see, for example, J. Parkinson, *Corporate Power and Responsibility* (1993); J. McCahery et al. (eds.), *Corporate Control and Accountability* (1993); S. Sheikh and W. Rees (eds.), *Corporate Governance and Corporate Control* (1995); K. Keasey et al., *Corporate Governance* (1997); and J. Charkham and A. Simpson, *Fair Shares: the Future of Shareholder Power and Responsibility* (1999).

42 That is, the problem is analysed as a consequence of the separation between ownership and control: for the classic exposition, see A.A. Berle and G.C. Means, *The Modern Corporation and Private Property* (rev. edn., 1967). For a detailed argument that it is misconceived to view shareholders as owners of the public company in any meaningful sense and accordingly that the separation of ownership and control is not the most apposite way to frame the governance debate as it overplays the narrow director/shareholder agency problem whilst underplaying the need for the wider social mechanisms of governance that are concomitant upon a radically reified or organizist view of corporate personality, see P. Ireland, 'Company Law and the Myth of Shareholder Ownership' (1999) 62 *Modern Law Rev.* 32, and J. Kay, *The Business of Economics* (1996) Part III.

43 There are in the region of 2,500 such companies quoted on the London Stock Exchange: DTI, op. cit (1998), n. 2, para. 2.1.

44 Though not exclusively so: see, further, report to the OECD by the Business Sector Advisory Group on Corporate Governance, *Corporate Governance: Improving Competitiveness and Access to Capital in Global Markets* (1998) ch. 1, para. 1.1:14. The same point is made in the preamble to the ultimate report, *OECD Principles of Corporate Governance* (1999), though it is interesting to note that it is somewhat narrower in focus overall and concentrates on governance issues arising from the separation of ownership and control.

45 The need to attain the appropriate level of regulation so as to remain attractive to indigenous companies and entice inward investment pervades government thinking in this area: see, in particular, DTI, op. cit. (1998), n. 2, paras. 3.8, 4.4, and especially 4.7, and DTI, op. cit. (1999), n. 2, para. 2.11. It should be noted that the autonomy of such companies is contestable as, in the eyes of some commentators, multinational corporations are just as 'hollowed out' as the state by the pressures of globalization. Consequently, whilst it is true that, '[i]n the global free market the instruments of economic life have become

the light of the latter point it is unsurprising (especially given the wider political scenario previously outlined) that the corporate governance discourse has been conducted primarily in the realm of self-regulation in both the domestic[46] and the international sphere.[47] Thus, although there is general agreement that some state intervention is necessary to provide a basic regulatory framework to the market,[48] the broad thrust of the corporate governance proposals is towards the flexibility and dynamism of self-regulation and to an invocation of a neo-liberal minimal state that will not place what are perceived as unnecessary hurdles in the way of wealth creation.[49]

At present it is widely acknowledged that the precise form and scope of the governance mechanisms of any system of self-regulation will need to map the specific culture of the host state[50] and it would seem that there is

dangerously emancipated from social control and political governance', such companies are nevertheless themselves operationally constrained by the very same environment: see, further, Gray, op. cit., n. 15, at pp. 63, 72–7, 234.

46 See, especially, *Report of the Committee on the Financial Aspects of Corporate Governance* (1992, chair, Sir Adrian Cadbury); *Directors' Remuneration* (1995, chair Sir Richard Greenbury); and *Committee on Corporate Governance: Final Report* (1998, chair, Sir Ronald Hampel). The result of all of this activity was the creation of the *Combined Code* (1998) comprising a set of principles of good governance and a more detailed code of best practice. Quoted companies are not compelled to apply the provisions of the Combined Code but, broadly speaking, the listing rules issued by the London Stock Exchange require any departures to be publicly identified and justified by the relevant company in its annual report. For an examination of the effectiveness of such sanctions, see A. Belcher, 'Regulation by the Market: The Case of the Cadbury Code and Compliance Statement' [1995] *J. of Business Law* 321, and for a critical appraisal of the Combined Code, see J. Parkinson and G. Kelly, 'The Combined Code on Corporate Governance' (1999) 70 *Political Q.* 101.

47 See, further, OECD, op. cit. (1998), n. 44.

48 For example, id., Chair's introduction, ch. 1, para 1.1:12; Blair, op. cit., n. 17, at pp. 8–11, and PIRC speech. The nature and extent of state involvement in 'free' markets is obviously contentious: for diametrically opposed viewpoints, see Gray, op. cit., n. 15, arguing 'free' markets can only be the product of strong states, and P. Minford, *Market Not Stakes: The Triumph of Capitalism and the Stakeholder Fallacy* (1998), favouring private ordering within a minimal state.

49 For example, see DTI, op. cit. (1999), n. 2, paras. 2.21–2.23. Indeed, even within a system of self-regulation such as that which pertains for the governance of quoted companies in the United Kingdom, concerns have been expressed that too much stress has been given to accountability to the detriment of enterprise: see, for example, Hampel, op. cit., n. 46, para. 1.1 and H. Short et al., 'Corporate Governance, Accountability and Enterprise' (1998) 6 *Corporate Governance* 151. More generally, the minimization of structural impediments to economic growth would seem to be one of the intended functions of the new Productivity and Competitiveness Cabinet committee announced in DTI, op. cit., n. 12, para. 5.5.

50 See the preamble to OECD, op. cit. (1999), n. 44 and Hampel, id., para. 1.4. For a comparative survey of the corporate governance systems in five states and the effect of the 'distinctive nature of each country's culture, history and institutions' thereon, see J. Charkham, *Keeping Good Company* (1995) and K. Lannoo, 'A European Perspective on Corporate Governance' (1999) 37 *J. of Common Market Studies* 269. An excellent historical comparative survey charting the significance of political culture in constituting corporate governance structures is given in M.J. Roe, *Strong Managers, Weak Owners: the*

general acceptance (at least in the United Kingdom business world) of two core ideas central to the Anglo-American paradigm: that a company's primary mission is to generate returns for the present and future shareholders and that the shareholders' rights are derived squarely from their private property interest in a company.[51] It follows that in one sense the effect of adopting a system of self-regulation in the United Kingdom which acknowledges the investors and directors as the principal legitimate actors in the company (thereby severely de-limiting the role of the state and other stakeholders in the formal governance process) has been to privilege a 'privatized'[52] view of the publicly traded company.[53] However, simultaneously and

Political Roots of American Corporate Finance (1994). On this theme see, also, D.A. Skeel Jr., 'An Evolutionary Theory of Corporate Law and Corporate Bankruptcy' (1998) 51 *Vanderbilt Law Rev.* 1325, who offers a stimulating discussion of the pressures exerted by the local corporate insolvency regime on the form of governance mechanisms adopted in different jurisdictions. The intersection with globalization at this juncture is perhaps worth noting as the above analysis would suggest that the business élite of the new world order is not, at least yet, operating within a 'hybridized' extra-territorial top culture but remains firmly rooted in praxis by the history and parameters offered by local/regional business culture: compare Z. Bauman, *Globalization: The Human Consequences* (1998).

51 See Hampel, id., paras. 1.16–1.18 and, in favour of the two principles generally, A. Alcock, 'Corporate Governance: A Defence of the Status Quo' (1995) 58 *Modern Law Rev.* 898 and OECD, op. cit. (1998), n. 44, ch. 2. The role of the institutional shareholder is thus viewed as increasingly central: see, for example, R.A.G. Monks, *The Emperor's Nightingale* (1998) who argues that investor activism (albeit conceived through a new language of sustainability which engages with other stakeholders' interests) forms the principal practical and legitimate axis of corporate governance. For a critique of this viewpoint arguing for the recognition of the corporation 'as a network of social and productive relationships' and '. . . the replacement of private, shareholder-centred mechanisms by more democratic, social mechanisms of governance . . ..' see Ireland, op. cit., n. 42, at p. 56 and, in the same vein, J. Maltby and R. Wilkinson, 'Stakeholding and Corporate Governance in the UK' (1998) 18 *Politics* 197. In any event, the extent to which governance by investor activism can be utilized in structurally and culturally inimicable environments would appear limited even in the case of very sophisticated investor institutions: see, further, T.J. André, Jr., 'Cultural Hegemony: The Exportation of Anglo-Saxon Corporate Governance Ideologies to Germany' (1998) 73 *Tulane Law Rev.* 69. It is interesting to note that the use of adverse publicity is suggested therein (p. 171) as one of the more effective ways in which such investors could influence the governance agenda.

52 That is, in contradistinction to a public or societal contextual perspective. When combined with economic globalization such a framework has profound implications for the very existence of civil society and democratic structures: see further U. Beck, *Democracy Without Enemies* (1998) ch. 5 and R. Dahrendorf, 'A Precarious Balance: Economic Opportunity, Civil Society, and Political Liberty' in *The Essential Communitarian Reader*, ed. A. Etzioni (1998) 73.

53 Hence, whilst Hampel, op. cit., n. 46 recognizes that good governance requires all the company's constituencies to be taken into account by the board with the objective of enhancing the shareholders' investment (paras. 1.3, 1.16, 1.18), the point is made most strongly that, although the board is responsible for relations with stakeholders, it is *accountable* only to shareholders (para. 1.17). A similar position is set out in OECD, op. cit. (1999), n. 44, principles III and V. Hampel states the reason for this distinction to be that if a multi-fiduciary duty was imposed on the board it would be impossible to find an appropriate benchmark against which to evaluate board decisions thereby perversely making

paradoxically, due not only to the employment of the twin principles of disclosure and accountability but due also to the desire to pre-empt state intervention,[54] another dimension arising from the use of self-regulation has been the placement of the governance debate firmly within the public sphere.

Clearly, the adoption of a 'pluralist model' as opposed to the present 'enlightened shareholder value model' would formally create a focused arena of a distinctive legal nature for public discussion concerning the business practice of company directors.[55] Such an approach would appear to resonate with the influential Royal Society of Arts inquiry, which commends corporations to take an inclusive approach to business, emphasizing notions of partnership and interconnectedness with other stakeholders, in order to both maintain their 'licence to operate' and maximize their long-term sustainable profitability to present and future shareholders.[56] However, although the DTI review recognizes that the present fiduciary duties require an inclusive approach, it clearly and categorically limits this duty to the latter objective.[57]

In very crude terms, the privatized axis is at present thus constituted as the dominant formal mode of discourse and is thus privileged over the public limb of 'inclusiveness' attaching to the notion of the 'licence to operate' which, in a formal legal sense, languishes barely distinguishable within its shadow (a fact which is undoubtedly exacerbated by the confusion within the enlightened shareholder model between short-termist and inclusive approaches).[58] However, on this axis it is the pre-emptive principle of self-regulation which ironically has thrown certain substantive business operations open for debate in the civic arena, for it permits and necessitates a discourse concerning the business practice of going concern companies as a means of legitimating and sustaining their societal 'licence to operate'.

directors even less accountable: for a vigorous academic defence of this argument, see E. Sternberg, 'The Defects of Stakeholder Theory' (1997) 5 *Corporate Governance* 3 (but compare Parkinson, op. cit., n. 41, and the essays in *Progressive Corporate Law*, ed. L.E. Mitchell (1995) which provide a more positive evaluation of various multi-fiduciary models). For a concise discussion of a range of governance paradigms in the corporate sphere, see D.P. Sullivan and D.E. Conlon, 'Crisis and Transition in Corporate Governance Paradigms: The Role of the Chancery Court of Delaware' (1997) 31 *Law and Society Rev.* 713, 714–20 and DTI, op. cit. (1999), n. 2, ch. 5.1.

54 See, for example, C. Villiers, 'Self Regulatory Corporate Governance – Final Hope or Last Rites?' (1998) 13 *Scottish Law and Practice Q.* 208, especially at 224–5.

55 These models are discussed as one of the central issues for examination in DTI, op. cit. (1999), n. 2, ch. 5.1.

56 RSA, op. cit., n. 6. This stance is also well illustrated by OECD, op. cit. (1998), n. 44, ch. 7 which, whilst explicitly recognizing the validity of societal interests and the role of corporate citizenship (ch. 7.6) nevertheless concludes by emphasising the pre-eminence of shareholders' interests (para. 143).

57 See DTI, op. cit. (1999), n. 2, paras. 5.1.19, 5.1.12, 5.1.28 respectively.

58 id., paras. 5.1.12, 5.1.20.

A prime example of this shift in the United Kingdom, which bears a close affinity to the name-and-shame campaign over rogue directors, is the ongoing public debate over levels of executive pay.[59] The topic of so-called 'fat cat' salaries, in particular in relation to senior executives of privatized industries such as Cedric Brown, chief executive of British Gas plc, has been constantly in the press in the last decade. Such pressures led to self-regulation through disclosure of information pursuant to the recommendations of an industry group.[60] However, it would appear that the recommendations contained in the Greenbury report may not be sufficient to forestall legislative intervention requiring shareholder approval of directors' remuneration levels if, as Stephen Byers put it in his PIRC speech, 'best practice does not succeed in delivering a greater link between pay and performance.' Subsequently, the topic has received an extended analysis in a DTI consultation document where the government has indicated its preference for the above measure together with the creation of new procedures to enable shareholders to move a resolution on directors' remuneration at the annual general meeting of the company.[61]

THE GOVERNANCE OF CORPORATE BUSINESS: PRIVATE COMPANIES

By way of contrast, the governance of private companies[62] is a subject which is rarely examined or even directly acknowledged as a field of enquiry in such terms.[63] Indeed, such companies have been traditionally placed for analytical purposes within a much more discrete frame of

59 For a substantive discussion of the issues, see C. Villiers, 'Executive Pay: Beyond Control?' (1995) 15 *Legal Studies* 260 and B.R. Cheffins, *Company Law: Theory, Structure and Operation* (1997) ch. 14. For an example of a name-and-shame table on the topic, see *Guardian*, 19 July 1999.

60 Greenbury, op. cit., n. 46.

61 DTI, *Directors' Remuneration* (1999) paras. 7.17 and 7.23 respectively.

62 Governance here is used in a general regulatory sense.

63 S. 459 of the Companies Act 1985 provides a potential forum for airing such matters, especially as a wide ambit has been given to the concept of unfair prejudice (particularly through supplementing the company constitution by reference to equitable constraints manifested by a member's legitimate expectations) by analogy with Lord Wilberforce's reasoning in *Ebrahimi* v. *Westbourne Galleries Ltd* [1973] A.C. 360. However, such expectations have been expressly stated to be inapplicable to listed public companies in *Re Astec (BSR) plc* [1999] B.C.C. 59, at p. 87D *per* Parker J, and recent decisions have been more restrictive in tenor even in the context of quasi-partnership companies: see, especially, *Re Saul D Harrison & Sons plc* [1995] 1 B.C.L.C. 14 (though compare *Re BSB Holdings Ltd. (No 2)* [1996] 1 B.C.L.C. 155, at 243e *per* Arden J) and *O'Neill* v. *Phillips* [1999] B.C.C. 600. In any event, the fact that the section concerns shareholder disagreements has given it a trajectory towards the resolution of specific private disputes with the result that the judges, in sharp contrast to the disqualification cases where the provisions are squarely informed by the public interest, seem to be chary of making generalized statements on

reference than listed public companies. This strongly private perspective is reinforced by a factual backdrop where there is rarely a separation of ownership and control as, unlike the majority of listed public companies, the owner-managers of a private company will almost invariably own or control the majority, if not all, of the share capital and voting rights of the company. Thus, as the small private company is viewed as being distinctively within the private sphere,[64] the analytical perspective associated with it has largely disregarded any broader civic, ethical or socio-political analysis, at least in relation to the *ongoing* governance of a company's business. Hence, the widely held view of corporate practitioners is that unanimous shareholder ratification is a near universal panacea at common law for any internal corporate irregularities (of a civil nature) arising in a solvent private company. The strong notion of shareholders as the utilizers of their own private property has undoubtedly been influential to this end, as one commentator has recently put it:

> Ownership . . . served to legitimate the corporate form itself. So long as it was owned by individuals the economic and political power of the company was both benign and a bulwark against the intrusion of the state.[65]

governance in this arena: for example, in terms of a director's duty of skill and care the courts have only very cautiously accepted that serious mismanagement might potentially constitute unfair prejudice: see *Re Elgindata Ltd.* [1991] B.C.L.C. 959 and *Re Macro (Ipswich) Ltd.* [1994] 2 B.C.L.C. 354. See, further, on the relationship between s. 459 and respectively, corporate governance principles and the common law duty of care and skill, S. Copp and R. Goddard, 'Corporate Governance Principles on Trial' (1998) 19 *Company Lawyer* 277 and A. Boyle, 'The Common Law Duty of Care and Enforcement Under s. 459' (1996) 17 *Company Lawyer* 83.

64 Whilst this characterization may be said to be true of company law as a whole, it is often argued that corporate law has a strong public law character (particularly in relation to public companies): see, for example, K. Greenfield, 'From Rights to Regulation in Corporate Law' in *Perspectives on Company Law: 2*, ed. F. Patfield (1997) 1. Indeed the overall position of corporate law on the public /private spectrum is very complex and multifaceted as well as being historically contingent: see, generally, H. Hartog, 'Because All the World was Not New York City: Governance, Property Rights, and the State in the Changing Definition of a Corporation, 1730–1860' (1979) 28 *Buffalo Law Rev.* 91 and D. Sugarman, 'Is Company Law Founded on Contract or Public Regulation? The Law Commission's Paper on Company Directors' (1999) 20 *Company Lawyer* 162. Such complexity is further evidenced by the lack of precise 'fit' with contemporary contractarian and communitarian debates in corporate theory: for example, see the lengthy argument in P. Cox, 'The Public, The Private and The Corporation' (1997) 80 *Marquette Law Rev.* 393. See, also, W. Bratton Jr., 'Public Values, Private Business, and US Corporate Fiduciary Law' in McCahery et al. op. cit., n. 41, p. 23, who acknowledges the various dimensions at play and therefore posits a mediative role for corporate law as a situs for dialogue between the private internal business values of the corporate actor and wider public community values.

65 R. Grantham, 'The Doctrinal Basis of the Rights of Company Shareholders' (1998) 57 *Cambridge Law J.* 554, at 554. Whilst Grantham is at pains to note that, due to the unitary nature of company law at a formal level, his wider argument, that legal doctrine has come to recognize that the shareholders have ceased to have any meaningful ownership claims over the company, technically applies just as much to quasi-partnership companies as to listed companies, he is clearly uncomfortable with this conclusion as matter of substance (556–7).

Clearly such sentiments were well fitted to the prevailing neo-liberal political and economic culture that characterized the majority of the Thatcherite era and in which the power of the state was in theory to be retrenched in order to allow maximum economic autonomy to individuals.[66] Accordingly, the extensive disquisition on the private limited company (which itself was strongly associated with this entrepreneurial freedom) in the last twenty years tends to have been conducted by way of a discussion of the appropriate facilitative structures to be adopted, in terms of deregulation initiatives and by way of an otherwise relatively discrete and technical legalistic discourse.[67] It is not obvious that this position will change, for whilst the company law review does consider private company governance issues both in the context of the scope of company law and in its own right, the former is considered largely irrelevant (within the context adopted) and the latter is primarily conceived in structural and facilitative terms.[68]

However, whatever the formal analytical legal position, as has been frequently noted, the putative corrosive tendency of untrammelled free markets within a desired minimal state has the paradoxical effect of enhancing the need for regulation,[69] whether sponsored by the state or in the form of self-regulation. Further, the regulatory processes employed are capable of thereby producing a 'complex set of legal fields'[70] in which it is not always easy to maintain transparency or to co-ordinate overall policy as each of the fields becomes more juridified and path-specific over time.

In particular, a high level of state intervention and regulation is found to be justified on the occasion of business failure (especially, as is the case for the overwhelming number of private companies, where the peculiar

66 For an exposition of this view connecting it with political freedom in a similar manner to Hayek and Friedman, see Minford, op. cit., n. 48 . For a more critical appraisal, see Faulks, op. cit., n. 25, chs. 4 and 5, and Kay, op. cit., n. 42, ch. 15.

67 An excellent review of the literature is given by J. Freedman, 'Small Businesses and the Corporate Form: Burden or Privilege?' (1994) 57 *Modern Law Rev.* 555; A. Hicks, 'Corporate Form: Questioning The Unsung Hero' [1997] *J. of Business Law* 306; and D. Sugarman, 'Reconceptualising Company Law: Reflections Upon the Law Commission's Consultation Paper on Shareholder Remedies; Part I' (1997) 18 *Company Lawyer* 226, at 233–7.

68 See DTI, op. cit. (1999), n. 2, paras. 5.1.48, 5.2.19–5.2.35.

69 See, for example, Sugarman, op. cit., n. 67, at pp. 230–1; Gray, op. cit., n. 15 , ch. 2; J. Braithwaite, *Crime, Shame and Reintegration* (1989) 171; and M. Power, *The Audit Society* (1997), especially ch. 3. It also leads to deep tensions within the neo-liberal theoretical account: see, further, Giddens, op. cit., n. 12, at pp. 33–41. For a specific application to corporate affairs, see S. Wheeler, 'Directors' Disqualification: Insolvency Practitioners and the Decision-Making Process' (1995) 15 *Legal Studies* 283, at 287–90.

70 Sugarman, id., at p. 233. Whilst this comment was made in the specific context of the financial markets the author thereafter speaks generally of, 'the complex dialectic of regulation, deregulation and re-regulation – of private and public law – which has characterised the regulation of companies, both public and private' (footnote omitted). For an illustration of this dialectic in company law see the detailed legal and economic analysis provided by the Law Commissions in *Company Directors: Regulating Conflicts of Interests and Formulating a Statement of Duties* (1998) and Sugarman, op. cit., n. 64.

attribute of limited liability is involved). It is primarily at this stage, since the legislative reforms of the mid-1980s, that the enclosed world of the private company is torn open and submitted to a retrospective judicial and public scrutiny by way of the insolvency and, where appropriate, disqualification processes. The considerable body of new jurisprudence that has thereby arisen has resulted in a dissonance between the traditional prospective rules of business behaviour required, which, in terms of the standard of skill and care expected of directors, tend to have reflected a *laissez-faire* approach whereby private actors are permitted a wide field of discretion, and the much more interventionist rules, reflecting the public interest, that are applied *ex post facto* on business failure.[71]

Hence, although the judicial treatment of issues in respect of this facet of the governance of the private company sector has not traditionally been imbued with a strong prophylactic aspect at common law, it may be argued that such an approach is increasingly to be found, to (mis)use Maine's famous phrase, 'hidden in the interstices of procedure' (or in more modern parlance, the designated fields of regulation) arising on business failure.[72] In fact this outcome is not too surprising given the Thatcher government's deliberate restructuring of the insolvency regime by licensing its operation to a new professional monopoly of insolvency practitioners and creating new punitive sanctions pursuant to the wrongful trading and disqualification regimes. Thus, it is undoubtedly the case that these major reforms were initiated in order both to police and to legitimate the market as a social (rather than simply an economic) institution.[73]

71 See, for example, the contrast between what is expected of a director according to the traditional approach in *Re Brazilian Rubber Plantations & Estates Ltd.* [1910] 1 Ch. 425 and *Re City Equitable Fire Assurance Co. Ltd.* [1925] Ch. 407 and the modern approach which is much more prepared to engage in standard setting as demonstrated in *Re D'Jan of London Ltd.* [1994] 1 B.C.L.C. 561. Whilst all these cases concern business failure, the earlier cases were undoubtedly decided against a background that was succinctly set out by Lord MacNaughten: 'I do not think it is desirable for any tribunal to do that which Parliament has abstained from doing – that is, to formulate precise rules for the guidance or embarrassment of business men in the conduct of business affairs': *Dovey* v. *Corey* [1901] A.C. 477, at 488. This rationale, and the lax prospective trajectory it suggests, were clearly fractured in favour of a more ex post interventionist approach with the enactment of both the wrongful trading provisions contained in s. 214 Insolvency Act 1986 and, as Lord Hoffmann noted in *Bishopsgate Investment Management Ltd.* v. *Maxwell (No 2)* [1994] 1 All E.R. 261, at 264b (C.A.), the Company Directors Disqualification Act 1986. For Lord Hoffmann's reconsidered position of the effect of this legislation upon directors' duties of skill and care, see n. 79.

72 For example, in the context of the disqualification jurisdiction, see the tenor of the judgments in *Re Continental Assurance Co of London plc* [1996] B.C.C. 888; *Re Westmid Packing Services Ltd* [1998] 2 All E.R. 124 and *Re Barings plc (No 5)* [1999] 1 B.C.L.C. 433.

73 See, further, Halliday and Carruthers, op. cit., n. 5.

A valuable aspect of New Labour's name-and-shame campaign therefore lies in its capacity to render explicit in the public domain the prospective dimensions of private company governance, thus facilitating the unification of the rules and values that have grown up (seemingly with scant reference to each other) in the two fields of regulation discussed above around the more objective test applied on corporate failure.[74] Further, it is also suggested that the effect of the name-and-shame policy would be likely to be enhanced if there was a statutory statement of the duty of skill and care clearly setting out the appropriate duty.[75] The duty would require to be stated in sufficiently flexible terms yet nevertheless be sufficiently clear to provide practical guidance. It is suggested that a similar provision to s. 214 of the Insolvency Act 1986 (as interpreted by Knox J in *Re Produce Marketing Consortium Ltd. No 2*[76]) is desirable. In broad terms, pursuant to this test, a director is expected to display the general knowledge, skill, and experience that may reasonably be expected of a person performing the same functions as the director in a similar company (the objective limb) in addition to applying any specific expertise that he/she may have (the subjective limb). It is pleasing to note that this is the option recently recommended by the Law Commissions.[77]

It is submitted that the transparency generated by these twin policy initiatives would have the benefit of promoting both a more general awareness and a deeper understanding of the responsibilities of a contemporary company director within society and thereby of reducing existing levels of confusion or ignorance on the topic. In addition, a public space would be created in which the appropriate governance principles for corporate business activities could be forged and elucidated.[78] As this task is central to the maintenance of the broad compact between companies, the multifarious corporate actors (principally comprising a company's directors, employees, creditors, and consumers), and the wider society, which constitutes the corporate 'licence to operate', there would seem to be no good reason why such a duty of skill and care should not also apply to the directors of

74 The fiduciary duties of company directors are also, of course, thereby brought into a public regulatory space.

75 See Braithwaite, op. cit., n. 69, at p. 79.

76 [1989] B.C.L.C. 520.

77 Law Commissions, *Company Directors: Regulating Conflicts of Interests and Formulating a Statement of Duties* (1999; Cm. 4436) part 5. For a succinct critique, see Hon. Justice Santow, 'Codification of Directors' Duties' (1999) 73 *Australian Law J.* 336.

78 Braithwaite, op. cit., n. 69, ch. 9.

publicly traded companies,[79] thus fusing the approach taken to this aspect of the governance of corporate business around this central pillar of ideas.

Such a stance in relation to the duty of skill and care is not one that has recommended itself to the judiciary who have traditionally eschewed any strong standard setting role in order to preserve an appropriate zone of business discretion; see, for example, the dictum of Lord Wilberforce:[80]

> There is no appeal on merits from management decisions to courts of law: nor will courts of law assume to act as a kind of supervisory board over decisions within the powers of management honestly arrived at.

Such a position is surely correct. It is clearly not for the courts to be engaged in the practice of running companies. However, as the recent decisions pursuant to the disqualification legislation indicate, the courts are nevertheless clearly engaged in at least setting the bounds of acceptable commercial behaviour.[81]

However, the advent of Peter Mandelson MP as the Secretary of State at the Department of Trade and Industry undoubtedly resulted in a further elaboration of the contours of the debate over the governance of corporate business in this respect when he directly raised the importance of societal attitudes and especially chose to stress the need to encourage the entrepreneurial spirit:

> We need to examine all our regulatory systems to ensure that they do not needlessly deter our entrepreneurs . . . Are we sure that they create confidence in enterprise and commerce? I don't think we are confident. I think we need fundamentally to re-assess our attitude in Britain to business failure. Rather than condemning it and discouraging anyone from risking failure, we need to encourage entrepreneurs to take further risks in the future.[82]

Such rhetoric has attracted a good deal of criticism due to its open-ended nature and, at first blush, certainly seems to run against the DTI's policy of naming and shaming rogue directors who have transgressed the bounds of

79 By way of contrast, the governance dichotomy between private and publicly traded companies evinced by the traditional stance in the United Kingdom is well evidenced by Lord Hoffmann's discussion in the fourth annual Leonard Sainer lecture: '. . . while the *Brazilian Rubber Plantations* rule is concerned principally with the relationship between the directors and the shareholders, the disqualification rules are concerned with the relationship between the directors and the proprietors of the business on the one side and their creditors on the other.' (1997) 18 *Company Lawyer* 194, at 197.

80 In *Howard Smith Ltd.* v. *Ampol Petroleum Ltd* [1974] A.C. (P.C.) 821, at 832 E–F.

81 See the cases cited in n. 72 , and for the development of this point in relation to the Insolvency Act 1986 and Company Directors Disqualification Act 1986, see Halliday and Carruthers, op. cit., n. 5.

82 See New York speech. In order to produce the desired change to the agenda the positive aspects of the entrepreneur clearly had to be stressed to the exclusion of the more negative issues connected with the idea: the concept itself perhaps remains underdeveloped, see, further, n. 84.

acceptable commercial behaviour.[83] However, from subsequent events it is clear that the sentiments expressed are part of a considered policy initiative which expressly looks to future law reform to improve corporate rescue procedures and to reduce the stigma of financial failure.[84]

The next Secretary of State at the DTI, Stephen Byers MP, has maintained the momentum whilst introducing a new character to replace Mr. Mandelson's 'serial entrepreneur': the director as a 'responsible risk taker'. It is suggested that this construct offers a rich linguistic resource[85] which may be drawn upon to develop a nuanced view of the company director's role and the pervasive interface with business practice and morality. Indeed, Stephen Byers has sought to do just this:

> To foster a climate of responsible risk taking, we must also tackle head-on the stigma attached to business failure in this country. At present our bankruptcy laws make no distinction between the responsible risk taker and those individuals who deliberately set out to cheat their creditors or abuse the system.[86]

Thus it is clear that for New Labour the notion of the company director as a responsible risk taker is central to the governance of business operations and to the maintenance of the corporate 'licence to operate' in the emerging global knowledge economy of contemporary informational societies.[87] What remain unclear are the institutional structures and processes by which the concept of the responsible risk taker will be fleshed out.

GOVERNANCE OF CORPORATE BUSINESS IN THE KNOWLEDGE ECONOMY

Returning to the theme of private limited companies, it is indeed unsurprising that government thinking should be orientated in the direction discussed

83 For example, see 'City Commentary' *Times*, 16 October 1998. The tone of the DTI press releases in the name-and-shame campaign certainly changed thereafter so as to stress the positive facets of the company director as an entrepreneur.

84 For example, see the subsequent speech to the CBI in London (2 November 1998); the integrated approach set out in the Chancellor's Pre-Budget Report (November 1998) ch. 3, especially paras. 3.46–3.48 and DTI, op. cit., n. 12, paras. 2.12–2.14. The latter report's conception of the entrepreneur is very similar in approach to the OECD's position as set out in *Fostering Entrepreneurship* (1998); for a stimulating alternative vision that rejects the Cartesian model of the entrepreneur in favour of a practically based dialogical model (drawn from the later works of Heidegger's philosophy) whereby individuals use their 'history making skills' to transform 'disclosive spaces' see C. Spinoza et al., *Disclosing New Worlds: Entrepreneurship, Democratic Action, and the Cultivation of Solidarity* (1997), especially ch. 2.

85 Though one which is also imbued with difficulties given that both risk and responsibility are sometimes rather imponderable concepts in a world of 'manufactured risk': see, further, A. Giddens, 'Risk and Responsibility' (1999) 62 *Modern Law Rev.* 1.

86 Extracted from Mansion House speech. See, further, 'Fostering Enterprise: the American Experience', report of the United Kingdom-U.S. Conference on Entrepreneurship (2 July 1999).

87 On informational societies, see Castells, op. cit., n. 11, vol. 1.

above, as the dynamism of the SME sector and its ability to develop the positive aspects of risk[88] are frequently stated by New Labour to be central to the development of the knowledge economy necessary to compete in the global marketplace. Following the New Labour model, it would seem that these twin pressures have brought about the need for economic restructuring so as to encourage small adaptive structures working in a bottom-up fashion in order to foster the necessary creativity and flexibility.[89]

Such thinking has led the Future Unit of the Department of Trade and Industry to develop two scenarios (which although not constituting an official statement of policy nevertheless will form a conscious aspect of departmental decision making) for the business world of the knowledge economy: 'built to last' and 'wired world'.[90] The former scenario envisages the dominance of large corporations (whose financial might will provide secure careers, good research and development facilities, structures to capture know-how and to exploit brands), whilst the latter more favoured model (picking up the current trend of business growth in the SME sector) posits a constellation of trust based networks of SMEs. It is acknowledged that the reality is likely to be an amalgam of the two positions but it is important to note that such an eventuality has significant structural implications, as Castells has put it:

> Under the conditions of fast technological change, networks not firms, have become the actual operating unit. In other words, . . . a new organizational form has emerged as characteristic of the informational global economy: the network enterprise.[91]

In such circumstances it is perhaps not surprising that there is concern that the traditional means of corporate governance (with their reliance upon the director/shareholder relationship within individual companies) are proving inadequate and that there is a much greater emphasis upon governance by way of business culture, in terms both of directors' practice and the relationship between companies and society.

Concomitant upon the above, it is New Labour's current view that the key to a government's success lies not in stakeholding,[92] at least in the

88 For a broad discussion and the possible origins of the responsible risk taker motif, see Giddens, op. cit., n. 27, especially at pp. 63–4 and 99–100.

89 Though not so explicitly stated, this would seem to be the import of the LBS speech. As a matter of broader social theory, the fragmentation of civil society evidenced by the proliferation of interest groups is perhaps one of the key elements of Beck's notion of 'individualization': see U. Beck, *The Risk Society* (1992) part II, especially ch. 5. In the political domain further elaboration is given through the concept of 'sub-politics' in the same author's *The Reinvention of Politics* (1997).

90 DTI: *Work in the Knowledge-Driven Economy* (1999).

91 Castells, op. cit., n. 12, vol. 1, ch. 3, at p. 171. See, also, Leadbeater, op. cit., n. 12.

92 See, further, on the diverse notions of stakeholding, G. Kelly et al. (eds.), *Stakeholder Capitalism* (1997); Driver and Martell, op. cit., n. 24, at pp. 51–60; W. Hutton, *The Stakeholding Society* (1999); Kay, op. cit., n. 42, part III; B. Pettet, 'The Stirring of Corporate Social Conscience' (1997) 50 *Current Legal Problems* 279; P. Ireland, 'Corporate Governance, Stakeholding, and the Company: Towards a Less Degenerate Capitalism?'

monolithic and corporatist manner in which it is generally conceived,[93] but in the more institutionally flexible and politically malleable notion of partnership. As such, the stakeholding idea, which was launched in Tony Blair's Singapore speech (8 January 1996) as an organizing principle of New Labour, has now been supplanted in this respect by the Third Way. Will Hutton gives a spirited defence of stakeholding against the charges set out above and defends the relevance of the concept: 'stakeholding represents the political economy that New Labour lacks to support its value and vision of the "Third Way".'[94] However, whilst Hutton fervently believes that stakeholding constitutes, 'the only current, practical way of pursuing progressive politics', he is forced to conclude regretfully that, as '[s]takeholding is one more expression of European social market capitalism; it will only succeed within an overall European framework constructed to defend the European model.'[95] As an indigenous political idea to the United Kingdom, stakeholding, therefore, seems dead. It seems unlikely that the company law review will mark an explicit re-vitalization of the concept (even if it is ultimately re-badged as the 'pluralist model' and applied principally in relation to publicly traded companies) in the United Kingdom corporate sphere.

By employing the new term 'partnership', New Labour is not, of course, seeking to limit the meaning to the legal definition of the concept but, rather, to use the word in its wide generic sense.[96] Such partnerships are consciously promoted as a means of delivering goods or services that would be considered too interventionist and expensive for the retrenched modern state alone.[97] However, the reconfiguration of the relationship between the state, business, and the wider community that is thereby entailed has had

(1996) 23 *J. of Law and Society* 287; and D. Campbell, 'Towards a Less Irrelevant Socialism: Stakeholding as a "Reform" of the Capitalist Economy' (1997) 24 *J. of Law and Society* 65.

93 See C. Leadbeater and G. Mulgan, 'Mistakeholding: Whatever Happened to Labour's Big Idea?' (1996).

94 Hutton, op. cit., n. 92, at pp. 267–74.

95 id., at p. 274. For European influence in this regard in relation to the governance of companies, see S. Wheeler, 'Enterprise and Community: New Directions in Corporate Governance' (1997) 24 *J. of Law and Society* 44, and J. Dine, 'Implementation of European Initiatives in the UK: The Role of Fiduciary Duties' [1999] *Company Financial and Insolvency Law Rev.* 218.

96 See, for example, Treasury press releases 'New Steps to Drive Forward Private Finance Initiatives and Public Private Partnerships' (2 February 1999) and 'Launch of the I.P.P.R. Commission into Public/Private Partnerships' (20 September 1999). The partnership concept is all-pervasive, applying to the private sector alone, its relations to the public sector, and its relations to the workforce: see, respectively, DTI, op. cit., n. 12, ch. 3 ('Collaborate to Compete') and DTI press releases, 'New Focus for the Future of Partnering in Business and Government' (25 November 1998) and 'New Civil Service Union a Model for Partnership' (26 November 1998).

97 See Tony Blair's speech on e-commerce (13 September 1999) where the modern state's role was expressly stated to be primarily facilitative and the greater use of self-regulation was encouraged.

the effect of blurring the traditional boundaries between the public and the private domain, and thereby of public and private law. In particular, there is some concern that the private law of contract is not an adequate vehicle by which to ensure representation of the public interest or to determine accountability.[98] Further, this is a matter which especially resonates in corporate law where there is a long heritage of suspicion of the private power wielded by corporations and it would seem that the question of corporate legitimacy will again come to the fore as a consequence of the greater concentration of erstwhile public power in ostensibly private entities.[99]

In addition, the broader governance problems raised by the multi-level interpenetrated formal and informal structures arising are notoriously difficult and complex.[100] Further, it would seem that, as public-private partnerships become more widespread, there is a real danger that some of the positive public service values of the traditional public sector will be eroded[101] (or at the least disappear from sight, which may have a similar effect). Rather disturbingly, when this factor is combined with a vigorous constellation of SMEs with a high sensitivity (and doubtless antipathy) to regulatory

98 See, for example, M. Freedland, 'Government by Contract and Public Law' [1994] *Public Law* 86 and 'Public Law and Private Finance: Placing the Private Finance Initiative in a Public Law Frame' in *Regulation and Deregulation: Policy and Practice in the Utilities and Financial Services Industries*, ed. C. McCrudden (1998) ch. 8; P. Craig, 'Public Law and Control Over Private Power' in *The Province of Administrative Law*, ed. M. Taggart (1997) ch. 10. For a very stimulating discussion of the dynamics of this relationship, see D. Oliver, 'The Underlying Values of Public and Private Law' in Taggart, id., ch. 11 and 'Common Values in Public and Private Law and the Public/ Private Divide' [1997] *Public Law* 630; G. Teubner, 'After Privatisation? The Many Autonomies of Private Law' (1998) 51 *Current Legal Problems* 393. For specific application to corporate law, see Sugarman, op. cit., n. 65.

99 Such issues have particularly exercised theorists in the United States: see, for example, J.W. Hurst, *The Legitimacy of the Business Corporation in the Law of the United States 1780–1970* (1970) and M.V. Nadel, 'The Hidden Dimension of Public Policy: Private Governments and the Policy-Making Process' (1972) 1 *Policy Studies J.* 2. See, also, A. Fraser, *Reinventing Aristocracy: The Constitutional Reformation of Corporate Governance* (1998) who argues for a re-politicization of the corporation through Republican political theory, and S. Wheeler, 'Towards A Feminization of the Corporation?' (1999) 52 *Current Legal Problems* 313 who sketches a theoretical model of the company based upon Aristotelian virtue ethics and an ethic of care as a way of grounding corporate legitimacy.

100 See, generally, J. Braithwaite, 'Accountability and Governance Under the New Regulatory State' (1999) 58 *Australian J. of Public Administration* 90. More specifically in the United Kingdom context, see R.A.W. Rhodes, *Understanding Governance* (1997) chs. 2, 3; P. Vincent Jones, 'The Regulation of Contractualisation in Quasi-markets for Public Services' [1999] *Public Law* 304.

101 This would appear to be the inevitable flipside of seeking to promote enterprise and risk in public services (as to the latter policy see the speeches of Tony Blair to the Civil Service Conference in London (13 October 1998) and the N.C.V.O. Conference in London (21 January 1999)) and led to the OECD adopting the recommendation *Principles for Managing Ethics in the Public Service* on 23 April 1998. For an examination of the sort of difficulties that might arise in the corporate sphere see S. Wheeler, 'Contracting Out in the UK Insolvency Service: the Tale of Performance Indicators and the Last Cowboy' (1997) 7 *Australian J. of Corporate Law* 227.

intervention,[102] the commercial environment becomes one in which there is a considerable risk of a governance vacuum.

In such a structural context it may be argued that there will be potentially a significant role for what has been termed 'moral intervention':[103] that is, the use of publicity sanctions by the state, as part of an orchestrated campaign to reinforce, inform or help determine the social values of market actors, as an alternative or supplementary, and relatively inexpensive, method of governance of the corporate business sector. Once again, the notion of the responsible risk taker may be utilized as the attitudinal touchstone by which the delicate balance between innovation and propriety may be drawn.

CONCLUSION

That the importance of developing an appropriate entrepreneurial culture is central to New Labour's approach to the governance of corporate business is well evidenced by Peter Mandelson's plea for '. . . an enterprise-orientated, risk-taking, failure-tolerant business culture that enables you constantly to innovate and constantly adapt to changing economic conditions . . .'.[104] However, whilst these facets are deemed essential within the globalized knowledge-driven economy of network enterprises which characterize the Blair government's political economy, that very same market situation also demands that the actors therein are subject to governance in order to maintain both its own integrity, and the legitimacy of such actors within the context of the wider society. It is suggested that these contradictory requirements are encompassed within the notion of the responsible risk taker and that this concept has the ability to fuse otherwise disparate strands within corporate governance and company and insolvency law.

102 See, for example, DTI press release 'Measures to Cut Red Tape and Reduce the Burdens on Business Announced' (3 June 1999). Better regulation is conceived in both qualitative and quantitative terms and the government is committed to improve the former and the reduce latter, especially as it is explicitly recognized that regulation puts a disproportionate burden on SMEs (see, for example, Better Regulation Task Force, *Regulation and Small Firms (Progress Report)* (1999); DTI, op. cit., n. 12, para. 2.28; and DTI consultation document, *The Small Business Service* (1999) s. 4. Considerable efforts have been made to this end: for example, the Regulatory Impact Unit of the Cabinet Office (advised by the independent Better Regulation Task Force) has instituted a Better Regulation Guide including not only a statement of general principles but also a Regulatory Impact Assessment process. For a discussion of some of the complexities and practical issues involved in regulation generally, see J. Kay and J. Vickers, 'Regulatory Reform: An Appraisal' in *The Law of the Business Enterprise*, ed. S. Wheeler (1994) 419, and McCrudden, op. cit., n. 98.

103 A term seemingly coined by E. Mayo, director of the New Economics Foundation: *Guardian*, 7 November 1998. On regulation by values rather than rules, see J. Kay, *Community Values and the Market Economy* (1997) ch. 2.

104 See New York speech.

Further, given New Labour's view of the structural changes wrought by globalizing processes and the reconfiguration of the relationship between business, state, and community thereby entailed, it is clear that the government has a preference for self-regulation or regulation through culture.[105] Such a device in terms of the governance of company directors may be seen as quite an encroachment into the what liberalism would describe as the private arena of the economic world. This is explicitly recognized by New Labour politicians, so (for example) Stephen Byers is quite conscious that in determining the appropriate balance for the responsible risk taker, 'we will be talking about the values that go to the very heart of the societies in which we live.'[106] This factor has led many commentators to worry about the potentially authoritarian nature of New Labour's communitarianism and, as Ireland succinctly puts it, there would seem to be a real danger that, '[u]nable to regulate the economy, the Party can be expected to regulate people instead.'[107]

Whilst alternative political and regulatory models are available in relation to a more positive and less authoritarian use of name-and-shame sanctions,[108] it is clearly evident from the example provided by phoenix companies that the mapping of morality and business regulation is in any event by no means straightforward.[109] Nevertheless, in conclusion, it would seem that the responsible risk taker motif does offer a useful starting point for discussion, and that a rigid distinction between the economic, social, and political realm is increasingly more untenable: it will be interesting to see how the debate evolves.[110]

105 For an extended analysis of how culture (backed by sanctions) can be invoked pursuant to a Republican model of dialogical democracy in order to check the private power of business, see J. Braithwaite, 'On Speaking Softly and Carrying Big Sticks: Neglected Dimensions of a Republican Separation of Powers' (1997) 47 *University of Toronto Law J.* 305.

106 Extract from speech at the United Kingdom–U.S. Conference on Entrepreneurship (2 July 1999).

107 P. Ireland, 'Endarkening the Mind: Roger Scruton and the Power of Law' (1997) 6 *Social and Legal Studies* 51, at 73. Similar sentiments are to be found in Minford, op. cit., n. 48, who refers to, 'communitarian thought police' and Driver and Martell, op. cit., n. 24 , at pp. 35–44. For some general difficulties, see A. Crawford, 'The Spirit of Community: Rights, Responsibilities, and the Communitarian Agenda' (1996) 23 *J. of Law and Society* 247.

108 See Braithwaite, op. cit., n. 69; Castells, op. cit., n. 11, vol. 3, at pp. 379–80; S. Wheeler and G. Wilson, 'Corporate Law Firms and the Spirit of the Community' (1998) 49 *Northern Ireland Legal Q.* 239, at 254–66.

109 Often it will be perfectly proper at law for a new company to take up the assets of a failed company even though both companies are controlled by the same individuals and this creates some resentment amongst other members of the business community: see National Audit Office, *Company Director Disqualification – a Follow Up Report*, HC (1998–9) 424, at paras. 3.35–36.

110 The recent move by the IOD to obtain professional recognition for company directors by way of the new chartered director status and the focus on substantive business practice in the Turnbull report, *Internal Control Guidance for Directors on the Combined Code* (1999) will doubtless provide subject matter, and the author agrees with Sugarman, op. cit., n. 64, at p. 183 that the trajectory of the debate will be towards a model of company law as public regulation.

JOURNAL OF LAW AND SOCIETY
VOLUME 27, NUMBER 1, MARCH 2000
ISSN: 0263–323X, pp. 178–217

Post-nationalism and the Quest for Constitutional Substitutes

DAMIAN CHALMERS*

Post-nationalism is suggestive of a number of transformations in the practice of both law and politics. In the case of politics, it implies an assertion of the salience of the organization of scale, time, and individual subjectivity in the practice of politics, yet a corresponding acknowledgement that traditional administrative structures have lost their hegemony over organization of these phenomena. In the case of law, it implies a legal pluralism caused in part by administrative differentiation, but also brought about an increase in the number and types of organization that have private 'law-making' capacities. These processes are particular disruptive for the modern constitution, which has traditionally been identified as a central instrument in the recognition, co-ordination, interaction, and self-legitimation of law and politics. This begs the question as to what processes are carrying out tasks that have traditionally been associated with the modern constitution. This essay argues that the fluidity and complexity of these processes entail that they must lie in the processes of interaction themselves. In particular, it argues that the central 'constitutional substitute' is the individual act of recognizing organizations as having political and legal attributes. For the process of recognition contains two structures which serve to organize and legitimize interaction. Any act of 'constitutional' recognition requires, first, a process of prior evaluation on the part of the observer that requires the organization to justify itself to the observer. The according of recognition, by contrast, entails that the observer respect the organization as having the autonomy to impose and represent itself politically. This respect allow the organization to order legal and political life.

INTRODUCTION

The post-national condition expresses a situation where the performance of law and politics is no longer configured around or constrained by the territorial structures of the nation-state. To be sure, to talk of post-nationalism

* *London School of Economics and Political Science, Houghton St, London WC2 2AE, England*

as a condition carries with it a whiff of exaggeration as it tends to understate the enduring importance of the nation-state. Yet, in so far as the emergence of post-nationalism is beginning to infect our understanding of the performance of politics and law, it problematizes, first and foremost, those institutions most closely associated with the nation-state, most notably the modern constitution. One response is to argue that in so far as processes such as globalization allow law and politics to operate on a scale which transcends the national structures of the modern constitution, these processes threaten the very existence of the modern constitution.[1] A counter-response is to argue that modern constitutionalism is sufficiently elastic to develop cosmopolitan features, which will allow it to adjust to these forces, with the European Community being given as an example of a constitution that has developed in an extra-national setting.[2] Central to both arguments is an assumption that post-nationalism is merely about a rescaling of politics and law. It involves no shifts in how law and politics are conceptualized or what is considered to be legal or political. The argument here rejects these assumptions by taking the paradoxical nature of the modern constitution as its starting point. As a formal instrument, even in this 'post-national age', the modern constitution continues to be resilient and its adoption ever more widespread. This persistence and vintage allow it to remain a powerful totemic force which continues to attract and stabilize many political and legal claims. As an organizational force, however, the modern constitution developed against the backdrop of an increase in the reach, intensity, and variety of government. It sought to accommodate this through differentiating itself from its mediaeval predecessor by entrenching, on the one hand, a particular vision of how law and politics were to operate and how they were to relate to each other and, on the other, requiring the polity to legitimate itself to its subjects through endowing the latter with legal and political claims against the polity. Central to this vision was the assumption that the modern constitution acted as a central mechanism which enabled the recognition, co-ordination, assimilation, and self-legitimation of the legal and political systems.

Post-nationalism, by contrast, signifies the proliferation and emergence of new forms of law and politics. It creates a backdrop, similar to that

1 For example, C. Himsworth, 'In a State no Longer: The End of Constitutionalism?' (1996) *Public Law* 639. This argument is part of a more wide-ranging critique which suggests that globalization threatens all structures which have emerged within the aegis of the nation-state. For a very critical analysis of this reasoning see J. Habermas, *Die post-nationale Konstellation* (1998) 91–169.

2 L. Ferrajoli, 'Beyond sovereignty and citizenship: a global constitutionalism' in *Constitutionalism, Democracy and Sovereignty: American and European Perspectives*, ed. R. Bellamy (1996); R. Bellamy and A. Warleigh, 'From an ethics of participation to an ethics of participation: Citizenship and the Future of the European Union' (1998) 27 *Millennium* 447.

which led to the modern constitution, of increased legal and political interaction. The post-national condition is therefore characterized by increased legal pluralism, on the one hand, and, on the other, by various forms of political disordering, leading to the emergence of new political arenas and a reflexive awareness by traditional political actors of their own limitations. This relativizes the modern constitution, which is unable to exercise its traditional organizational hegemony over these forms of legal and political unbounding. Paradoxically, in this, post-nationalism expresses a desire for increasing amounts of human activity to be legally and politically organized. The multifarious, fluid, and interlocking nature of much of this activity may prevent it from being organized through any central point or even through any form of external steering mechanism. Yet the impulse towards organization suggests the need for 'constitutional substitutes' which can carry out the processes traditionally performed by the modern constitution of recognizing, co-ordinating, assimilating, and enabling self-legitimation of this legal and political activity.

Such substitutes can only exist within the process of legal and political interaction themselves. The final section of this paper considers the two forms of interaction that can take place, communication and recognition. Such processes reside in the subjective and intersubjective activities of the individual. It argues that models centred around communication are unable, *per se*, to generate sufficient programming and evaluative processes, as their requirement of intersubjectivity both overstates the degree of cognitive convergence between actions and forecloses certain forms of evaluation. This paper argues, however, that recognition of legal and political measures and identities can and does act as a constitutional substitute in relation to this post-national activity. In particular, as only organizations have the resources to make law or politics, the principal argument of this paper is that the central 'constitutional substitute' is the recognition of an organization by an individual as having either political or legal attributes. This process of recognition carries an internal dualism, which generates similar organizational structures to those predicated by the modern constitution. On the one hand, as the act of recognition presupposes autonomy on the part of the recognizer, organizations can do no more than press a claim for recognition of these attributes. The duty to justify themselves, both to earn recognition and to prevent derecognition from observers, generates a priori conditions for organizations to meet concerning their actions, decision-making procedures, distribution of internal power, and relations with third parties. This process of justification thereby creates important structures of evaluation, legitimation, and accountability. On the other, an act of recognition implies a commitment to respect the attributes of the organization. This, in turn, generates those others structures important to political and legal organization, those of co-ordination and assimilation.

Modern constitutionalists like to portray the modern constitution as having a heritage which extends back to Aristotle's discussion of the *politeia*.[3] The term 'constitution' did not, however, exist in ancient Greek. The *politeia* (polity) was a more embracing concept, which served to constitute both the public sphere (*polis*) and the private one (*oikos*). The word 'constitution' can rather be traced back to the second century AD. A *constitutio* was a legal enactment, distinguishable from other forms of *lex* by reason of its being enacted by the emperor.[4] Writers such as Cicero and Seneca also used it to refer to the entire body politic.[5] The term, however, fell into disuse. Within such a context, as Lloyd has observed, early arguments for institutional checks on power lay within the sphere of resistance theory rather than constitutionalist thought.[6] McIlwain finds, therefore, no reference to the term 'constitution' until 1610.[7] The term began, increasingly, to be applied to the sphere of government during that century as a result of the increasing application of biological analogies (for example, the human constitution) to politics.[8] For most of the century, however, constitution was used interchangeably with the term 'government'. It was only with the advent of the Glorious Revolution that it is endowed with autonomous binding qualities of its own with James II being accused of subverting the 'constitution of the kingdom'.[9]

It was in the eighteenth century that the 'modern' meaning of the term came into more habitual use. In 1733, in his book on *The British Constitution; or the Fundamental Form of Government*, Bolingbrooke stated:

> By constitution we mean, whenever we speak with propriety and exactness, that assemblage of laws, institutions and customs, derived from certain fixed principles of reason, directed to certain fixed objects of public good that compose the general system according to which the community hath agreed to be governed.

Understanding of the modern constitution was informed, above all, by the attempts to enshrine the settlements that emerged from the United

3 C. McIlwain, *Constitutionalism: Ancient and Modern* (1947) 25 and following; D. Castiglione, 'The Political Theory of the Constitution' in *Constitutionalism in Transformation: European and Theoretical Perspectives*, eds. R. Bellamy and D. Castiglione (1996).

4 McIlwain, id., pp. 44–5.

5 H. Lloyd, 'Constitutionalism' in *The Cambridge History of Political Thought 1450–1700*, ed. J. Burns (1991) 244–5.

6 id., p. 256.

7 McIlwain, op. cit., n. 4, at p. 27.

8 G. Stouzh, 'Constitution: Changing Meanings of the Term from the Early Seventeenth to the Late Eighteenth Century' in *Conceptual Change and the Constitution*, eds. T. Ball and J. Pocock (1988) 38–42.

9 id., p. 43.

States War of Independence and the French Revolution into relatively immutable texts.[10] Subsequent imitations and rationalizations of these eighteenth-century events resulted in the modern constitution coming to be given a relatively settled meaning. It is seen as a foundational law which first purports to set out the objectives of a political community in terms that correspond to the interests of that political community and, secondly, distributes and constrains administrative power.[11]

In this the modern constitution came to have explicit structurating qualities. It inherited from the 'mediaeval constitution' a belief in its ability to describe accurately the make-up and operations of the political and legal systems. It was distinguished, however, from its predecessor through a self-conscious attempt to programme the operation of politics and law. It does this, on the one hand, through governing the terms of their interaction. In this, as shall be seen, it not only acts as the gatekeeper through which each can code the performance of the other,[12] but also makes the operation of each contingent upon the structures of the other. Yet, to characterize the modern constitution as no more than a fulcrum between the political and legal systems is misleading. If a metaphor must be used, it is that of a parergon.[13] The parergon is compared to the frame of a painting. It is serves to constitute something, but is simultaneously distinct from it. As the capacity of the modern constitution to govern interaction between law and politics is premised upon its ability to bound and describe them, it purports, above all, to impart a particular understanding of the operation and nature of law and politics individually. The central attributes of each, their limits, and for whom each acts are thus set out. In short, the modern constitution set itself out as not merely central but constitutive to the recognition and understanding of law and politics. So what did this vision contain?

1. *Constitutional understandings of law*

The modern constitution understands law as the unity between two different types of text. There is constitutional law, an immutable corpus of law not subject to change by the political settlement, and other law, most

10 On the contribution of these to the understanding of the modern constitution, see Lloyd, op. cit., n. 5; Stourzh, op. cit., n. 8; P. Onuf, 'State Sovereignty and the Making of the Constitution' in *Conceptual Change and the Constitution*, eds. T. Ball and J. Pocock (1988); J. Tully, *Strange Multiplicity: Constitutionalism in an Age of Diversity* (1995) 91–8; P. Kahn, *Legitimacy and History: Self-Government in American Constitutional Theory* (1992).

11 Some academics have also tried to argue that modern constitutions also provide for guarantees of representative democracy; G. Sartori, 'Constitutionalism: a preliminary discussion' (1962) 56 *Am. Political Science Rev.* 853; Castiglione, op. cit., n. 2, at pp. 22–3.

12 N. Luhmann, 'Operational Closure and Structural Coupling: The Differentiation of the Legal System' (1992) 13 *Cardozo Law Rev.* 1419, at 1436–7.

13 On this term taken from I. Kant, *The Critique of Judgment* (1951), see J. Bartelson, *A Genealogy of Sovereignty* (1995) 51 and following.

notably legislation, which is subject to change by the political settlement provided this is carried out according to procedures deemed valid by the constitution.[14] It was this unity that allowed other attributes associated with the liberal conception of law to emerge.

One is law's formal autonomy. Through the constitution, law is provided with its own internal structures of authority. Constitutional law provides the parameters for its own modification through the setting out of procedures by which this can be carried out. It also regulated the operation of other law. The central question now for legislation became one of legal validity – was it enacted in accordance with the constitutional arrangements rather than whether it was an act of the political sovereign.

This differentiation within the modern constitution between constitutional law and other law also allowed all law to share the attribute of normativity. All law stabilizes expectations by providing that where such conduct deviates from the legal expectation, it is the conduct not the expectation that is wrong.[15] This normativity contains within it further assumptions about the attributes of law. Law is considered to be supreme in that it recognizes no limitations on the spheres of authority it can regulate. It is also considered to be comprehensive in that it claims to be authoritatively binding on all those it regulates.[16] Prior to this, normativity had not been associated, by contrast, with earlier practices of public law. Public law only began to have an 'immediate impact on legal practice' in the middle of the sixteenth century.[17] At that time it was a self-limitation of rule by the political sovereign which contributed to the latter's hegemony within the public sphere and a coda to demarcate the public sphere from the private one.[18] It was thus characterized by its exclusion of judicial intervention from the business of government[19] and by the contrast between it and the use of custom to regulate the private sphere.[20] Within such a context public law was reduced to being the will (*volontas*) of the political sovereign. By providing for the subjects of constitutional law and other law to be different – the institutions of government in the case of the former, and extra-political actors in the case of latter – the modern constitution deprived the legal subject of the opportunity for auto-interpretation. There was no possibility for the mutual accommodation of the norm and the conduct in question, which could place the normativity of the provisions in question by making it correspondingly difficult to separate legal expectation from the conduct of the subject.

14 N. Luhmann. 'La Constitution comme Acquis Evolutionnaire' (1995) 22 *Droits* 103, at 114.
15 N. Luhmann, *Risk: A Sociological Theory* (1993) 54.
16 J. Raz, *The Concept of a Legal System* (2nd edn., 1980) 151, 213.
17 R. van Caernegem, *An Historical Introduction to Western Constitutional Law* (1995) 2.
18 Used in this context in the sixteenth-century meaning of state-related activity.
19 van Caernegem, op. cit., n. 17, at p. 3.
20 Lloyd, op. cit., n. 5, at p. 269.

Despite the autonomy and unity granted to the legal system by the modern constitution, the former was rendered dependent by the modern constitution for its performance upon the political system in three ways. The concept of the political, as a permanent, secular administrative apparatus with coercive powers over its subjects was informed by two events – the Reformation[21] and the growth of centralized bureaucracies, associated with the emergence of the territorial state.[22] In turn, however, the differentiation which lay at the heart of both law's autonomy and its normativity was folded around it. Constitutional law was therefore concerned with bounding political power whilst legislation was a manifestation of political power. Secondly, within the modern constitutional settlement, political power is not just externally juxtaposed to the legal system, but is presupposed by law.[23] As no legislation can be enacted without action by the political system, the modern constitution posits the latter as the locus of agency for the differentiation of law. This allows the political system to infect secondary legislation not simply through the latter enacting the programmes of particular parliaments, but by the political system being the provider of those deeper structures which permeates all legislation. Legislation came therefore to contain a number of features that representative institutions had inherited from their predecessors in the seventeenth century public sphere. These include publicity – legislation will have been the subject of public debate and have been published; permanence – it remains in force until formally repealed; abstraction – it governs a generic set of situations; and universality – it recognizes no limitations, other than those imposed by constitutional law, on its authority over its subject community.[24]

Finally, the coercive facilities of the state are necessary to organize and sanction the enforcement of the regime of legal rights.[25] Law increasingly became an administrative regime – the administration of justice – with its own specialized apparatus, in the form of the courts, and its own specialized technocracy, in the form of lawyers and judges, acting as the interlocutors of this regime. Within this, legislation became a central instrument of the apparatus of government for the bringing about of internal pacification. A breach of legislation was never, thus, just a challenge to the external interests or values presented in the legislation: it was also a challenge to the political system's ability to regulate or administer. This 'bureaucratization' of law increasingly infected its function. Its centre of gravity shifted

21 C. Nederman, 'Conciliarism and Constitutionalism: Jean Gerson and Mediaeval Political Thought' (1990) 12 *History of European Ideas* 189; F. Oakley, 'Nederman, Gerson, Conciliar Theory and Constitutionalism: Sed Contra' (1995) 16 *History of Political Thought* 1; C. Nederman, 'Constitutionalism – Mediaeval and Modern: Against Neo-Figgisite Orthodoxy' (Again) (1996) 17 *History of Political Thought* 179.

22 H. Spruyt, *The Sovereign State and Its Competitors: An Analysis of Systems Change* (1994) especially 158–82.

23 id.

24 J. Habermas, *The Structural Transformation of the Public Sphere* (1989) 52–3.

25 J. Habermas, *Between Facts and Norms* (1996) 134.

from judicial dispute resolution to being increasingly invested with norms and being concerned with providing common denominators that enabled 'normalization'. Within this context Moscovici has noted how legislation suggests two forms of conformity which mirror the administration/regulation differentiation within the political system.[26] Repressive conformity configures legislation around the metaphor of national security. It becomes concerned with either the protection of the administrative apparatus's interests[27] or protection of central symbols or practices, for example, criminal law, immigration law, laws on blasphemy and obscenity.[28] In either instance, it operates as an administrative process of subjection in which the legal subject is treated as a passive object. It is enforced, principally through punishment, 'in such a way as to make the members of the group binds themselves even more to the type of collectivity and stress their mutual similarities.[29] This is to be contrasted with restitutionary conformity.[30] This pivots around the division of labour rather than any collective primordial norm. Legislation is concerned here with generating conditions which allow a series of private relationships (market transactions, professional activities, the employment relationship, the family) to operate. This entails, necessarily, that it set out conditions detailing the circumstances in which such institutions can be created and terminated. It is also concerned with preventing the operation of these processes from being disrupted.[31] It contours itself around these institutions, providing them with recognition and support, Breaches of legislation are correspondingly viewed through the prism of the damage done to the institution itself. In these circumstances legislation induces conformity through a subtle interplay. On the one hand, it relies upon the autonomous disciplining processes to generate patterns of conformity and forms of collective consciousness. On the other, it prevents the dispersion and multiplicity of such institutions generating a centrifugal counter-dynamic of their own through the centralized recognition and co-ordination it confers upon these institutions.

26 Within the Weberian tradition politics were conceived partly as a coercive administrative order (administration) and partly as directed towards sustaining external activities (regulation), M. Weber, *Economy and Society: Outline of a Theory of Sociology* (1978) vol. I, at 51–2.

27 On this, see B. Wright, 'Quiescent Leviathan? Citizenship and National Security Measures in Late Modernity' (1998) 25 *J. of Law and Society* 213, at 226–7.

28 S. Moscovici, *The Invention of Society* (1993) 84–5. From a different tradition which also noted this development, see F. Ewald, 'Norms, discipline and the law' (1990) 30 *Representations* 138.

29 This is, thus, brought out in the language which emphasizes the inhuman nature of many criminal offenders, the alien qualities of refugees, and altruistic nature of 'out of area' military actions, id., p. 87.

30 id., pp. 89–93.

31 B. Hindess, 'Politics and Governmentality' (1997) 26 *Economy and Society* 257, at 266–7.

2. *Constitutional understandings of administrative power*

For the political system the modern constitution represents a form of administrative rationalization which is highly paradoxical in its nature. On the one hand, the modern constitution represented a process of assimilation and centralization in that the only administrative power countenanced was that recognized in the constitution. The legislative apparatus set out there had a monopoly over law-making; the judicial apparatus over adjudication, and the executive over the legitimate monopoly of violence. Thus, the modern constitution reinforced the hegemony of administrative institutions over powers that were acquired only relatively recently, most notably that of law-making, the administrative monopoly over which had only developed with the onset of the territorial state.[32] On the other, it appeared to bound and limit administrative power. It did this functionally through its arrangement of the formal powers of the different units of the administration and its placing of constraints upon their exercise of coercive power. Certainly, this is the most noted form in all the literature that examines the modern constitution as offering a series of checks, balances, and guarantees.[33] The modern constitution enacted another division, however, by providing for some rotation of offices, be it through election or appointment. This enabled a distinction to emerge between political office and political programmes, the importance of which is captured below:

> The code function of the leading offices – the fact that their occupation by one person excluded that by another – was not yet differentiated from the program function, ie not distinguished from the question of by whom and according to which programs is the government to be executed properly. Only the separation of these questions makes the popular will – expressed in political elections – function as a criterion, while the code value of office-holding . . . loses its value as a criterion. In a clearer conceptual sense one can say that the holders of governmental offices today do not possess authority any longer, ie, can no longer presume to act correctly as office-holders.[34]

Within the modern constitution government ceased to be generalized obedience to some external institution – be it the *raison d'état*, a monarch or the Church – and became caught up with the interests and its representation of this institution.[35] Instead, this lack of authority signifies that politics has become characterized by the quality of difference. The political system allowed for any administrative decision to be contested, with the difference between programme and office allowing for opposition to be embedded in the structures of the political settlement.

32 E. Ehrlich, *Fundamental Principles of the Sociology of Law* (1936) 14–38.

33 Sartori, op. cit., n. 11.

34 N. Luhmann, *Ecological Communication* (1989) 87.

35 Hindess, op. cit., n. 31, at pp. 259–60; M. Foucault, 'Politics and Reason' in *Politics, philosophy, culture: interviews and other writings, 1977–1981, Michel Foucault*, ed. L. Kritzman (1988).

Yet this administrative settlement was dependent upon the structures of the legal system to stabilize its operation in a number of ways. These endowed the administrative settlement with a number of further attributes.

It was the relatively immutable structures of constitutional law which stabilized expectations of the political settlement. Interpretation of constitutional provisions became central to determination of the polity. Much of politics became a form of inscriptive politics through which 'the polity could memorialise, preserve, interpret, enforce and rewrite its fundamental political commitments'.[36] It was, in particular, through this process of inscription, that the polity came to be understood across space and time. In temporal terms each interpretation of a constitutional provision provides a precedent which must be negotiated by subsequent interpretations. In this way every interpretation of the constitution must articulate not just the scenario at hand but all previous interpretations of prior scenarios and build them into a story-line, which acts as a coherent depiction of that part of the polity that it is considering. The unfolding of the past in the present requires that acts in the 1990s must be analogized alongside acts of the 1800s. In this way, constitutional law endows the political settlement with continuity. A similar spatial bounding takes place. The invocation of a provision to cover a particular situation requires that it be analogized with all other situations which that provision has been successfully invoked to protect. In this manner, assertion of a freedom of expression provision, for example, in a case on advertising, means that provision must be rationalized in a manner alongside cases on political dissent and pornography.

The bounding of the administrative settlement by constitutional law also allows political settlements to describe themselves as value-oriented, and politics to be seen as the authoritative allocation of values. The use of constitutional law as the instrument through which claims can be articulated entails that the administrative apparatus can never close itself off, a priori, to claims about the nature of the political settlement. A corollary to the normativity of law was that law always has the ability to acquire different meanings.[37] Any legal statement will thus contain within it a dichotomy. There is on the one hand a duty to acknowledge, explicitly or implicitly, previous legal statements. Yet a legal statement will also not be directly observable, in the sense that it cannot be empirically tested. The invocation of law involves not merely its application to a particular situation but also an 'idealising moment of unconditionality that takes its beyond its immediate context'.[38] A claim about or interpretation of constitutional law is thus never just a description of the political settlement but, also, a

36 J. Rubenfeld, 'Legitimacy and Interpretation' in *Constitutionalism: Philosophical Foundations*, ed. L. Alexander (1999) 218.

37 For example, a bald legal statement that 'theft is wrong' would transmutate, to prevent falsification, when confronted with the situation of the person who steals to survive, either by providing a justification or by modifying the definition of theft.

38 W. Rehg, 'Translators Introduction' in J. Habermas, *Between Facts and Norms* (1996) xiii.

prescriptive assertion of what the administrative apparatus of government ought to be.

This lack of direct observability is also shared by values. These are 'conceptions of the desirable . . . with a particular relevance for behaviour'.[39] They prompt rather than describe action. They are also never self-standing. An understanding of a value requires an understanding of its field of action. Their operation is always embedded in their social environment.[40] The validity of constitutional law – to borrow Habermas's terminology – suggests a series of deontological ideals which precede and structure political actions. For any constitutional claim to succeed, it must therefore be couched in terms which are not fully directly observable, and prescriptive. Meanwhile, the other half of the dichotomy of constitutional law, its facticity – its immersion in concrete scenarios – provides the necessary context for the embodiment of values.

Despite its being sufficiently malleable to allow oppression of all kinds,[41] these features allow the modern constitution always to offer the possibility that it will be receptive to the claims of outsiders.[42] It is this possibility of reasoned renewal which provides the answer to the question as to why successor generations should feel constrained by their predecessors' politico-legal arrangements. It has also allowed Weber to distinguish the rational authority of law from other forms of authority[43] and Raz to argue that morality 'underdetermines' constitutions.[44] A paradoxical relationship is forged, however. The possibility of almost infinite political reform is offered but only if it is crafted as the perfection of existing formal norms and structures.[45] A continuity is provided between existing and future settlements through the imposition of a priori duties upon any act or debate to refer back to existing structures for it to be recognized as constitutional.[46] This is found most strongly in the discourse of constitutionalism which emerged in the nineteenth century as a belief-system which simultaneously both sustains

39 J. van Deth and E. Scarborough, 'The Concept of Values' in *The Impact of Values*, eds. J. van Deth and E. Scarbrough (1995) 22.

40 id., p. 30.

41 For example, Tully, *Strange Multiplicity: Constitutionalism in an Age of Diversity* (1995) ch. 3.

42 Namely, the eagerness of writing on feminism: L. Kerber, *No constitutional right to be ladies: women and the obligations of citizenship* (1998); on environmentalism: M. Sagoff, *The Economy of the Earth* (1988); and on consumerism: D. Schneiderman, 'Constitutionalizing the Culture-Ideology of Consumerism' (1998) 7 *Social and Legal Studies* 213, to appropriate constitutionalist discourse.

43 Weber, op. cit., n. 26. at pp. 853–5.

44 J. Raz, 'On the Authority and Interpretation of Constitutions: Some Preliminaries' in *Constitutionalism: Philosophical Foundations*, ed. L. Alexander (1999). For a fairly devastating critique as to why neither this nor the Weberian form of authority constitutes a new form of legitimation see J. Habermas, *Legitimation Crisis* (1973) 111–17.

45 J. Rubenfeld, 'Legitimacy and Interpretation' in Alexander, id.

46 R. Posner, 'Against Constitutional Theory' (1998) 73 *New York University Law Rev.* 1.

and reviews the modern constitution.[47] Law, politics, and ethics are reduced within it to a rationality unity in which any ethical claim can ground a new legal-politico arrangement, be it based upon individual rights;[48] forms of pre-commitment from decision-making;[49] cosmopolitanism; the securing of collective goods;[50] or theories of representation which adjudicate upon who can participate and what can be represented.[51]

If constitutional law serves to bound politics, rendering it, at least in part, inscriptive and value-oriented, the mutability of legislation *vis-à-vis* political actors, and its authority and immutability for other actors stabilizes a dualism within which it is the administration that represents and these other spheres of action which are represented. This endows the administration with capacities of co-ordination, recognition, and assimilation. For, as a series of textual communications, legislation acts as an authoritative mapping process which identifies, projects, and contours relationships.[52] It sets out the scale of the operation of the programme, defines its limits and organization, highlights those 'social facts' that the programme will address, and co-opts participants through establishing shared dependencies and linkages of interests.[53] To be sure, this can be done through political texts, such as action plans, communications, statements, which are not strictly legislative in nature. But legislation carries a particularly intense transliterative function as it is something that *requires performance*. Just as the legal subject presupposes the presence of legislation, it is doubtful whether legislation can persist without its performance by the legal subject. It enables the administration to set in motion what Latour calls 'circulating entities'.[54] The acting out of the legislative duties, rights, powers, and so on requires the entry into new relationships or alteration of existing ones, which generate new dependencies, attributes, and patterns of internal organization. In short, patterns of transformation occur to the

47 Lloyd, op. cit., n. 5, at p. 254. For a detailed analysis of this 'originalism', see P. Kahn, *The Cultural Study of Law* (1999) 88–90.

48 R. Rawls, *Political Liberalism* (1993); J. Waldron, 'A Rights Based Critique of Constitutional Rights' (1993) 13 *Oxford J. of Legal Studies* 18; R. Dworkin, 'Constitutionalism and Democracy' (1995) 3 *European J. of Philosophy* 2.

49 S. Holmes, *Passions and Constraint: On the Theory of Liberal Democracy* (1995).

50 C. Sunstein, *The Partial Constitution* (1993).

51 R. Rawls, 'The Idea of an Overlapping Consensus' (1987) 7 *Oxford J. of Legal Studies* 1; Habermas, op. cit., n. 25.

52 B. de Sousa Santos, *Toward a new Common Sense: Law, Science and Politics in the Paradigmatic Transition* (1995) ch. 7.

53 B. Latour, 'The Powers of Association' in *Power, Action, Belief*, ed. J. Law (1986); N. Rose and P. Miller, 'Political power beyond the State: problematics of government' (1992) 43 *British J. of Sociology* 176, at 189–90; H. Lefebvre, *The Production of Space* (1991) at 40–6; de Sousa Santos, id., at pp. 462–72.

54 B. Latour, 'On recalling ANT' in *Actor Network Theory and After*, eds. J. Law and J. Hassard (1999) 17–18.

point where it becomes increasingly difficult to generate an individual understanding of any parties separate from this relationship.[55]

The modern constitutional settlement also enables legislation to endow the administration with representative powers in another sense. In this context, Murphy has argued that law had, since the early mediaeval period, come to be the instrument through which a knowledge of pre-society constituted itself.[56] Things came into being socially through their exposition in legal texts. By the time of the advent of the modern constitution, the hegemony of legal knowledge over this was displaced. The emergence of statistics and economic provided more empiricist, cumulative techniques through which the social as a plane for action could be understood – a displacement that has been exacerbated exponentially with the advent of the computer. This did not result in law's role here being eradicated altogether. Its persistence, instead, allowed the administration to put forward a series of understandings. A legal understanding of society lost its scientific pretensions, however, and became, in Goodrich's words, a 'religious knowledge' which appeals to 'an imaginary order of collective truth'.[57] It becomes a form of representation rather than a form of knowledge of the social economy. It offers a series of understandings of society which are perhaps less falsifiable, but also more accessible and more affective than those offered by empiricist methods. In this, it allowed the administration to generate cross-cutting identities more easily than was possible through statistical methods. Thus, understandings of such institutions as the family, nationhood, and the workplace were heavily influenced by legal conceptions of these institutions. The modern constitution increased legislation's allegorical powers in a number of ways. It gave it a foundational aura by binding it to a settlement which usually articulated a strong sense of collective identity – a settlement that claimed to speak on behalf of 'we, the people'. Modern constitutions often expressed a series of collective ideals or aspirations that were heavily totemic in nature. Finally, through the monopoly of representation they conferred upon the administration, they set it up as the storyteller-in-chief. It becomes, in an allegorical sense, the 'centre of society'.

3. *Constitutional understandings of government*

As a paragon, the modern constitution also served to inform understandings of law and politics more generally. The centre of gravity of government was no longer compulsion of subjects, but rather the management of a political community of free citizens whose autonomy it had to respect and

55 An example in point is whether it is possible to treat British courts' relations with the executive or legislature without considering the position of the European Court of Justice, and vice versa.

56 W. Murphy, *The Oldest Social Science? Configurations of Law and Modernity* (1997) at 114–18.

57 P. Goodrich, 'Social Science and the Displacement of Law' (1998) 32 *Law and Society Rev.* 473, at 486.

in whose terms law and politics had to justify itself. Central to this, as Habermas has observed, are the principles of individual autonomy and popular sovereignty, which have informed normative self-understandings of the modern constitution right through to the present day.[58] Yet the interpretation of each these principles is conditioned by the other. The principle of individual autonomy served, on the one hand, to allow the exercise of private individual will from governmental constraint. Yet individual autonomy was considered to be an equal entitlement of all members of the political community. It was therefore not merely reducible to the exercise of private will, but was centred around a notion of public autonomy within which each agrees to limit his or her freedom so as to ensure the freedom of others. This right to an equal distribution of liberties and constraints could only be given concrete shape through the exercise of government in response to changing circumstances which is collectively understood as oriented to the common good.[59]

The dialectic between these principles influenced the organization and bounding of administrative power. Rights-based theories of constitutionalism point to the presence of Bills of Rights within modern constitutions constraining the exercise of government power. The most formalized modern constitutional settlements also created civil codes, separate from the legislative process, which partitioned off the administration from civil society.[60] Republican models, by contrast, take popular sovereignty as the focus of modern constitutions, pointing to the opportunities modern constitutions provide through representative and participative institutions for involvement in the exercise of government.[61]

Yet these principles informed not just the organization of government but also the practice of government, law, and politics. This followed from their transcendental nature which required all governmental conduct to legitimate itself in these terms, and provided the measure of review for the self-legitimation of the modern constitution. The modalities of this varied, however, for politics and law. In the case of politics, it has already been noted that the modern constitution centred politics around the enactment of particular programmes. The principles of individual autonomy and popular sovereignty entailed that these programmes legitimate themselves and open themselves to contestation in terms of how they contribute to individual welfare. The phrase 'government for the people' was thus synonymous with government being directed towards sustaining, arranging and 'perfecting' those routines, disciplines and institutions which provided for the conduct of stabilized everyday life – be they the market, the

58 Habermas, op. cit., n. 25, at p. 94.

59 id., at p. 125.

60 J. Habermas, 'Law as Medium and Law as Institution' in *Dilemmas of Law in the Welfare State*, ed. G. Teubner (1986); Murphy, op. cit., n. 56, at pp. 44–5.

61 An introduction to civic republicanism can be found in J. Pocock, *The Machiavellian Moment* (1975).

employment relationship, the professions or the family. Politics became conceived, increasingly, as a regulative rationality which perfected itself by reference to those processes which stood outside the political system but could be represented, co-ordinated and co-opted sufficiently by it that, over time, a politics of the family, the economy, the workplace, and so on could emerge.[62]

By contrast, in the case of law these features requires that law could no longer simply be approximated in terms of command but had to legitimate itself in terms of legal subjectivity. Whilst legal subjectivity preceded the modern constitution, the central contribution of the modern constitution in this regard was that it required all laws to be capable of being rationalized in terms of legal subjectivity. Legislation enlarged and redefined legal subjectivity, in that its provision of rights and duties created new ways for the legal subject to act upon others. A link was therefore established between the amount of legislation and the degree of freedom enjoyed by an individual through the legal rights and powers she or he enjoys.[63] It also protected autonomy by bounding off areas – either through the provision of individual privileges or of collective goods – that could not be encroached upon by others. The starkest form of this was the proportionality principle, which declared any measure illegal that, in the absence of a public interest, encroached upon individual interests. Less obviously, all legislation preserved some individual autonomy through only seeking to regulate interaction. In this, the liberal vision of law and the liberal vision of politics acted as counterbalances to one another. The latter focused on stabilizing an institutional backdrop which allowed individual behaviour to be tolerated by providing the conditions of security within which freedom could be tolerated. The former sought to curb this leading to a settlement that was too over-totalizing by offering an alternative vision that was less aggregative which allowed always for the circumstances of individual cases to be pleaded.

THE GROWTH OF CONSTITUTIONAL DISORIENTATION

Understandings not just of how law and politics interact, but also of many of the attributes of law and politics is premised upon the manner in which they have been organized and delineated via the central Place d'Etoile that is thc modern constitution. In this, the performance of the unity of each is premised upon the unity of the other. The performance of constitutional law is contingent upon the presence of a single administrative system which only it has the

62 M. Foucault, 'Governmentality' in *The Foucault Effect: Studies in Governmentality*, eds. G. Burchill, C. Gordon, and P. Miller (1991); N. Rose and P. Miller, 'Political power beyond the State: problematics of government' (1992) 43 *British J. of Sociology* 176.

63 The above intimates how the modern constitution resolves for itself the contradiction between political action and private freedom. The extent to which this actually happens is not considered.

authority to recognize. The unity of the legal system thus requires a centred political system which can enact legislation recognized by constitutional law. Similarly, many of the attributes of law – its state-based nature, the forms of conformity it requires – come from its close associations with the administration. The unity of the political system is, conversely, premised upon the liaison between constitutional law and legislation acting as a structure through which the very principles which constrain the administrative organization of the political system also stabilize and structure its performance.

The presence of modern constitutional structures is now so widespread[64] that it has been observed that it is unclear whether a polity will now be recognized without the presence of a modern constitution.[65] It may thus seem unwise to doubt the hegemony of their influence over understandings of law and politics.

To be sure, the omnipresence of the formal structures of modern constitutions are widespread. This omnipresence can be put down in part to the resilience of the nation-state, the central (and possibly the only) scale within which the modern constitution has been developed.[66] Constitutions are, in addition, by their nature difficult to amend. They are also difficult to overturn. Their programmatic structures can inculcate a resistance to chance. In part, this may be through participation leading to a sense of appropriateness about the settlement on the part of central political protagonists. The structuring of activity around the modern constitution also results in any revision introducing high opportunity costs for 'insiders' which will always result in some opposition to change. Modern constitutions are, finally, also highly adaptive structures. All contain 'abeyances'[67] – gaps and ambiguities which allow for politically divisive matters to be left unresolved but also give space to the constitutional settlement to evolve alongside the evolution of the polity.

All this ensures that modern constitutions continue to remain powerful points of organization of legal and political expectations and understandings. Yet the modern constitution creates its own paradox. Despite the presence of 'abeyances', it claims to offer such a universalistic paradigm, that it is only necessary for limited recognition to be afforded to other forms of law and politics for its claims to be problematized. A central argument of this essay is that post-nationalism symbolizes a break-down of this

64 For a survey, see S. Huntington, *The Third Wave: Democratization in the Late Twentieth Century* (1991).

65 U. Preuss, 'The political meaning of constitutionalism' in *Constitutionalism, Democracy and Sovereignty: American and European Perspectives*, ed. R. Bellamy (1996).

66 The only other scale has been that of the EC, which, highly debatably, is endowed by some academics but very few political practitioners with having its own constitution. The most well-known analysis of EC 'constitutionalism' can be found in J. Weiler, *The Constitution of Europe: essays on the ways and means of European Integration* (1997).

67 M. Foley, *The Silence of Constitutions* (1989) at 9–11.

boundedness. This has led to the modern constitution being increasingly unable to exercise its co-ordinatory function or to fulfil its role as a meaning-generating process. Because of their intellectual debt to the modern constitution, this leads, in turn, to traditional assumptions about many of the attributes of politics and law having to be reconsidered. This breakdown has taken a number of forms.

1. *The pluralization of regulatory authority*

The performance of political power under the modern constitution was premised upon an understanding that whilst power was decentred, it could be corralled sufficiently for problems to be defined and addressed from a single point, albeit that the sites and techniques used would be heterogeneous. This assumption relied upon all problem-fields being 'negotiable'. That is to say that the administration could identify actors who could represent interests and act as the relay for the organization of these interests so that:

> they can be worked out in the multilateral negotiating system, with the participation of the state. This increasingly concerns the legal design where the governmental agent is primarily left with the central control of the context'.[68]

This negotiability has been placed in question by a series of disordering processes which have dislocated understanding of the political system.

(a) The disordering of political subjectivity

The subject of the modern constitution was, in Touraine's words, a 'product of institutions'.[69] Politics relied upon the subject primarily as a relay for government. Central to this was a conception of subjectivity as self-disciplining, as something which submitted itself to the instrumental rationalities of the market place, the work place, the family, and so on. The security provided by the individual for these institutions was, in Foucault's view, the precondition for individual freedom.[70] Increasingly, subjectivity as a political phenomenon, is conceived, however, not in terms of self-discipline but in term of its contestation of political power. It now:

> comes into being through its combined resistance to instrumental rationalities, be they economic or political, and to 'suffocating' communitarian norms which require homogenous 'social' behaviour.[71]

68 G. Böhret, *'Die Handlungsfähigkeit des Staates am Ende des 20. Jahrhunderts'* (unpublished manuscript) cited in U. Beck, *The Reinvention of Politics* (1996) at 141.
69 A. Touraine, *What is Democracy?* (1997) 128.
70 M. Foucault, 'The Subject and Power' in *Michael Foucault: Beyond Structuralism and Hermeneutics*, eds. H. Dreyfus and P. Rabinow (1982) at 219–22.
71 Touraine, op. cit., n. 69, at pp. 128–9.

The most forthright analysis in this regard is that of Beck who talks of the growth of individualization.[72] This analysis claims that it is the side-effects of industrialization, which dismantles the previous taken-for granted storylines of political economy. This 'disintegration of the certainties of industrial society' leads to a disembedding of the individual – individualization – so that she or he becomes the 'actor, designer, juggler and stage director of his biography, identity, social networks, commitments and convictions'.[73] As individuals increasingly have the property over their own networks, these can, of course, be less easily negotiated. Such analysis has rightly been criticized on grounds of its over-generalization, excessive materiality, reluctance to problematize the relationship between organization and infrastructure,[74] and ahistoricity.[75]

Notwithstanding this, analyses focusing more carefully on the grammar codes of political reason have, however, detected a similar shift. Charles Taylor has suggested such a tension was always present in modern liberalism. For the right to recognition of individual dignity that it conveyed implied not merely a politics of universalism based on equality but also a politics of difference in which the unique identity of any individual or group is called to be recognized.[76] Governmentality literature suggests a renewed emphasis on the latter has been prompted by disillusion with the financial costs and colonizing tendencies of welfarism, on the one hand, and the development of new technologies, such as social insurance and audit, on the other. It therefore talks of the onset of advanced liberalism whereby practices of government are increasingly governed by the rationalities of competition, entrepreneurialism, and consumerism.[77] These induce the individual both to retake responsibilities for provision of goods (for example, prevention of crime, old-age and health care provision) previously supplied by the administration[78] and to mistrust and challenge traditional disciplining processes.[79] Rose notes that this preoccupation with individual subjectivity has led to the growth of therapeuticization. Events

72 U. Beck, *Risk Society* (1992) 127–9; Beck, op. cit., n. 68, at pp. 94–7; U. Beck, 'World Risk Society as Cosmopolitan Society? Ecological Questions in a framework of manufactured uncertainty' (1996) 13 *Theory, Culture and Society* 1.

73 Beck, op. cit., n. 68, at p. 95.

74 J. Alexander, 'Critical Reflections on "Reflexive Modernisation"' (1996) 13 *Theory, Culture and Society* 133.

75 M. Dean, 'Foucault, Government and the Enfolding of Authority' in *Foucault and Political Reason: Liberalism, neo-liberalism and the rationalities of government*, eds. A. Barry, T. Osborne, and N. Rose (1996).

76 C. Taylor, *Multiculturalism: Examining the Politics of Recognition* (1994) 37–8.

77 G. Burchell, 'Liberal Government and Techniques of the Self' (1993) 22 *Economy and Society* 266, at 273; N. Rose, *Powers of Freedom* (1999) 138–47; M. Dear, *Governmentality* (1999) at 164–71.

78 F. Ewald, 'Insurance and Risk' in *The Foucault Effect: Studies in Governmentality*, ed. G. Burchell et al. (1991).

79 M. Power, *The Audit Society: Rituals of Verification* (1997).

such as job change, divorce, or debt acquire a far more salient psycho-analytic dimension, where, in addition to other planes of analysis, they are viewed in terms of their effect on self-esteem.[80]

In all this, it is the individual's ability to reorganize and contest power which becomes central.[81] In so far as this shift takes place, this leads to a disordering. Politics becomes more dependent on individual subjectivity as individuals become more pro-actively engaged in the management of their own government. Individual subjectivity becomes less negotiable, however, as it generates unpredictable vectors of action which render it more resistant to external representation and organization.

(b) The spatial disordering of political performance

The spatial disordering of the performance of politics goes under the euphemism of globalization. Transnational flows of information and factors of production are, it is argued, decentering and disembedding 'territorial and place-based' socio-institutional forms and identities.[82] National boundaries are becoming porous; urban geographies reconfigured; traditional administrative apparatuses disempowered; 'social structures' disrupted; meanings and identities reconfigured. Against this it can be observed that the presence of autonomous, transformative, transnational networks of organization is not a new phenomenon. The whole sorry institution of New World slavery, rooted largely in the processes of civil society, is perhaps the most unfortunate, enduring, and significant example.[83] Furthermore, it has been observed that economic interdependence is no greater now than at the beginning of the century.[84] A parallel tendency, based on identical methodological assumptions, has therefore grown which, in its emphasis on the endurance of statal institutions, argues that globalization's claims are at best overblown.[85]

The materialistic underpinnings of this debate obscure globalization's importance as a political phenomenon. The use of globalization in political

80 Rose, op. cit., n. 77, at pp. 89–93.

81 R. v. Krieken, 'Proto-governmentalization and the historical formation of organizational subjectivity' (1996) 25 *Economy and Society* 195; P. O'Malley, 'Risk and Responsibility' in Barry, Osborne, and Rose, op. cit., n. 75.

82 For example, S. Lash and J. Urry, *Economies of Signs and Spaces* (1993); K. Ohmae, *The End of the Nation State* (1995); M. Castells, *The Rise of the Network Society* (1996) ch. 2; Beck, op. cit., n. 72; N. Brenner, 'Globalisation as Reterritorialisation: The Re-scaling of Urban Governance in the European Union' (1999) 36 *Urban Studies* 431.

83 R. Blackburn, *The Making of New World Slavery: From the Baroque to the Modern 1492–1800* (1997) especially 5–12.

84 A. Kleinknecht and J. ter Wengel, 'The myth of economic globalization' (1998) 22 *Cambridge J. of Economics* 637.

85 P. Hirst and G. Thompson, *Globalization in question: the international economy and the possibilities of governance* (1996); M. Mann, 'Has globalization ended the rise and rise of the nation-State' (1997) 4 *Rev. of International Political Economy* 472.

discourse – of which there is plenty – implies an acknowledgement by administrators and policy-makers of the non-negotiability of processes traditionally regulated by the administration. It describes both the slipping away of entities if government requires their performance of political programmes and the disruption of political programmes by extraterritorial processes – be it through electronic communication, mobility of capital or straightforward regulatory competition. These effects are generated through a political preoccupation with scale. The regulatory programmes of the nation-state imposed national territorial scales on markets through the establishment of national legal codes, national energy and transport infrastructures, national systems of exchange.[86] Globalization privileges the organization of scale in political performance by describing a dialectic between the emergence of a deterritorialized 'space of flows', characterized by patterns of interaction and exchange between actors in physically disjointed positions, and the reterritorialization of relatively fixed territorial structures (or 'spaces of places'). The central organizers of scale within this process, however, are world cities, the internet, and so on.[87] The importance of the organization of scale in politics is increased, but administrations – be they national, local or supranational – are no longer acknowledged as pivotal to this process of organization. This results in scale becoming something to be contested. A politics of scale emerges whereby in so far as the organizational scale of one process inevitably cuts across and thereby disrupts the organization of another process, it comes to be constructed as a threat to all those objectives which are politically valued by the latter.[88]

(c) The temporal disordering of political performance

The metaphor used for temporal disordering is that of risk. Risk indicates that one cannot determine in the present how other will behave or phenomena unfold in future situations.[89] If globalization illustrated a concern with the political organization of scale, risk, by contrast, illustrates a concern with the political organization of consequences and a corollary acknowledgement that the organization of consequences is both more central to politics and impossible to organize administratively. To be sure, a concern with the consequences of political programmes has been a central concern of politics since politics became concerned with the organization of its own performance, and is manifested in the traditional reflexivity of the political process. There is also nothing new about the notions of contingency, hazard, and uncertainty.

86 Lefebvre, op. cit., n. 53, at pp. 278–82.

87 S. Sassen, *The Global City* (1991); Castells, op. cit., n. 82, ch. 3.

88 N. Smith, 'Remaking scale: competition and co-operation in prenational and post-national Europe' in *Competitive European Peripheries*, eds. H. Eskelinen and F. Snickars (1995); Habermas, op. cit., n. 1, at pp. 94–6.

89 Luhmann, op. cit., n. 15, at p. 59.

The internalization of risk into political discourse suggests a new double bind, however. Political programmes are held responsible for the calculation and anticipation of consequences which it is acknowledged they cannot predict. The reasons given for risk moving more centre-stage in politics vary,[90] and it is not clear how much of the practice of politics is indeed dominated by the concept of risk. Yet the novelty of the increased political discussion of risk, and the temporal disordering that it expresses, is that its use enfolds both the past and the future in the present. It implies a more intense intergenerational responsibility on the part of the present to discount for the future, albeit in a manner that will always be deemed to fail. Equally, unintended consequences of the past are no longer nobody's responsibility, they are to be attributed to poor planning or negligence on the part of somebody in the here and now. This disordering has led to new reterritorializations of politics.

First, risk renders politics dependent upon the technologies of calculation, be they economic forecasting or physical science. As Beck has observed, this leads increasingly to functional co-ordination rather than functional differentiation. Changes in understandings of science or economics bring about changes in politics.[91] Similarly, failures in these disciplines – be they BCCI, BSE, collapses of housing during the Turkish earthquake – are also seen as regulatory (that is, political) failures. As a corollary of this, there emerges a double enfranchisement of locales where this expertise is concentrated. The activities of these locales becomes, on the one hand, politically important. Yet, on the other, developments in local knowledge and specialization of expertise has led to regulatory authorities being increasingly unable to review the activities of these locales. In areas as diverse as integrated pollution control and financial services, these locales become therefore political entities which are not fully negotiable.[92]

Temporal disordering also reterritorializes political counterdynamics around the politics of anxiety.[93] Risk provides a rationalization for anxiety. Yet whereas risk liberalizes present action to affect future situations, anxiety constrains present action for fear of future consequences. Thus, by taking a risk, I allow myself to do something now (buy a house with a highly levered mortgage) irrespective of future consequences. Anxiety, by contrast, constrains me. I do not buy the house now for fear of the future inability to make repayments. The politics of anxiety is thus inevitably the politics of resistance and constraint.[94] It focuses around the objects of its fear – fields of

90 Compare materialist analyses which attribute it to the growth of unintended consequences brought by industrialization: Beck, op. cit., nn. 68 and 72, and more genealogical approaches which attribute it to the advent of new calculative technologies, which allowed for the detection of increased inter-temporal dependencies, see Ewald, op. cit., n. 78.

91 Beck, id., n. 68, at p. 27.

92 K.-H. Ladeur, 'Towards a Legal Theory of Supranationality – The Viability of the Network Concept' (1997) 3 *European Law J.* 33.

93 Luhmann, op. cit., n. 34, pp. 89, 127–9.

94 id., p. 90.

genetically modified crops, the City of London, Shell oil pumps – rather than around the administrative apparatus of government, thus contributing to the reterritorialization of politics. Centred as it is on constraining the present, it, paradoxically, does the opposite of risk by folding the present into the future. Expositions of the future by the ecological movement, therefore, rely heavily upon the sacralization of existing places, the extolling and historicization of current identities, and the extolling of 'traditional' ways of life.[95]

The political significance of these three disordering processes lies not simply in their non-negotiability, but in their carrying out of tasks essential to the performance of politics – for example, the organization of political subjectivity, scale, and consequential responsibility. In this they represent more than some external challenge provoking the need for administrative readjustment. They break down the subject-object dualism within which responsibility for the political representation and configuration of 'non-political actors' lies with the administration. New processes of programming emerge under the aegis of these phenomena which relativize the art of administration. In the case of individualization, it is a simple retrenchment of the administrative capacities to programme. In the case of globalization, political administrations are reduced to 'entrepreneurial agencies' seeking to 'enhance the locational advantages and productive capacities of their territorial jurisdictions as maximally competitive nodes within the world economy'.[96] In the instance of risk they are reduced to dealing with the unfortunate consequences of other actors' programmes. All this leads to an erosion of the distinction between who is governing and who is governed. Lash therefore discusses the era of globalization in terms where objects take on capacities associated with subjects, 'powers of judgment, of measuring, translating and interpretation'.[97] The homogenous responses of capital traders, dictated almost exclusively now by computer programmes, to changes in short-term interest rates leads to the market in a very real sense governing administrations. Latour similarly analyses how natural objects acquire powers of articulation, translation, and so on precisely because damage or anticipated damage to them – the inherent corollary of risk – necessitates a policy response.[98]

It is a question merely of semantics whether these processes generate new sites of politics or sub-politics. If this is seen simply as overloading the term, it cannot be denied that they constitute new forms of regulatory authority. As if there were any doubt about this, these processes are infected with their processes of publicity. Instrumental rationality is no longer sufficient. Instead, the sites of globalization, risk, and subjectivization increasingly accommodate pluralistic rationalities, principles of transparency, and due

95 D. Harvey, *Justice, Nature and the Geography of Difference* (1996) 299–313; P. Macnaghten and J. Urry, *Contested Natures* (1998) 245.

96 Brenner, op. cit., n. 82, at p. 440.

97 S. Lash, *Another Modernity: A Different Rationality* (1999) 342 and following.

98 B. Latour, *We have Never Been Modern* (1993); Latour, op. cit., n. 53.

process. With subjectivity this takes the form of the institution of community imposing a series of cross-cutting, horizontal, and multiple responsibilities upon the individual. In the instance of globalization, it is through the development of world culture – the emergence of universalistic norms and associational processes, which inform political understanding and action across much of the world.[99] In the case of risk one finds the opening-up of the locales where this expertise is gathered through the generation of structures of corporate governance, the provision of procedures of ecological communication over land development, the responsibilisation of lending institutions, increasingly, for the non-material consequences of their loans. All three thus become sites for new forms of contestation, confrontation, and coalition.[100] There is a genuine pluralization of regulatory authority which happens outside the constitutional settlement. This authority is not susceptible to any form of network management, 'smart regulation', or regulatory design from any central point.

2. *Internal differentiation of administration*

The modern constitution's ability to code administrative power depends upon its ability to provide a map which describes the various entities' and sub-entities' relations *vis-à-vis* one another. This acts as a process of synthesis that enables the modern constitution to create a 'rational unity' of the different administrative units, which both stabilizes expectations about the distribution of power within the administration and also provides normative expectations about what administrative conduct is acceptable and what is not. The ability of the modern constitution to map administrative power has been problematized by administration's absorption with its problem-solving capabilities. Problem-solving requires that the administration can not legitimate itself simply on input-oriented grounds of conformity with constitutional procedures but must increasingly legitimate itself in terms of its output.[101] In particular, it must 'answer to that range of common interests that is sufficiently stable and broad to justify institutional arrangements for collective action'.[102] This has led to both increased formal and functional differentiation within administrations as these adapt to the demands imposed upon them by their environment. A crude quantitative measure of this is provided by John Boli who, in a survey of 419 constitutions between 1870–1970, found that both administrative jurisdiction over social life and mechanisms of implementation doubled during the period to, on his methodology, fifty-six and forty-five respectively.[103] Qualitatively, it

99 J. Meyer et al., 'World Society and the Nation State' (1997) 103 *Am. J. of Sociology* 144.
100 Beck, op. cit., n. 68, at pp. 150–2.
101 F. Scharpf, *Governing in Europe* (1999) 10–23.
102 id., p. 11.
103 J. Boli, 'World Polity Sources of Expanding State Authority and Organization, 1870–1970' in *Institutional Structures: Constituting State, Society and the Individual*, eds. J. Thomas, J. Meyer, F. Ramirez, and J. Boli (1987) 72.

is found in the increasing homogeneity in national constitutional structures, educational systems, environmental policies, demographical instruments, welfare systems, and development-oriented economic policies.[104]

This formal differentiation leads to new demarcations which render co-ordination increasingly difficult. Administrative units/sub-units develop their own autonomous pathologies of rent-seeking, problem-solving, and clientelism which bring them more often than not into competition with other administrative sub-units.[105] This will not be detected by the modern constitution and, in one sense, does relativize its ability to stabilize expectations and give normative guidance. Yet, in so far as such differentiation is 'internal' to institutions set out in the constitution, it does not problematize it formally. Whatever internecine conflicts take place, their outcomes still have to be enacted through the formal constitutional arrangements.

The position is more complicated in relation to institutions or configurations whose establishment was unforeseen by the modern constitution. The formal basis for the establishment of these procedures is always some variant of the delegation principle (for example, the development of administration or quasi-legislative powers to regulatory agencies). The principal-agent relationship is too crude to generate detailed normative expectations which guide the day-to-day conduct of the agent for the simple reason that the granting of agency presupposes a degree of autonomy which can never fully be determined or guided. It is no longer a pre-given that all the rules which govern the principal's behaviour will also govern the agent's. In the case of such arrangements the constitution may, thus, continue to describe the distribution of power but it is no longer able to 'exercise determinate judgment' over the conduct of these bodies. They are simultaneously agencies subject to the constitution but also different from the agencies set out in the constitution. Analogical rationality is applied to govern the conduct of such institutions. The universal rules of the modern constitution do not necessarily apply to them, but, as these institutions are *sui generis*, regard will be had to what 'functions' they are performing or the 'quality of the acts' they are adopting.[106] The universal qualities of the modern constitution become subsumed in the particular qualities of the individual agency rather than, as the case with the original institutions, their conduct being primarily determined by a set of pre-given rules.[107]

The most severe form of administrative disordering is found in post-national settlements. Such arrangements which provide for the geographical redistribution of power, either supra/internationally or sub-nationally, have proliferated, locking most national constitutional arrangements into

104 Meyer et al., op. cit., n. 99, at pp. 152–3.

105 C. Offe, *Modernity and the State* (1996) 60–4.

106 To give an example in the field of EC law, it is unclear whether and what general principles of law apply to the many regulatory agencies set up or to the activities of private standard-setting bodies such as CEN and CENELEC.

107 Lash, op. cit., n. 97, at pp. 2–3.

a web of 'confederal arrangements' in which the existence of self-rule and shared rule become premised upon each other.[108] The feature of such arrangements is that they posit the existence of autonomous loci, other than the national constitution, which contribute to the distribution of administrative power. Such arrangements generate not only new configurations of normative expectations, which cut across those of the constitution but also new configurations which redistribute administrative power. This redistribution occurs not so much from one process trumping the other but from the operational tension between the administrative mechanisms for shared rule and the administrative mechanisms for self-rule. Such tensions exist not only, as with the EC, where the supranational regime claims some form of formal sovereign authority. In other cases, in the absence of domestic mechanisms which provide for the trumping effects of international agreements or regional or local assemblies, the national constitution may prevail in individual cases. Yet, even here, it is not feasible for states to remain in a regime where they are more often in breach than conformity. The regime either collapses under the weight of countermeasures or the state either exits in a *de iure* or *de facto* manner from the regime. The persistence and relative operational authority of most regimes suggests that, in general, neither happens, but rather there is an operational redistribution of administrative power.

Functional differentiation further reduces the mapping capabilities of the national constitution. It reorganizes administrations around the carrying out of a particular task. This creates new divisions and allegiances within administrative units and sub-units between those carrying out and those who are not. It, however, also creates new interdependencies and allegiances across formal administrative demarcations. This occurs partly through the functional dependence of each administration upon the other, which requires a process of mutual recognition whereby each has to have regard to the interests and attitudes of other if the task in hand is to be achieved. It also occurs through a 'fusion' of administrative interaction, whereby the central dialectic for an administrative sub-unit occurs not with other parts of its unit but with sub-units dealing with the same problem in other administrative apparati.[109] This can generate new synergies, processes of adaptation, and meaning-structures, which provide a configuration of organization of tasks and normative expectations quite separate from that set out in the constitution.

3. *The emergence of legal pluralism*

The modern constitution's ability to organize the social economy centred upon the enactment of legislation as a central tool for the disposal of

108 D. Elazar, *Constitutionalizing Globalization: The Postmodern Revival of Confederal Arrangements* (1998) ch. 9.

109 W. Wessels, 'An Ever Closer Fusion? A Dynamic Macropolitical View on Integration Processes' (1997) 35 *J. of Common Market Studies* 267.

administrative power. Legislation's qualities both facilitated and legitimated the exercise of social control and generated a self-representation of society which was to provide a orientation for and patterning of socio-economic relations. The autonomous qualities of legislation also facilitated the capacity of the constitution to code and bound this power, as legislation could only be adopted in accordance with the constitution and only recognized the authority of the constitution. Legislation's qualities as an organizational tool have been weakened by an increase in the scale of non-administrative forms of organization, which contribute to the reconfiguration of the social economy in ways that are both disjointed and not anticipated by the constitutional settlement. Example of these include new social movements, corporate codes, trade union rules, the *lex mercatoria*, standard-setting bodies, NGO treaty regimes. A feature of all these is that they contain processual characteristics which allow them to generate rules and coerce or induce compliance.[110] Powerful ties of mutual obligation emerge, which it is argued, deflect the operation of 'external (state) law'.[111]

At their most inchoate, these semi-autonomous fields of organization take the form of 'cultural sources of continuity and coherence'.[112] Powerful symbols or totems are disseminated across a wide variety of fora – industry, art, music, sports, patterns of consumption – to generate, emphasize, and exploit common allegiances and dependencies. In other instances, more clearly recognizable forms of legal pluralism emerge where either 'the regulation of the field is differentiated from the rest of the activities in the field and delegated to specialized functionaries'[113] or there is provision for:

> a body of regularised procedures and normative standards, considered justiciable in a given group, which contribute to the creation and prevention of disputes, as well as to their settlement through an argumentative discourse coupled with the threat of force.[114]

Whilst legislation can, and frequently does, hook up to these allegiances, insofar as they are cross-cutting, they deflect the operation of legislation by providing more powerful inducements for compliance and a more resonant map of participants' relations than those offered by legislation.

The increase in these modes of organization has been ascribed by Offe to the capacities of modern political economies and technological systems both to displace conflict and to increase the scope of the impact of failures.[115] This is caused, in part, through solutions to conflicts externalizing

110 S. Moore, 'Law and social change: the semi-autonomous social field as an appropriate subject of study' in *Law as Process: An Anthropological Approach*, ed. S. Moore (1978) 57–8.

111 J. Griffiths, 'What is Legal Pluralism' (1986) 24 *J. of Legal Pluralism* 1, at 38.

112 C. Offe, 'Challenging the boundaries of institutional politics: social movements since the 1960s' in *Changing Boundaries of the Political*, ed. C. Maier (1987) 93.

113 Griffiths, op. cit., n. 111, at p. 30.

114 de Sousa Santos, op. cit., n. 52, at p. 112. For a survey of the literature on legal pluralism, see W. Twining, 'Mapping Law' (1999) 50 *Northern Ireland Legal Q.* 12.

115 Offe, op. cit., n. 112, at p. 85.

some or all of the costs of agreement onto third parties – a process that creates new sites of conflict and negotiation.[116] Offe also agrees with the school of reflexive modernization by arguing that conflict displacement has been caused by these institutions and technologies being 'all powerful' in controlling and producing their environments but being 'largely helpless to address the self-paralysing consequences of their use of such power'.[117]

Both these features contribute to the new sites of confrontation and new belief-systems that underlie the development of the so-called new social movements (for example, environmentalism, feminism, the peace movement, consumerism, anti-racism).[118] It is often remarked that these constitute a new self-limiting form of politics, which is not interested in traditional forms of political participation. Another, possibly more accurate, characterization is that these movements are concerned with establishing an alternate form of legal organization. The question of externalization of costs leads to a counterdynamic which seeks freedom from the imposition of costs. This centres these new forms of organization around the protection of particular places and identities in a far more particularistic manner than any administration could seek to achieve. The feature of the risk society also renders this organization oppositional in nature. It is centred around the criticism of particular institutions rather than individual interests or parties. Whilst reliant in many ways upon the institutions it criticises, it consciously situates its organization and meaning-systems on the 'outside' of these institutions.

Such creation of new semi-autonomous fields is also enhanced by new dynamics of internalization. Offe describes this as the invention of new disciplining processes which produce 'new social relations'.[119] He points, in particular, to increased control over information and processes of symbol-formation as the cause for this. Examples of this would include the patterning of consumer behaviour through mass advertising or supermarket rebate cards; management techniques which centre the lifestyle of the employee (health, family, friendships) around the workplace; the co-opting of neighbourhoods into acceptance of industrial practices through the manipulation of the undertaking's green or community image. A feature of such practices is that they must adaptive. In all the examples, industry must therefore continually be seen to be responsive to the concerns of neighbourhoods, consumers, employees. This leads both to the development of new standards of conduct (for example, on those on advertising or

116 Disputes about land use are therefore resolved through NIMBYISM. The industrial costs of competition to shareholders are resolved through mergers, which displace these costs onto the workforce. Disputes about consumption of risky products (for example, GMOs) are resolved through consumption of products with other risks (for example, intensive farming).

117 Offe, op. cit., n. 112, at p. 85.

118 For a fine survey of the considerable literature on this, see P. Donati, *Environmentalism, postmaterialism, and anxiety: the new politics of individualism* (1996).

119 Offe, op. cit., n. 112, at p. 86.

eco-auditing) and new institutional links between parties which generate their own self-organizing practices.[120]

This would not, alone, problematize the representational or necessarily the performative abilities of legislation – many of these modes of organization are after all longstanding in nature – were it not for the latter being counterfactual in nature. They require a leap of faith – something proselytized by the modern constitution – on those participating. This leap of faith has, on the one hand, indeed allowed these semi-autonomous fields to be rendered invisible and marginalized so that they do not problematize the constitutional monopoly over legislation. These modes of organization only challenge belief in legislation's capacity to organize in so far as they bring about an awareness in their presence and significance that leads to a process of reflexive self-doubt. Yet the more manifest these become and the wider their embrace, so the harder it becomes to sustain this disbelief. Some argue rather unconvincingly that the cumulative generation of transnational patterns of organization of globalization is bringing this about.[121] There is little evidence this is so. A particularly dynamic form of legal pluralism is the *Movimiento sem Terra*, a Brazilian land movement, which has brought about the redistribution and organization of property title in land for about 400,000 Brazilians in the last fifteen years. Its impact is such that it is to be seen as the central node for the organization of and siting of conflict in land in Brazil. Yet such an organization is rooted very much in the particularities of the Brazilian domestic situation.[122] Similarly, it is probably accurate to state that one of the most recognized forms of 'private law-making' is the longstanding one of gypsy law.[123] More subtle arguments imply, however, that globalization may still be significant. As a paradigm, in so far as it suggests spatial disordering, it may prompt an awareness and receptiveness to new forms of spatial organization.[124] This argument avoids the weaknesses of the infrastructural arguments, addressing the point of legislative self-belief far more directly. And yet if this is so, suspension of this disbelief, like globalization, remains an uneven process. The centrality of administrative law is doubted by nobody and its exclusivity still upheld by some.[125] Yet the

120 A prominent example of the latter is *Business in the Community*, a corporate entity, consisting of 400 members, including 75 of the companies in the FTSE Top 100, which sets out codes its members with which its members agree to comply, on 'corporate social responsibility' and 'Corporate Community Investment'. For further details see <http://www.bitc.org.uk>.

121 de Sousa Santos, op. cit., n. 52, ch. 4.

122 For an autobiography of this movement, visit <http://www.sanet.com.br/~semterra>. For an early introduction see H. Veltmeyer, 'The Landless Rural Workers Movement in Contemporary Brazil' (1993) 26 *Labour, Capital and Society* 204.

123 W. Weyrauch and M. Bell, 'Autonomous Lawmaking: The Case of the "Gypsies"' (1993) 103 *Yale Law J.* 323; Symposium on Gipsy Law (1997) 45 *Am. J. of Comparative Law.*

124 G. Teubner, 'Breaking Frames: The Global Interplay of Legal and Social Systems' (1997) 45 *Am. J. of Comparative Law* 149; G. Teubner, 'The King's Many Bodies: The Self-Destruction of Law's Hierarchy', ARENA WP 97/22, <http://www.sv.uio.no/arena/>.

125 For example, P. Morton, *An Institutional Theory of Law: Keeping Law in Its Place* (1997).

increase in the growth and awareness of these new forms of organization has corroded belief in legislation's ability to map and to organize. This corrosion can only grow, and even now problematizes the assumptions of the modern constitution. Yet the paradigmatic shift is not so great that if belief in administrative legislation is akin to a religious belief one can talk about a new found atheism; it is, rather, an indecisive agnosticism.

THE QUEST FOR POST-NATIONAL CONSTITUTIONAL SUBSTITUTES

The disordered and decentred nature of post-nationalism does not signify an inevitable descent into the vortex of relativism. The modern constitution served as a fulcrum through which politico-legal processes of assimilation, co-ordination, recognition, and rational self-critique and renewal could emerge and be sustained.[126] The need for (or presence of) some form of constitutional substitute can only be dismissed if it can be argued that either such politico-legal processes no longer exist or that the internal development and external roles of politics and law are so autarkic from one another that no structures are necessary to mediate their relationships. There is little evidence that either argument can be convincingly sustained. The disordering outlined earlier does not constitute a denial of the presence of the politico-legal processes of co-ordination, recognition, and so on but, rather, emphasizes their centrality by suggesting that their contestedness has led to their reorganization. The increased reference to a new form of atomistic political subjectivity may make it harder for political subjects to be managed or aggregated from a set of central points. But it does not lead to the return of the unencumbered self. Instead, it results in individuals having to enter increasing numbers of arrangements and adopt larger, more multifarious numbers of political and legal identities.[127] In this it suggests an expansion of politico-legal arrangements rather than the reverse. The task of any constitutional substitute is, therefore, to subject all political and legal interaction within this context to processes of co-ordination, assimilation, recognition, and rational self-critique.

The condition of disordering presupposes that such interaction takes place in the presence of considerable *organizational pluralism*.[128] Interaction will take place between organizations; between organizations and their membership; organizations and non-members; and between individuals. As very few of these jurisdictions are exclusive, so the tasks, roles, responsibilities, and identities produced by these organizations are not merely multiple but frequently overlapping and occasionally interdependent. This generates

126 Tully, op. cit., n. 10, chs. 2, 3.

127 Murphy, op. cit., n. 56 at pp. 214–17.

128 K.H. Ladeur, 'Post-Modern Constitutional Theory: A Prospect for the Self-Organising Society' (1997) 60 *Modern Law Rev.* 617.

conditions which are not merely diverse but also volatile in the sense that organizational loyalties can also be fluid and conflicting.[129] The multifarious, unstable, and unpredictable nature of political and legal interaction engendered by this renders it impossible for any external mechanism to subject all such interactions any form of purposive rationality which requires such interaction to meet certain substantive ends. For, within its own terms of reference, it will be impossible for any such mechanism to locate responsibility for attainment of these ends, control who is subject to it, and produce substantive goals that are both acceptable to and have resonance for its subjects.

Deprived of strong external steering mechanisms, constitutional substitutes can only rely upon the processes of legal and political interaction themselves to engineer processes of co-ordination, assimilation, and rational self-critique. Such interaction takes two forms. It may take the form of communication or dialogue. Alternately, it may be less intersubjective and be based on recognition. Within either, 'constitutional substitutes' rely upon structures of subjectivity or intersubjectivity that are rooted deep within the subject. It is beyond the scope of this paper to explore in detail the limitations of the former. Instead, the final section considers how individual processes of recognition act as the functional substitute for the modern constitution in their regulation of legal and political interaction.

The most forthright advocate of a politics of recognition is probably the historian Jim Tully.[130] Tully takes cultural identity as central to self-knowledge and self-realization. It is, however, aspectival and fluid – formed through the experience of the overlap, negotiation, and interaction of different cultures.[131] This fluidity contributes to cultural identity being marked by cultural difference. Such identity cannot fully know itself. It takes 'the form of a subject only in the non-identity with itself'.[132] This inherent instability prevents any form of rational consensus premised upon communication from being an attainable ideal. Tully believes, however, that recognition confers meaning upon other actors. He agrees with Taylor's argument that recognition is central to the creation of self-identity. Thus, 'we define our identity always in dialogue with, sometimes in struggles against, the things our significant others want to see in us.'[133] In so far as recognition creates some form of mutual accommodation, it brings about limited processes of co-ordination and assimilation. This process of mutual accommodation enables law and

129 M. Dorf and C. Sabel, 'A Constitution of Democratic Experimentalism' (1998) 98 *Columbia Law Rev.* 267, at 286.

130 In particular, he differs from liberal advocates of the politics of recognition. For a survey of the latter's work, see S. Tempelman, 'Constructions of Cultural Identity: Multiculturalism and Exclusion' (1999) 47 *Political Studies* 17.

131 Tully, op. cit., n. 10, at pp. 13–14. For an application of Tully's work to a European Union context see J. Shaw, 'Postnational Constitutionalism in the European Union' (1999) 6 *J. of European Public Policy* 579.

132 J. Derrida, *The Other Heading: Reflections on Today's Europe* (1992) 9.

133 Taylor, op. cit., n. 76 at 32–33.

politics to be identified, understood, and constituted not on the basis of any common, transcendent understanding but through the prisms of each party's cultural identity.

Recognition is thus central to politics as it generates not merely patterns of exclusion and inclusion but also constrains how actors 'conduct themselves in order to count as players'.[134] Types of knowledge, standard forms of conduct, and relations of power are therefore all premised upon relations of recognition, even though they help to reconstitute these relations. Tully argues that this often leads to oppression through the politics of non-recognition and misrecognition, which prevents parties from participating equally and freely in the practice of politics. Tully does not explain, however, how his politics of recognition can enable critique of politics and law. He argues for a politics of mutual recognition of cultural identity in which different cultural identities are more broadly recognized, yet does not explain what cognitive structures enable this. Furthermore, the boundaries and process of the nature of recognition is left very vague. This generates further problems.

Whilst relations may be created which are more inclusive than others, recognition is something finite which is always premised upon the right to differentiate between whom one recognizes and whom one does not. Universal recognition is simply not possible. The power of recognition comes from the patterns of inclusion and exclusion it bestows – for example, I recognize X rather than Y as the appropriate person to plumb my flat – and its enabling of those recognized. Recognition can also take a number of forms and demand a number of different things. Habermas, for example, contrasts the demands of feminism with those of oppressed ethnic minorities. The case of the former 'concerns interpretation of gender-specific achievements and interests'.[135] Recognition of feminism's claims therefore *directly* affects men's own self-understanding. Such a high level of self-understanding is not called for in a claim for a state to recognize minority rights. In like vein, Habermas observes that the mode of recognition called for will differ whether it is minority rights or nationhood being sought.[136] From this it follows that high and varied demands are placed upon the individual making the recognition, for recognition, properly conducted, will require the entry into a series of subsequent actions or relations. As any act of recognition will be done from the perspective of, and often call for reflection upon, the observer's own cultural identity, it will be always an act of misrecognition. As cultural identities are fluid and context-dependent, the claims those identities will make will not be stable and will vary in accordance with the context of interaction. In talk of a politics of recognition, simply, there is a danger of reification of these identities, with individuals being too 'tightly scripted' to these identities.[137]

134 J. Tully, 'The agonic freedom of citizens' (1999) 28 *Economy and Society* 161, at 172.

135 J. Habermas, 'Struggles for recognition in the Democratic Constitutional State' in Taylor, op. cit., n. 76, p. 117.

136 id., p. 118.

137 K. Appiah, 'Identity, Authenticity, Survival: Multicultural Societies and Social Reproduction' in Taylor, id., pp. 159–60.

These arguments are not necessarily fatal to recognition being a constitutional substitute. They suggest, however, that more attention be given to how the immediate context constrains and configures the quality of recognition granted and that the normative qualities of any act of recognition are tied far more deeply to the internal structures of the process of recognition than has been acknowledged.

1. *The cognitive demands of recognition of legal and political acts*

As a constitutional substitute, only a particular genus of measure and identity is being recognized, political and legal ones. This imposes cognitive constraints on what can be recognized and the modes that recognition can take. For whilst the boundaries of law and politics are highly contested, there are certain attributes which are central to each.

Post-national politics implies a form of politics that exists outside administrative apparatuses. In this context, politics is normally understood as the 'process of . . . conflict over power-sharing and power-positions'.[138] Whether power is taken to be a resource or merely the ability to act upon the actions of others, it is probably too broad to equate politics absolutely with the struggle for and the exercise of power. A further element is necessary which is implicit in the Aristotelian concept of politics being the art of adopting collectively-binding decisions. For Aristotle this involved taking decisions upon the basis of collective argument and opinion. In a more materialized age, Beck has noted that politics, conventionally, involves only collective actors. By which he means that to engage in political action, individuals must subscribe to 'large-scale categories', which recognize other large-scale categories.[139] Central to either definition is that a decision is political if it negotiates with 'difference'. It must bridge a gap between the decision-makers' internal values and interests and other external values and interests. Rose thus describes political power as 'taking as it object the conduct of its subjects in relation to particular moral or secular standards'.[140] Politics may do this through ensuring the hegemony of one value or interest over the other or mediating between the two but in any case it must confront this 'otherness'. It was precisely the state's perceived loss of this monopoly over negotiation that contributed to the disordering of politics.

If it was ever possible to make sovereignty a precondition of legality, with the onset of greater legal pluralism that era has now passed. Legal and social theorists recognize a number of cumulative features endemic to law. The first is *normativity*. Laws regulate conduct and stabilize expectations through maintaining a clear division between what is and is not permissible, that is, legal. Normativity carries with it a number of features, which have already been mentioned in this essay, those of supremacy, comprehensiveness, and

138 Beck, op. cit., n. 68, at p. 103.
139 id., p. 23.
140 N. Rose, op. cit., n. 77, at p. 7.

non-falsifiability.[141] In this context, these suggest a quality of law that there be no limitations on either its authority or its jurisdiction other than those it recognizes, and that if there is no convergence between behaviour and a norm, it is the behaviour that is labelled non-conformist or deviant and not the norm. A second feature of any law is its *formal-legalism*. First suggested by Weber, this distinguishes legal claims from either ethical or moral ones by designating zones of authority, relatively unmediated by norms. This carries a presumption that an individual is unconstrained and free to pursue their own subjective interests and values unless legal norms intervene. The bestowing of individual subjectivity in this manner results in the possibility of strategic interaction between norms and individuals being a feature of any legal system.[142] The third feature of any legal system is *legal validity*. There must not be full compliance with the norm, but the norm must be sufficiently effective that, in Habermas's words, there is 'average compliance' with it.[143] The final feature of law is, to use Habermas's terminology, the *second dimension of legal validity*. Any law must invite 'the addressees to follow them from the non-enforceable motive of duty'.[144] Whilst there is disagreement as to the extent to which this implies a moral content to the nature of law, there must always be the possibility for people to obey laws out of respect for them.

2. *The centrality of organizations to law and politics*

As both law and politics are collective enterprises applied to finite situations, the presence of these qualities is dependent upon the creation of collective 'explicit knowledge'. In this context knowledge contains a number of elements. It involves:

> beliefs and commitment. Knowledge is a function of a particular stance, perspective or intention. Second, knowledge, unlike information, is about action. It is always knowledge to 'some end'. And third, knowledge, like information, is about meaning. It is context-specific and relational.[145]

Furthermore, as legal and political measures are dependent upon processes of formulation and communication, they rely predominantly upon 'explicit knowledge' – knowledge that is transmittable in formal, systematic language.[146]

These features entail that organizations are central to the constituting of law and politics. Organizations can take many forms and vary considerably in size and power, but all are bodies that define their own jurisdiction

141 id.
142 Weber, op. cit., n. 26, at pp. 311–16, 666–8; Habermas, op. cit., n. 25, at p. 31.
143 id.
144 id.
145 I. Nonaka and H. Takeuchi, *The Knowledge-creating Company* (1995) 58.
146 id., p. 59. This is contrasted with tacit knowledge which is personal and context-specific. The distinction is taken from M. Polanyi, *The Tacit Dimension* (1967).

and contain procedures for their own governance and reconstitution. To be sure, not all organizations engage in political or legal acts. Yet, only organizations have the resources to create the 'social facts' central to the making of law or politics.

The decision-making structures within the organization provide it with resources unavailable to other institutions, such as norms. It allows them to rely upon the cognitive capacities of the individuals who are part of the organization. This is central as knowledge-creation is dependent upon the interaction between forms of tacit and express knowledge.[147] Decision-making processes, by endowing organizations with a 'collective consciousness' also allow them, like individuals, to transfer information into knowledge. For it gives them the necessary strategic ability to acquire, create, accumulate, and exploit knowledge.[148]

Organizational decision-making processes also give them advantages over individuals. The first advantage is that of informational redundancy.[149] This refers to the sharing of information by individuals or a group with other individuals who do not need the information immediately. This promotes shared tacit knowledge, and is only possible in a patterned, regularized manner within organizations. The other advantage organizational decision-making processes have over individuals is access to informational variety, which allows them to adapt more easily to complexity.[150] There is a final advantage unique to organizations. Like individuals, they have the ability to externalize information by transforming information into explicit concepts. Organizations are thus pivotal to the externalization, and hence common identification, of cultural identities and different belief-systems. Yet, because any organizations exercise a jurisdiction over a membership, these concepts automatically acquire the status of 'social facts' or common denominators. They are taken to represent collective meaning-structures through which behaviour can be orientated. Even individuals not participating directly in or negotiating directly with organizations will, thus, be interacting against a backdrop of political and legal meaning that has been largely provided by the organization.

Constitutional recognition is therefore centred around the recognition of organizations. Indeed, it implies a presumption in favour of recognizing any organization as having inchoate law-making or political qualities. These are, however, only inchoate. Constitutional recognition requires, in addition, that organizations are endowed with political or legal qualities. Recognition of an organization as political attributes to it the capacity to exercise power collectively in a manner that negotiates with difference. Any 'political act' taken by it must also have these attributes. Similarly, to attribute an individual (or a group) a political identity is to suggest both

147 id., pp. 62–73.
148 id., pp. 74–5.
149 id., pp. 80–2.
150 id., pp. 82–3.

that its 'difference' is affected by measures of the institution and that she or he has the right to participate in the struggle over the exercise of this power. In the same way, to recognize an organization as having law-making powers recognizes that it can take measures, which are normative, valid, and formal-legal in nature. Similarly, an organization grants an individual a legal identity in its addressing any norm to her or him and recognizing her or his right to contest that norm.

3. *Recognition as mediation between evaluation and respect*

Some organizations with political and legal qualities can, of course, coerce recognition. The most obvious of these is the administrative state with its 'monopoly of legitimate violence'. They cannot, however, coerce 'constitutional recognition'. In passing, one might note that post-nationalism suggests a dethroning of such coercive relations with their being replaced by adaptive relations. More crucially, the distinction between the modern constitutional state and its predecessors was that the former constructed in terms of its acting for its free subjects. It thus always left open the possibility that political and legal action that did not observe these did not require recognition or obedience. An organization with political and legal qualities can do no more, therefore, than make a claim for constitutional recognition. It can not demand it. This allows for recognition to be used as an instrument of evaluation of all political and legal action. That the act of recognition can be so used is due to its possessing two immanent structures within it, which invariably render it a tool of critique – those of evaluation and respect.

The imminence of evaluation within recognition stems from the necessity for reflection before recognition can take place. For the ability to recognize carries also with it the capacity not to recognize and with it the need to make a choice. This choice is all the more weighty as the act of recognition transfers certain resources – be they symbolic or material – through the empowerment of the recognizee, and thus engenders an ethical responsibility on the part of the recognizer for the subsequent consequences of the recognizee's actions.[151] To be sure, this evaluation can vary in its intensity and in its explicitness. Taylor, thus, distinguishes between simple cost-benefit analyses (weak evaluation) and the application of a series of idealizations to the case in hand (strong evaluation).[152] Yet within this, the necessity to identify legal or political attributes of any organization renders any act of constitutional recognition relatively explicit. Thus, whilst it has been observed that strong evaluation demands a high level of reflexive self-understanding

151 If, for example, I employ a paedophile as my plumber who then spends the money earned on child prostitution, I bear some responsibility for this, as the subsequent payment enabled him, in part, to commit those acts.

152 C. Taylor, 'What is human agency?' in *Philosophical Papers I: Human Agency and Language* (1985).

for day-to-day interaction, it does not seem an excessive threshold in this instance.[153]

A decision to recognize something or somebody carries with it an implicit duty of respect, as an autonomy, capacity, and responsibility for action is accorded to the person or body recognized. The notion of respect implies certain further context-transcendental duties, which may never be fully recognized in any act of recognition, but are at least immanent in any such act in that there is a commitment to them. First, it carries a duty to enter into positive relations with the organization. This is not an obligation to support it. I can, for example, recognize a political party with whose views I disagree. It implies a requirement, however, to negotiate with that organization. By recognizing an organization, one recognizes its ability to organize, represent, and articulate certain interests. One acknowledges its political and legal attributes. Secondly, recognition implies a cognitive openness to the claims of the organization being recognized, whilst any recognition will be a form of misrecognition, coloured as it is by the observer's own cultural identity. Recognition, in this context, is different from other forms of misrecognition as it opens the observer up to the claims of those that have been recognized. It might misunderstand the arguments of those it recognizes. But recognition suggests a both receptiveness for advocates of those arguments to put their case, thereby opening up new terrains of struggle and organization, and a willingness upon the part of the recognizer to reform itself in the light of the arguments it hears. Finally, recognition implies a duty to acknowledge that the organization should be free from oppression and domination from either oneself or others. This can take a number of forms: exploitation, where the resources of one group are transferred to another without a fair return; marginalization, where members of one organization are denied participatory rights in other activities of social co-operation and access to the means of the consumption; powerlessness, where members of one group are accorded a lack of authority and sense of self in other contexts; cultural imperialism, where a dominant group or organization's experience is universalized so as both to stereotype other groups and to render their experiences invisible; and finally, direct violence – in this case targeted against somebody on account of their group membership.[154]

These twin structures of evaluation and respect imply certain a priori qualities to any political or legal organization recognized and to any relations that it enters into with individuals or other organizations. The first is that, as any organization can only make a demand for constitutional recognition, to satisfy the process of evaluation it will need to present a justification for recognition. Indeed, it will have to go further by presenting justifications, which are shared by those recognizing its jurisdiction.

153 D. Weinstock, 'The political theory of strong evaluation' in *Philosophy in an Age of Pluralism: The Philosophy of Charles Taylor in Question*, ed. J. Tully (1994) 73–4.

154 I. Young, *Justice and the Politics of Difference* (1990) ch. 2.

A person buying goods from a company might want to make sure that it has its own codes on child labour or genetically modified crops. Tourists might not want to stay at state-run hotels of governments who provide for no observance of fundamental rights.

The requirement to justify itself imposes an a priori condition on an organization to have mechanisms in place which enable it to critique its own actions. For the ability to formulate such justifications requires reflexive re-evaluation upon the part of the organization and the validity of any norm within an organization is also dependent upon its structuring organizational learning. It is the structure against which subsequent circumstances are tested and in the light of which prior cases are considered. Secondly, the capacity to formulate justifications presupposes not simply that argument must precede any measure, but that there must be an internal relationship between the argument and the decision taken. This is not a commitment on the part of the organization to accept the argument which commands the highest degree of validity. It is, rather, a requirement that any measure taken must negotiate with these arguments, either through accepting or rejecting them or mediating between them. All this entails that there must be structures within the organization which connect the process of internal dialogue to decision-making. If the argument is not to be a charade, furthermore, and not more than a procedural formality, there would also have to be structures within the organization, which allow for the possibility of decision-making power to be redistributed within the organization.

A requirement of shared justification imposes a clear danger of cultural imperialism, of outsiders telling organizations how to run themselves and the meaning-structures they should use. The principle of respect implicit in recognition entails that constitutional recognition only allows the recognisor to require an organization to acknowledge the validity of a particular norm or justification for action.[155] An organization would have to do no more than show that it acknowledged as valid the norms considered by the observer to be central to rational self-critique.[156] It would, however, be incompatible with the concept of recognition for the observer to determine the application of the norms. It could not govern the appropriateness of norms to particular contexts nor would it govern how these norms are tailored in those circumstances. In addition to the normativity of context, the risk of cultural imperialism would be assuaged through it always being open to the recognized organization to have other justifications for action (in so far as these were not a flat denial of the shared justifications in question) which might be more appropriate in certain circumstances. Thus, a shared commitment to freedom of expression may have to balanced in

155 On this, see K. Günther, 'A Normative Conception of Coherence for a Discursive Theory of Legal Justification' (1989) 2 *Ratio Juris* 157. But on the difficulty of separating validity and application see R. Alexy, 'Justification and Application of Norms' (1993) 6 *Ratio Juris* 157.

156 This is not the same as shared understanding and implies no intersubjectivity.

some societies with protection of the dignity of religious belief. Prohibition of a text because it was blasphemous would not be a case for derecognition.

The second a priori condition imposed on an organization for it to be constitutionally recognized concerns its manner of government. A feature of modern constitutionalism was that a polity legitimated itself in terms of its membership, which resulted in its granting certain political and legal claims against it. Whilst it may be possible to recognize an organization, politically or legally, which does not do these things, it is difficult to see how it could be granted constitutional recognition. A condition for an organization to be constitutionally recognized is, therefore, that, at the very least, an organization commits itself not to oppressing or marginalizing its membership. Whilst no organization ever fully attains this ideal, this would involve the granting of legal and political claims to its membership which allows them to test its commitment.

The third a priori condition for recognition is a propensity on the part of the organization to polyarchy. Polyarchy in this context signifies the transfer by the organization of resources – be they material or non-material – to other jurisdictions and to actors outside its jurisdiction.[157] Such a requirement does not impose a duty upon the organization to transfer resources to anyone or anything outside its jurisdiction but merely a duty to consider the matter. Three features render this requirement immanent within the process of recognition. There is the condition of interdependence. The only 'asocial' beings are the hermit and the anarchist. Organizations will, therefore, invariably, be in a series of interlocking and interdependent relations with outsiders. Their survival is predicated upon the mediation of these relationships, which requires, at the very least, transfer of resources on their part through the recognition of these relationships. Secondly, constitutional recognition would preclude acts of recognition that are necessarily exploitative. In so far as recognition empowers, and thereby involves some transfer of resources, the relationship would necessarily be exploitative in so far as it was shown that there was no transfer of resources by the organization. This does not require a transfer of resources to the recognizer, but could be to some third party. To be sure, the transfer may be to the organization's own members (for example, aid granted to a state gripped by famine). Yet the condition of interdependence would suggest that the transfer of resources to outsiders be, at least, a possibility. The final condition is that of accountability. Recognition is not a one-off act, whose effects, once exercised, are immutable and continuous, but something that needs to continue to be asserted, explicitly or implicitly. It therefore always includes the possibility of derecognition. The recognized organization is, thereby, continuously held to account. Derecognition must include amongst its grounds that of transgression of shared justification. An organization has committed some act or failed to do some act, which violates the grounds, which it

157 Dorf and Sabel, op. cit., n. 129, at p. 320.

used to gain recognition. The requirement of (in)action will result in this being manifested either through a failure to transfer resources to those to whom it has committed itself to transfer resources or a transfer of resources to those whom it has committed itself not to transfer resources.

CONCLUSION

The central argument of the last section was that the constitutional substitute that has emerged is a process. This process resolves around a dualism whereby, on the one hand, organizations with political or legal attributes seek recognition from individuals and other organizations, and, on the other, recognition of their attributes is granted when these organizations present justifications for their action that are accepted as valid by those recognizing them. This latter requirement will necessarily involve constitutionally recognized organizations having decision-making processes that are both capable of structuring their actions and subjecting those actions to critique; a commitment not to oppress or marginalize their membership; and, finally, a propensity to polyarchy

Critics of recognition-based approaches have argued that these would give rise to political systems that are too atomistic and fragmented.[158] One riposte to this is to argue that this need not necessarily be so. There is no argument for some form of fatuous parity between organizations. Each will have different levels of political and legal resources, dependent, in particular, upon the level of recognition cultivated. If only one organization was universally constitutionally recognized, therefore, there would be no relativism or seperatism. Furthermore, a post-national polity is fragmented. This paradigm merely reflects that. For this, one need only examine organizations that purport to govern but make no claim to possession of a monopoly of legitimate violence. Whether it be the European Union or models of corporate governance, the central tenet of government is that relations will not be entered into with outsiders by such bodies unless certain requirements are met.

A further concern might be that the thresholds demanded by constitutional recognition are too weak. Many bodies which behave egregiously, particularly in their treatment of outsiders or in their denial of membership, might be recognized under this model. It might also be argued that even the explicitly 'postmodern' constitutional theory of Ladeur, which is also centred upon organizational power, seems to impose greater constitutional demands upon organizations, namely those of experimentation, innovation,

158 D. Ivison, 'Pluralism and the Hobbesian Logic of Negative Constitutionalism' (1999) 57 *Political Studies* 83, at 86–87.

long-term horizons and flexibility, than are suggested here.[159] In a post-national, fluid order, not only will the egregiousness of an organization's behaviour temper its ability to induce constitutional recognition, but the structures proposed are immanent ones, which provide the recognizer with almost unlimited opportunity to interpret their exigency before granting recognition. The mechanisms demanded of organizations open them to critique over their ends, their decision-making processes, their internal distribution of power, and their relation with third parties. Moreover, in so far as constitutional recognition requires that they address these issues in some form, it implies that they will have a cognitive capacity to respond to such critique. The demands imposed of organizations are therefore as high as the subject wishes them to be.

It may, finally, be considered, paradoxical to argue for the centrality of subjectivity in an age where it is impossible to divorce the individual from the social relations or organizational networks in which she or he is enmeshed.[160] Yet it is precisely those relationships which create the dialectic necessary for the emergence of this subjectivity. On the one hand, they create systems of rationality in which the individual becomes so highly instrumentalized that she or he becomes no more than an 'actant' in an network, something which only has attributes (and therefore only exists) through their articulation by other objects in the network.[161] It is the alienation and perpetual misrecognition this provides, however, that allows individuality to thrive, however, by providing a resource off which subjectivity can thrive and discover itself.[162] Paradoxically, therefore, the greater the organizational pluralism, the more intense the development of networks, the more opportunities will emerge for the discovery of individuality. In this regard, the innovation of the legitimating responsibilities that modern constitutionalism imposed in the eighteenth century upon the polity was the reformulation of law and politics around a dialectic between the subject as institutional artifice – a term to be acted upon and upon whose behalf the polity acted – and the active subject who through her or his praxis pursues legal and political claims against the polity. Post-nationalism merely carries this dialectic forward to legal and political organizational structures beside the administrative ones of the nation-state.

159 Ladeur, op. cit., n. 128, at pp. 628–9; K.H. Ladeur, 'The Liberal Legal order and the Rise of Economic Organizations – Towards a Legal Theory of Proceduralization' in *Liberal Institutions, Economic Constitutional Rights, and the Role of Organizations*, ed. K.H. Ladeur (1997) 195–8. It will be clear from what was stated earlier that, in conditions of great fluidity, unpredictability, and interdependence, to subject organizations to any external steering criteria and to determine the content of these criteria will be highly problematic.

160 Touraine, op. cit., n. 69, at pp. 125–6.

161 For example, Latour, op. cit., nn. 53, 54.

162 G. Kateb, *Hannah Arendt: Politics, Conscience, Evil* (1984) 188–9.